NO WOMEN [illegible] OUT!

Trade Unions Past, Present and Future

Edited by Craig Phelan

Volume 17

PETER LANG
Oxford • Bern • Berlin • Bruxelles • Frankfurt am Main • New York • Wien

NO WOMEN JUMP OUT!

Gender Exclusion, Labour Organization and Political Leadership in Antigua 1917–1970

Christolyn A. Williams

PETER LANG
Oxford • Bern • Berlin • Bruxelles • Frankfurt am Main • New York • Wien

Bibliographic information published by Die Deutsche Nationalbibliothek.
Die Deutsche Nationalbibliothek lists this publication in the Deutsche Nationalbibliografie; detailed bibliographic data is available on the Internet at http://dnb.d-nb.de.

A catalogue record for this book is available from the British Library.

Library of Congress Control Number: 2012952374

ISSN 1662-7784
ISBN 978-3-0343-0863-2

Hochfeldstrasse 32, CH-3012 Bern, Switzerland
info@peterlang.com, www.peterlang.com, www.peterlang.net

Printed in Germany

For my mother
Arnelda Silvia Joseph

In memory of
Selma and Lucy (grandmothers)
Ann and Adelaide (great-grandmothers)

Contents

Tables

INTRODUCTION

Gender Exclusion, Labour Organization and Political Leadership in Antigua 1917–1970

This book explores the twentieth century history of the British Caribbean islands of Antigua and Barbuda, focusing on labour organization, political leadership and gender exclusion from 1917–1970. At the heart of this book is the critical role of gender – the social construction of identity based on sex – in the development of trade unionism and in local level leadership. Trade unions developed during the transition from colony to nation in the eastern Caribbean islands of Antigua and Barbuda, formerly members of the British administrative unit called the Leeward Islands. In the 1990s as a graduate student conducting research on trade unions and politics in Antigua and Barbuda, I encountered a collective amnesia about women's role in both of these institutions. This book addresses this neglect and exclusion from the memory and from the literature of Antigua and Barbuda scholars. Both Patrick Lewis and Novelle Richards, scholars of Antigua labour and political history, have focused their work exclusively on the role of Antiguan men both in trade unions and in politics. These works have further contributed to the belief of many men and women, professions and working class alike that women didn't do 'those sorts of things.' However, when I interrogated both primary and secondary sources, the evidence of women's central role is clear.[1] Women were the islands' majority population throughout the colonial period, and still are. As a result of their demographic position and their labour occupation they had a significant impact in the region's economy and society, and made

1 Both men and women interviewed and in casual conversations insisted to me that 'women didn't do those sorts of things', in reference to labour conflicts with landowners, colonial administrators and union organization and activism.

enormous contributions to labour and political developments. Despite the absence of documentation local union records or and monographs, of women's active roles in the economy and society of Antigua and Barbuda, I had only to interrogate union members, authors and historians about organizational structures, support networks and agricultural production to uncover the active role of women. Antigua and Barbuda labour and political history is the story of both men and women acting together. The oral sources, interviews with men and women of the island, have provided the most crucial evidence of women's participation in labour and political activism in Antigua, leading up to the acquisition of autonomous political rights in the 1970s.

This book also exposes the central role of the trades union in the island's social transformation, from a colony ruled by the small landed oligarchy, with full control over the society and economy, to one with an active working class majority which then claimed control from the minority. An organized working class in Antigua emerged only after the legalization of trades unions in 1940. The post emancipation nineteenth-century history of Antigua and Barbuda, 1834–1838, is a significant time period for regional labour history. While much has been written on the issues of labour conflict, labour organization and trade unionism in the British Caribbean, these earlier works have mainly focused on the twentieth-century labour history. More specifically they do not extend much past the 1930s labour unrest, nor has there been much examination of the role of gender in the twentieth century labour and nationalist movements. Antigua and Barbuda are of central importance in the history of free labour in the British West Indies, because they were the only islands where slave owners voted to forego the Apprenticeship option and adopted Immediate Emancipation in 1834. They therefore became the proving ground for post slavery labour laws, and the site of the first conflicts between large numbers of former slaves and former slave-owners. It was to Antigua and Barbuda that other islands including its Danish neighbours in the Virgin Islands, turned, modelling the labour codes and social controls instituted in Antigua and Barbuda in 1834. The significance of this role for Antigua and Barbuda has been overlooked in Caribbean labour history.

The history of free labour on the islands of Antigua and Barbuda begins with full emancipation in 1834, the only Caribbean islands where the planter class voted for free labour over apprenticeship, the period of transition which was to have lasted six years. The almost complete monopoly of land, by the white oligarchy and former slave owners in Antigua and Barbuda, kept ex-slaves extremely dependent on land owners for survival. This complete monopoly was broken only during World War I when the colonial government organized the first land redistribution scheme. The 1916 scheme was a response to the abysmal conditions among the black population, which suffered starvation and increasing numbers of suicide. Redistribution led to the emergence of a small class of peasants and proto-peasants, a class which by 1918 organized public protests in response to pay rate changes by estate owners. This protest marks the second watershed in the history of labour in Antigua and Barbuda following the islands' historic leap to full emancipation in 1834.

The period 1918–1951 marks the high and low points of white Creole hegemony in twentieth-century Antigua and Barbuda. By expanding the timeframe to include the 1970s, I show the dramatic social change that the 1951 political shift to universal adult suffrage allowed. The 1960s was a period of dramatic political developments as the British government moved to transfer political control to the Caribbean majority. By 1967 the British ceded political control over Antigua and Barbuda, allowing the small nation to make application for individual independence.

Part I of this book includes Chapters 1 and 2 where I address the legacy of sugar monoculture and post emancipation labour conditions. Historical developments after emancipation in 1834 are the bases from which these islands' economies and societies emerged in the twentieth century. Chapter 1 provides a crucial overview until World War I. The chapter explains how as the only British Caribbean colony in which the planter class voted for full emancipation in 1834, Antigua and Barbuda avoided the apprenticeship system imposed upon the other Caribbean slave societies. In post-emancipation Antigua and Barbuda, the white oligarchy (mostly plantation owners) established a number of laws directly targeting the island's newly freed population. Contract acts demanded that labourers enter into long-term binding agreements with land-owners; vagrancy acts limited movement and required the rural black population to be resident on estates or in free villages; family and labour laws were designed to protect the state from financial responsibility for the destitute, passing the burden for care of the ill, the elderly and the very young to the impoverished black population. These laws, beginning in Antigua and Barbuda in 1834 and adopted elsewhere in the region after 1838, would be used throughout the nineteenth- and twentieth-century colonial period, to control the lives and labour of the Caribbean working people.

The post-emancipation history of Antigua and Barbuda is a history of political consolidation by the nineteenth century plantocracy. This period, described as 'massa day' by historian Eric Williams and acknowledged by Antiguan peasants as representing a period when 'massa kill king and rule country' was a period in which a new hegemony was established over the island's labour force. Both *de jure* practices exposed and analysed by Mindie Lazarus-Black, and *de facto* practices described by Antiguan informants, explains why trade union leader V. C. Bird, had described the island of Antigua as having the quiet of a graveyard, prior to the legalization of trade unions. Laws and common practices limited the freedom of the island's masses and created an environment of fear and submission that was not lifted until the establishment of trade unionism in 1940.[2]

In Chapter 2, I analyse the disruptions in the British Caribbean sugar economy following emancipation. Many islands had chosen diversification of agricultural production following emancipation and some had successfully ended their dependence on sugar cane by the twentieth century. This was not the case for Antigua and Barbuda, where sugar monoculture continued to dominate the economy into the mid-twentieth century. Because Antigua remained an island primarily focused on sugar cane, its society and economy reflected the peculiarities of sugar economies. A small peasant class, economic dependence on one crop, a heavily coerced labour population and insecure work conditions, remained central features of the economy through the first half of the twentieth century.

2 Mindie Lazarus-Black, *Legitimate Acts and Illegal Encounters: Law and Society in Antigua and Barbuda* (Washington, DC: Smithsonian Institution Press, 1994) (hereafter *Legitimate Acts*).

The primary social peculiarity of sugar monoculture was the dominance of the minority planter and merchant class over the economy and the society. The Antiguan case is compared to that of the island of Jamaica, where immediately following the end of apprenticeship the economy and the concentration of labour shifted from sugar production. This shift from production of sugar to that of fruit, including bananas, greatly impacted the political economy of Jamaica through the late nineteenth century. Whereas economic diversification and the emergence of an independent peasantry were important features of post-emancipation Jamaica, the economy in Antigua and Barbuda remained unchanged through the mid-twentieth century, a sugar monoculture with a small peasant class.

In addition to the comparative discussion between the post emancipation economies of Antigua and Barbuda and Jamaica, Chapter 2 examines the relationship between the Colonial office and the business interests of Antigua and Barbuda, the island's elite of landowners and merchants. Having succeeded by 1898 in wresting control away from the local oligarchy, the Colonial Office attempted to make good its promises to improve the economy of the small island colony. But because the local oligarchy resisted colonial recommendations for agricultural diversification and land redistribution, the Antiguan economy suffered from high unemployment and food shortages. These conditions became more extreme during World War I when all economic activities including sugar production decreased. The colonial office could do nothing to improve the economic conditions on Antigua, without the participation of land and estate owners, and this group was resistant to the recommendation from this office that small plots of land be made available to labourers. little could be done to reduce the economic crisis on the island. The landowning class, the island's oligarchy, resisted diversification projects by the colonial office until 1916, when they finally relented. They agreed to allow small parcels of land to be distributed to some labourers. Land distributions would occur sporadically over the next two years, and contributed to the rise of a peasant class by 1918. However, overall the peasant class remained a very small one. They had no political access and no legal right to organize for collective interest. In addition, much of the small plots of land distributed were barely adequate to support basic subsistence farming or to alleviate hunger.[3]

Working class activism on the island became evident in the World War I period as economic conditions deteriorated and employers sought to protect their interests by lowering wages and changing pay conditions. Workers and peasants responded with protest and vandalism. The colonial administration sought to protect the peace and employers' interests by using local militia to break up strikes and marches. In addition, a series of regulations including the *Defense of the Presidency Ordinance* threatened imprisonment to workers who refused to work and to anyone else who encouraged such behaviour.[4] The threats and growing vigilance of employers and state militia to suppress organized protest failed, however, to stop revolts both in St. Kitts and Antigua and Barbuda in 1917 and 1918. In addition to labour protest over lowering wages, limited opportunities for work and shifting pay conditions, Caribbean workers also protested the hostile treatment and poor conditions experienced by black and coloured soldiers of the West India Regiment. The regiment had been mobilized in 1915 and comprised over 15,000 volunteers from the British Caribbean colonies. Two hundred twenty nine of these volunteers were from the Leeward Islands. Returning volunteers described rampant racism and discrimination by fellow white volunteers and from military personnel. Many who returned to the Caribbean following the war would become active labour and political leaders and advocates of Black Nationalist ideologies. Movements such as the one led or inspired by Marcus Garvey, which called for fuller participation for black and coloured men in their societies, had large support from these World War I volunteers and from others inspired by their activism.[5]

3 Land settlement schemes were begun on Antigua in 1916 and continued for some seventeen years 'Plan for Development and Welfare' (1949): 12.

4 Posted in the *Leeward Islands Gazette*, 7 March 1918.

5 W. F. Eklins, 'A Source of Black Nationalism in the Caribbean: The Revolt of the British West Indies Regiment at Taranto, Italy'. *Science and Society*, 35:1 (1970): 99–103.

Part II of this book begins with Chapter 3, which focuses on the society and economy of the island colony, looking at demography, origins of labour organization and the role of women in it. In Chapter 3, I use census reports, prison reports and bluebooks (these were reports which included administrative overviews, and information from prison reports and census), to evaluate Antigua and Barbudan society and analyse the impact and meaning of colonial policies on the everyday lives of the working people of the island colony. The society described in colonial documents is far from the full story and these colonial documents, along with oral and written sources by Antiguans themselves, are analysed in an effort to provide a more complete picture of the society. I am grateful to social historians and in particular to Verene Shepherd (1999), Lisa Douglass (1992) and Leith Mullings (1997), and to pioneer gender and feminism scholar Joan Scott (1988, 1996), for providing both theories and histories that demonstrate how much the story changes when women and their unique experiences are factored into history.[6]

The diminishing economy in the twentieth century resulted in population shrinkage. The majority of those who left the island were male, and their exodus further increased the sexual imbalance that had long been a feature of the island's economy from the eighteenth century. The female population on the island actively participated in the sugar industry and in the young cotton industry that was begun during World War I. By the 1930s, cotton fields were worked primarily by women and children.[7]

6 Lisa Douglass, *The Power of Sentiment: Love, Hierarchy and the Jamaican Family Elite* (Boulder, Colourado: Westview Press, 1992); Leith Mullings, *On Our Own Terms: Race, Class and Gender in the Lives of African American Women* (New York: Routledge, 1997); Joan Wallace Scott, *Gender and the Politics of History* (New York: Columbia University Press, 1988); Verene Shepherd, *Women in Caribbean History: The British Colonized Territories* (Princeton, New Jersey: Markus Weiner, 1999). While not all of these scholars have examined Caribbean societies their works have focused on women, some specifically on black women. The scholarship they have produced has been generated by questions relevant to women's experience irrespective of class, colour or national identity.

7 West India Royal Commission Report (London: His Majesty's Stationery Office, 1945) (hereafter 1938 Royal Commission Report); Novell Richards, *The Struggle and*

Gender is an important analytical category in this book. Most women in Antigua were employed in agriculture and domestic service. As the majority of the workers on the island colony, they suffered poverty as a result of the fluctuations in the colonial economy and the social limitations that were placed on women's participation. Of the eighteen occupations on the island, they were in only eight. Gendered wage structures ensured that female-headed households, that were the vast majority, lived in poverty. Women earned lower wages than men in areas of work in Antigua and Barbudan society, and, in both urban and rural areas these women struggled to support their families. In addition, because of the low wages paid to adult workers, child labour was the norm on the island throughout the 1950s, despite restrictions, passed in the 1930s setting age minimums for young labourers.

Interviews and oral histories included in this book, shows the active roles women played in Antigua and Barbuda society following emancipation. These are important for adding women's experiences into the records. The voices and the perspectives of the female informants are crucial in shedding light on other aspects of colonial Caribbean society. As a group whose historic role has been overlooked in other versions of the region's history, this book supports Verene Shepherd's point, 'the view of history changes when women are included in the historical account.'[8] I am aware of the challenges of using oral sources, particularly of the ways in which memory can impose its own influence on the recalled events. Guided by this knowledge, I have given these sources no central place as historical evidence without corroboration from sources of other types.[9] Many of these informants spoke freely of their childhoods and their family history,

---

the Conquest: Twenty five years of Social Democracy in Antigua (Antigua: Published by the author, 1981; New York, Seaburn Publishing, 2004). Conditions also described in Keithlyn B. Smith and Fernando C. Smith, *To Shoot Hard Labour* (Scarborough, Canada: Edan's Publishers, 1986) (hereafter Smith and Smith).

8 Verene Shepherd, *Women in Caribbean History*.

9 The questionnaire, constructed under supervision of my advisor and the CUNY-GC IRB board, asked subjects to talk about gender and images of women and their memories of the 1930s.

especially about their mothers and other women who influenced their lives. These narratives include my own family history, as told by my grandmother and two of her sisters. Through the evidence of my informants and the few written histories of other Antiguans, I have attempted to provide a more complete history of the rural life of the men, women and children whose lives revolved around labour in the sugar and cotton fields, mills and estate houses.

The mating and reproductive patterns of rural Antiguans differed from that of urban Antiguans in post-emancipation Antigua and Barbuda. In addition to location, race and class influenced the general patterns of life of residents. Colonial laws had a profound impact on working people, not only defining work conditions, but also establishing familial relations, and limiting access to resources. These laws affecting labour and family were constructed and modified from 1834 onwards, and by the twentieth century had a strong influence on Antiguan society. Scholars such as Mindie Lazarus-Black and Elsa Goveia have provided valuable monographs on this topic.[10]

The dynamics of the everyday lives of the working people not captured in colonial documents is exposed in the personal interviews I conducted in Antigua and Barbuda and the US Virgin island of St. Croix during 2002 to 2005. These interviews put a personal face to the people impacted by the business decisions of land owners and the administrative and legal policies endorsed for Antigua and Barbuda by the colonial government. In order to compete in the global sugar market and to ensure profits, no matter the global or local conditions, land owners and employers in Antigua and Barbuda established a three tier wage system based upon gender and age, and by hiring large numbers of women and children who fit into the lower wage scale of the three tier wage system, they reduced their wage costs and were able to post profits.

10 Mindie Lazarus-Black, *Legitimate Acts*; Elsa Goveia, *Slave Society in the British Leeward Islands at the end of the Eighteenth Century* (New Haven: Yale University Press, 1965); *The West India Slave Laws of the Eighteenth Century* (Barbados: Caribbean Universities Press, 1970).

In Chapters 4 and 5, I examine the role of British politics in particular British labour politics in the opening up of Caribbean society for mass participation. Although the landed oligarchy dominated almost all aspect of Antiguan society in addition to their control of the economy, their ability to maintain full dominance began to erode after the 1940s. This erosion is tied to the creation of Trade and Labour unions by the British Trades Union Congress (TUC). The Royal Commission of 1938 (hereafter the 1938 Royal Commission), and particularly Commissioner Walter Citrine played a critical role in turning around the labour and social conditions on Antigua and Barbuda and other Leeward Islands. Citrine recorded his role in the Caribbean in his diary and letters, documents in which he outlined the objectives of the TUC in organizing Caribbean labour. These objectives were not that far removed from those of the 1938 Royal Commission, to witness conditions and to make recommendations to the British government. The recommendation and support for trade unions would create the opportunity for real social and political change in Antigua and Barbuda and other British Colonies.[11]

Chapter 4 also introduces trade union foundations in Antigua and Barbuda. The Antigua Trades and Labour Union (ATLU) roots are embedded in British trade unionism, with the Trades Union Congress (TUC) in particular. It was the TUC whose institutions, laws and ideology were imported into Antigua and Barbuda with the formation of the ATLU in 1940. In Antigua and Barbuda, a particular male-focused leadership pattern had emerged among the free black population, and this pattern expanded among the larger black population in the post-emancipation period. This pattern of male-focused leadership continued into the mid-twentieth century, with village and grassroots organizations whose leaders were exclusively male. Because leadership had become identified in the society as a male

11 In my effort to keep the book focused on the Leeward Island of Antigua and the labour history of Antigua, I have constructed no place for a fuller study of Walter Citrine, a significant British labour actor. Readers interested in Walter Citrine can find a rich source of information available including his two volume autobiography *Men and Work* (Connecticut: Greenwood Press, 1976, c1964) *Two Careers* (London: Hutchinson, 1967).

activity prior to 1940, the TUC's own gender exclusive practices reinforced this gender hierarchy within the ATLU leadership structure. The TUC had a gendered division of participation based in its history representing a primarily male industrial workforce in Britain.[12]

Trade union masculinity and political leadership are addressed in Chapters 6, and 7, which make up Part III of this book. V. C. Bird as the representative of organized labour is a central actor in this work in order to demonstrate the changing political dynamics on Antigua and Barbuda between 1940 and 1970. Local level leadership and the influence of the TUC impact on gender exclusion, is the focus of Chapter 6, the lead chapter in this section. I combine both a history of local level leadership and an examination of trade union masculinity. For much of the nineteenth century in Antiguan society, gender ideology, with strong emphasis on the division of labour that confined leadership to males, had primarily been practiced by the coloured middle class and the small white elite. This pattern would expand to the working people after the 1940s largely as a result of the formation of ATLU as the working man's organization. This gender exclusion built upon earlier efforts begun in the 1920s by the colonial administration and the church, to change the behaviour of the working people and to enforce middle class ideology of gender, work and family on this population. Yet, the thirty year period, from 1940 to 1970, is a time of political activism when women's participation in local unions and political parties was extensive. Despite their heightened participation in these institutions, trade union rhetoric by the 1970s began to play down and exclude women's role. Women's historical role as labour activists, trade union members and leaders has become victim of a cover over. This process was conducted within the union itself, but it is my contention that it also had outside impetus and models.

Chapter 7 focuses on the changing political dynamic in Antigua and Barbuda from the 1940s as working class black and coloured men as trade

12 Walter Citrine distributed copies of Tolpuddle Massacre Literature to Caribbean Trade unions, and they embraced Red Flag anthem and other European labour traditions.

union leaders began to challenge the landed oligarchy. I have focused on several key events in this chapter, the legalization of trade unions; the removal of some of the punitive labour laws such as that banning the formation of labour unions and the opening up of political participation to the black and coloured majority.

Of primary focus in this book is the relationship between men in Antigua and Barbuda from the 1940s to the 1970s. The central issues are industrial relations, race and social class, and the conflict between Creole men for the control of the state. I allowed the evidence to dictate the direction of this chapter and was surprised that the Minority Report, the local labour contribution to the larger Soulbury Report documenting the most recent industrial unrest on the island, emerged as the central document for this chapter. This report, as well as letters and other communications originating from the Colonial Office, reconstruct the last battles over control in the Leeward Island colonies. Women's absence is palpable in the deliberations between the Colonial Office, employers or trade union leaders, yet gender is everywhere in the documents. Consequently I have used this chapter to discuss and evaluate the operation of masculinity in the Antiguan context.

Recent studies on gender, the social construction of identity based upon sex, have made possible a new approach to looking at relations between men and women in Caribbean society. Additionally, the emergence of masculinity studies, have exposed the complexity of race and class in societies described by scholar Rafael Ramirez as 'structured on asymmetrical gender and power relations.'[13] More than femininity studies, masculinity studies is multi-dimensional and focuses more attention on power and sexuality in the construction of identity. Moreover, in the construction of masculine identity the uneven power in relations among men is evident. Both masculinity and femininity as constructs include a socially and culturally specific set of symbols and meanings.

13 Rafael L. Ramirez, 'Foreword', in Rhoda E. Reddock, ed., *Interrogating Caribbean Masculinities: Theoretical and Empirical Analyses* (Kingston, Jamaica: University of the West Indies Press, 2004): ix.

Methodological Introduction

Many of the primary sources are from the UK National archives in London at the Public Records Office (UK Archives/PRO) and from the Antigua archives in St. Johns (Antigua Archives) and the Antigua and Barbuda Museum. The Trades Union Congress archive in London (TUC Archives) introduced me to Walter Citrine and to the partnership between the TUC and Caribbean trade unions. I visited these locations several times to collect from the reports, censuses, private letters and other communications the information I needed to fill in the gaps in the Antigua and Barbuda history. In the United States, visits to the Library of Congress (LOC) as part of a sponsored seminar for Community College professors in the summer of 2001 gave me access to maps and to the literature and scholarship on Empire studies.

It became quite clear when I began talking about my interest in writing about both men and women in labour and politics in Antigua and Barbuda, that I would need to pursue oral sources in order to be able to include women's role into the history. The memory of women's contributions had been so thoroughly erased that even historians and trade union activists insist initially that women were not there. Yet, when prodded further they are able to retrieve shadowy female figures at the forefront of protest marches, and in union organizing.

The oral sources that I have compiled as a result of the research for this book have contributed to my own family history. I had conversations with family members on and off the record, many of these conversations were not part of the research process but were nonetheless informative and helped to mould the direction of my IRB questionnaire. Oral sources, some of which are included in this book are invaluable in this particular context, because they represent the only primary sources on the historical role of women in Antiguan trade unionism and of women's role in nation building from 1951. Additionally, many of the Antiguan rural population through the 1960s were poor people who had been exposed to limited education. Their oral records have added to the very small collection of primary sources on the experience of peasants and workers in the British Caribbean in the twentieth century. These oral sources greatly enhanced the archival sources and secondary sources; they have assisted to fill in the gap and to answer important questions about agency and role played by men, women and children in the sugar economy that dominated the life of the Antiguan working people through much of the colonial twentieth century. I am indebted to the people, both men and women of Antigua who took the time to answer my questions and to let me share their memories and history. This work is dedicated to all of them.

In addition to historical resources I have made use of gender studies and social history, to better document the history of Antigua and Barbuda and expose the causes and outcome of women's exclusion from local labour and political history. Also included are a range of other sources and discussions that are connected to the resources listed above but are distinguished from them by having very specific focuses. The colonial structuring of Antigua and Barbuda involved demographic history, which is very much a focus in Chapters 2 through 4. In addition the political history of Antigua and Barbuda and the Leeward Islands includes the study of colonial political institutions through 1970.

At the heart of this book is my concern with the policies of the colonial administration in Antigua and Barbuda toward women, workers and the political access and performance of the ruling male Creoles, a group which was primarily white until the 1950s. I invoke intellectual history through the discussion of the Soulbury Report and labour union contributions via the Minority Report.[14] The nature of Antigua and Barbuda and Leeward Islands nationalism is invoked particularly in the final two chapters of this book. It is evident that gender analysis is crucial in this book, as everywhere in the accounts race, class and gender are clearly interlocked.

Gender and in particular, masculinity, studies in the Caribbean region have been an emerging field for the past ten years, with more scholars beginning to direct the focus of gender to the male sex, away from women, who had long been assumed to be the only group with gender. It is becoming

14 Soulbury Commission Report hereafter CO 152/520/4.

increasingly clear that for Caribbean scholars, 'men have gender too', – a point women's history scholar and Professor Barbara Welter insisted in making in my first women's history class at The Graduate Center, CUNY in the 1990s. Part III which includes the final two chapters of this book brings the labour history up to the 1970s. Colonial Office communications, memos, letters and other reports form the basis of primary source materials for this book. The conflict between Creole groups dominated the records, as white, black and coloured men struggled for control of the island colony.

What made these oral sources all the more important was the weakness or absence of trade union sources for Antigua and Barbuda. I found out in 2002 when I began my research that no archives existed with documents for the ATLU. My only access to ATLU materials was from the limited holdings of the Antigua Archives and the TUC Archives in London. I was also shocked and dismayed to find in 2002 that V. C. Bird, a central actor in this book, had left no papers. In fact, a former labour Minister in the Labour Party who had agreed to act as my go-between with the Bird family relayed to me the news that V. C. had, in fact, destroyed all his records before his death. However, despite that attempt to control history through destruction of primary sources (from which a different story could be told), my research for this book was not derailed. Other labour leaders and participants provided important information that has yielded a fuller history, one not completely tainted by the nationalist objectives of black Creole men. It is clear from the existing written sources by labour and trade union activists that their objective has been to paint an image of their roles so large and overwhelming that no room was left on the pages for others, especially women's roles. My task has been to begin the correction of this misconception.

PART I

Backgrounds

CHAPTER I

Historical Overview: Labour and Social Conditions, 1834–1917

Because Antigua and Barbuda are peripheral islands in the Caribbean region little analysis has been done by historians on labour, gender or political leadership in these islands. This chapter concentrates on the labour and political systems of Antigua and Barbuda moving from the contract Acts of 1834 to the transfer to Crown Colony government by the end of the nineteenth century. The labour laws encoded in the Contract Acts of 1834 dominated the labour and social conditions on Antigua and Barbuda to the mid-twentieth century. Contracts and other restrictive legislation directed at the rural workforce came to dominate not only working conditions between estate owners and workers but social conditions between the largely white estate and factory owners and the majority black and coloured workforce. Contract acts and restrictive labour laws defined class and race relations between white and coloured employers and black and coloured workers. These were the theoretical antecedents to labour conditions in twentieth-century Antigua and Barbuda.

The islands of Antigua and Barbuda were colonized in 1632 and 1661 by the British. By the eighteenth century Antigua had been transformed from a fledgling settler colony into a successful plantation slave economy and remained a slave economy until the granting of immediate emancipation to the estimated 29,000 slaves on the island in 1834. An estimated payment of £425,549 was paid in compensation to the slave owners of Antigua. This compensation did not include the 500 slaves in the neighbouring island of Barbuda. Christopher Codrington, the patriarch of the Codrington family in the Caribbean, had immigrated to Barbados from England in 1649 where he became a rich sugar planter. His son, also named Christopher arrived in Antigua in 1674 to run the estate which he had been given in 1668. Named Betty's Hope, it was a large estate on some of the most fertile land on the island. Using the knowledge acquired in Barbados of sugar cane production the younger Codrington transformed the island from a fledgling sugar producer into one of the most productive of eighteenth century British Caribbean colonies.[1]

In addition to their estate on Antigua, the Codrington family enjoyed a lease of the small island of Barbuda, sister island to Antigua. While Barbuda was the property of the British crown, it was leased in the seventeenth century to the Codrington family and remained under lease to the family for the negligible sum of one fat sheep per year until 1870.[2] Barbuda was neither large enough nor suitable physically to be used for sugar cane production or for large-scale settlement. The worth of the island lay in its location, and the opportunities it offered for the salvage of shipwrecks. In addition to the revenues they received for salvage operations, the Codrington family used the island to provide essential services including labour and livestock to the family estates in Antigua.[3]

The colonial government's commitment to the plantation sugar economy would place estate owners and the state in direct conflict with the black and coloured labour force who envisioned for themselves and their children a better future in post-emancipation Antigua and Barbuda. Estate owners had envisioned a labour shortage to be the immediate outcome of emancipation. They had predicted it as a matter of fact in their opposition to the emancipation proposal by the British Government. Their concerns regarding labour were acknowledged by the Colonial Office, which elected to give them the choice between full-emancipation or gradual

1 Brian Dyde, *A History of Antigua: The Unsuspected Isle* (London: Macmillan Education Ltd, 2000): 30–47; Mrs. Lanaghan, *Antigua And Antiguans: A Full Account Of The Colony and its Inhabitants From The Time Of The Caribs To The Present Day*. Reprint in two volumes (London, UK: Saunders and Otley, 1844 London, UK: Macmillan Education Ltd, 1991).

2 Ibid.

3 Brian Dyde, *A History of Antigua*, 30–37; Douglass Hall, *Five of the Leewards*. (Aylesbury: Ginn and Company, 1971): 54–95; *The Codrington Correspondence, 1743–1851* Compiled by Robson Lowe (London: 1951).

emancipation with a system of apprenticeship. The system of apprenticeship, which was put in place in all British Caribbean colonies except Antigua and Barbuda in 1834, bound ex-slaves to estates for an additional six years. Only in Antigua and Barbuda did planters opt for immediate emancipation. In addition to apprenticeship, the Colonial Office also approved a plan for the importation of indentured labourers into several Caribbean islands. Labourers were imported to the British Caribbean colonies from India, China, Madeira and Africa to compete in the labour market with black and coloured estate labourers.[4]

The system of Apprenticeship, as it was applied elsewhere in the former British Caribbean slave colonies, redefined the relations between the ex-slaves and their former owners. This new relationship was one of apprentices to employer. To protect the economic interests of estate owners and merchants in the plantation society, the system established the work week at forty hours, beyond which wages were to be paid to apprentices by their employers. It also defined new boundaries where treatment, in particular punishment, of apprentices was concerned. It provided an oversight committee in the form of magistrates to listen to the complaints of the workers, and with the power to end the contract of apprentices in cases of excessive abuse.

The system was fraught with problems. It denied both groups their aspirations. Estate owners were denied the complete control of labour and the ex-slaves were denied their true freedom. With neither side benefiting the system ended prematurely in 1838. Initially designed to last six years from 1834–1840, it ended in 1838. The British Apprenticeship system clearly demonstrated that the attempt by the colonial administration and landowners to maintain their full control of labourers was to be one of the greatest challenges of post-emancipation Caribbean societies.[5]

4 Susan Lowes, 'The Peculiar Class: The Formation, Collapse, and Reformation of the Middle Class in Antigua, West Indies, 1834–1940' (Columbia University, 1994): 47; Brian Dyde, *A History of Antigua*, 162; Douglas Hall. *Five of the Leewards*, 22–23.

5 Douglas Hall, *Five of the Leewards*, 30–31; Susan Lowes, 'The Peculiar Class'; O. Nigel Bolland, *The Politics of Labour*, 29–33.

The society and economy of post-emancipation Antigua and Barbuda remained much the same throughout the nineteenth century, despite the adoption of immediate emancipation. The growth of sugar-cane for export to European markets remained the dominant industry of the islands, despite various recommendations by the colonial office for diversifying production in the region. The Antigua and Barbudan labour force, though 'free', by 1834 was heavily coerced into selling their labour to estate owners.[6] Antiguan estates, therefore, while heavily indebted and encumbered prior to emancipation, survived immediate emancipation and the expenses of wages, largely as a result of their ability to reduce their purchase and maintenance costs and labour costs. A cost analysis for post-emancipation Caribbean, estimates that labour represented half of the operating costs for estate owners. The ability of estate owners on Antigua and Barbuda to keep wages low in the post-emancipation period, came at the expense of labourers. It was partly a result of low wages that many floundering estates were able to remain in operation.[7]

While the other colonists gladly embraced gradual emancipation in the form of the apprenticeship, in Antigua and Barbuda the planters did not believe that this system would provide them with the best opportunity to reduce their operational costs. When they voted to give full freedom to their slaves in 1834, it was because they had been convinced by one of their own that their expenses would be greatly reduced by such a decision. Like their counterparts in the other British Caribbean colonies, the Antigua and Barbudan planters were in 1833 actively planning their protest against the impending act, until the argument of one of their members resulted in a complete reversal of their position. The Antigua and Barbudan planters were convinced by Samuel Otto Baijer that they stood to benefit from free labour. Assemblyman and estate owner Samuel Otto Baijer's argument was simple, full freedom would cut costs for planters. He informed his fellow planters that he had come to the conclusion that they would be able to reduce the cost of running their estates by making freedmen of

6 Douglas Hall, *Five of the Leewards*, 128–164.

7 O. Nigel Bolland, *The Politics of Labour*, 35.

their slaves rather than apprentices, as apprentices would have to be fed, housed and cared for whether they were productive labourers or not.[8] For a community of men much concerned with lowering the cost of their business, especially at a time when most of them were heavily indebted, the argument for lowering cost was a convincing one and while the other colonies were drafting Apprenticeship bills, the Antiguan assembly drafted a bill offering immediate, entire and universal emancipation. Ensuring the continued existence of the sugar economy required an unlimited labour force for the sugar estates and refineries. It was because of their belief that they could assure themselves such unlimited labour that the Antigua and Barbudan estate owners voted for immediate emancipation in 1834. They would use the small size of the island, the lack of other options to estate labour and their command of the legal system to avail themselves of the labour of the ex-slaves.[9]

Under immediate emancipation planters were freed from their former obligations to provide for their slaves. Food, clothing and housing became the responsibility of the ex-slave population. Estate owners were able in addition to free themselves from all obligations to those slaves who were no longer capable of selling their labour. The old and infirm and the very young became the responsibility of family members. In some cases the state assumed such responsibility, but this was a last resort as new detailed family and labour laws placed the responsibility and the burden in the lap of family members, many, still incapable of providing for their own basic needs.[10]

The Antiguan Emancipation Act of 1834 abolished the old system of bondage and sought to create a new system based on free labour. As such, many of the tensions of pre-emancipation Antigua remained, and in some cases these tensions were heightened by the resistance of the labourers to

8 Brian Dyde, *A History of Antigua*, 23 The much referenced section of Baijer's speech that cites the economic motive states 'that I have ascertained beyond a doubt that I can cultivate my estate at least one-third cheaper by free labour' was available on the website for the Antigua Museum in December 2005.

9 Ibid., 18–31.

10 Mindie Lazarus-Black, *Legitimate Acts*, 102–111; Caroline Carmody, 'First Among Equals'.

the new laws. While the laws and the systems of control remained firmly on the side of estate owners the labourers developed their own systems of resistance, and found ways to renegotiate wages and work conditions. Because of this response the tensions in post-emancipation Antigua and Barbuda remained centred around labour.[11]

Contract Acts and Other Techniques

The two most dramatic events in Antigua and Barbuda's nineteenth century history were emancipation and the island's conversion to Crown Colony status. Emancipation in 1834 required some reorganization of labour and personal relations to deal with the change from a slave society to a free plantation society.

Despite the confidence with which Antigua and Barbudan estate owners had supported immediate emancipation, it was not their only plan for reducing their expenses and responsibilities where the ex-slave population was concerned. Estate owners sought in addition to stack the deck in their favour by use of the law. Contract acts, vagrancy acts and family and labour laws were introduced in the small colony by a local government intent on maintaining their control over the society and in particular the labour of the island's majority.[12]

By the late nineteenth century, planters and other employers on Antigua and Barbuda were the first masters of techniques for labour control. They were the first to introduce the use of contracts between labourers and employers. The 1834 Antiguan Act, the first of such labour acts in

11 Douglas Hall, *Five of the Leewards*, 15–17. The contributions of the West Indian scholar and politician the late Dr. Eric Williams to the scholarship on slavery and abolition in the Americas, must be acknowledged. While his thesis is dated, *Capitalism and Slavery* has been the basis upon which many contemporary arguments have been built.

12 Douglas Hall, *Five of the Leewards*, 26–28.

the Caribbean was passed in the Antiguan legislature on 29 December 1834. The Act made rural labourers wards of the estates immediately upon entering into contract with estate owners. Clearly high illiteracy among the labourers made written contracts quite unworkable, and to accommodate this challenge the law stated that labour contracts need not be written and oral contracts between employers and employees were deemed legal and binding if made in the presence of two witnesses. It is obvious that the vast majority of contracts made between slaves and estate owners in 1834 were oral. Whether oral or written contracts tied wages to the use of estate 'cottages' and to gardens where workers grew food crops and raised animals including pigs, chickens and sheep. The law made work absence subject to severe whipping as well as hard labour sentences in state prison. Labourers under contract were held responsible for their employers' property and their conduct, whether at work or in estate housing, was heavily regulated by the law and by the estate owners. Severe punishment was metered out for offences including drunkenness and careless use of fire.[13]

The law severely limited the freedom of ex-slaves and in Antigua and Barbuda it was responded to by protest from ex-slaves and their supporters. In response to these protests the British government disallowed the 1834 Act and heavily scrutinized its replacement. The 1835 revised Act was less severe in its violation of the freedom of labourers. The Act established the workday at nine hours days, with a day off weekly or every two weeks. Wages were set for estate workers at 9d daily. In addition to establishing the work week and wages, Antigua and Barbudan estate owners also introduce a first in the wage system of the region, 'the wage rent' system.

Wage rent allowed estate owners to reduce wage costs by tying wages to housing accommodation. The small dilapidated accommodations of the slave quarters were offered as part of the wage package. Some estates only hired workers who were also residents in order to reduce their labour costs. For ex-slaves who remained on estates where they had been enslaved, wage

13 Smith and Smith, *To Shoot Hard Labor*: 39–48. Brian Dyde. *A History of Antigua*: 154; O. Nigel Bolland, *The Politics of Labour*, 33–54 and Susan Lowes, 'The Peculiar Class', 41–47.

rent was a difficult arrangement as well as a relief. They had constructed and maintained these accommodations and worked the small plots of land into fertility. In addition many of them had spent their entire lives in these houses and despite their dilapidated condition and the cost now being assessed by estate owners against their wages; they had developed emotional attachments and were unwilling to leave.[14]

The fact that workers created other alternatives to estate labour and found ways to resist the more restrictive and violent aspects of the contract act made some estate owners offer fairer work conditions to attract competent workers and raise the morale of the work force. One means of improving work conditions and attracting good workers was the introduction of the English system of general hiring. Under general hiring workers lived on estates where their housing and gardens were rent-free and they received medical care. The daily hiring wage was 6d sterling for able-bodied males. All other adults and children were paid at a lesser rate. General hiring agreements between estate workers and estate owners could be cancelled by either side with notice given one month prior. Many estates allowed workers access to land for garden cultivation in post-emancipation Antigua and Barbuda, but the size and quality of such land used for garden plots were reduced to an estimate of fifty feet square. In addition estate owners established limits to how much and what workers could produce for themselves in these gardens. The limits were designed to ensure that workers could not become self-sufficient and would remain dependent upon the wages of the estate to supplement their food needs.[15]

14 Douglas Hall, *Five of the Leewards*: 27–28; Novelle Richards, *The Struggle and the Conquest: Twenty Five Years of Social Democracy in Antigua* (St. Johns, Antigua: Published by Author, 1981); Keithlyn Smith and Fernando Smith, *To Shoot Hard Labour*, 37–88; Neville Cleofoster Brown, *The Emergence of a Bishop; Memoirs of Neville Cleofoster Brown: Bishop of the Moravian Church* (Trinidad and Tobago: Granderson Bros. Ltd, 2000): 1–14. Well into the twentieth century, Antiguan informants described similar workplace conditions and told stories of abuses of power experienced by workers, at the hands of estate owners and managers, as well as in the sugar factory and mills.

15 O. Nigel Bolland, *The Politics of Labour*, 54–63.

Yet despite their use of coercive mechanisms which they built into the Labour Act, the expectation of a completely dependent work force that had driven their vote for full emancipation was not completely realized. Workers in post-emancipation Antigua and Barbuda were not all fully dependent upon the estate owners for wages and housing. Independent villages, occupied by workers who were largely independent of estate owners, began to be established in Antigua and Barbuda by 1840. These villages emerged despite the attempts to discourage land sale to workers. Many of these land purchases were facilitated by third parties such as churches and other groups who supported workers quest for independence from estates. From the start the villages reflected the determination of workers to escape the control of estate owners – these villages allowed them to have their first real experience of freedom, and to introduce alternative products into local and export economies of the region. Village life allowed for the emergence of a proto-peasantry in the region, as many villagers sold their labour seasonally to the estates in exchange for cash, while they subsisted for most of the year on their own produce. These labourers were drawn to seasonal estate work only by the need for cash to operate in the larger economy of the island.[16] Village life allowed for the introduction of alternative economic models for Leeward Island societies. The commitment to sugar cane production was maintained in post-emancipation Antigua and Barbuda and this commitment allowed for colonial administrators and for estate owners to move quickly to stifle plans for economic alternatives to sugar, even viable ones. The refusal to consider and or support alternative economic models to sugar plantation production would contribute to the economic crisis which the region faced throughout the nineteenth century.[17]

16 Smith and Smith, *To Shoot Hard Labour*: 55–70; Susan Lowes. 'The Peculiar Class'; O. Nigel Bolland, *The Politics of Labour.*

17 Franklyn Knight, *The Caribbean: The Genesis of a Fragmented Nationalism* (London: Oxford University Press, 1990), 184–185.

Government Strategies to Control Labour

Slave emancipation required an almost complete reorganization of power and the class structure in Antigua and Barbuda. The laws in the colony through the nineteenth century had been designed to govern slaves, servants and free persons. A free society required new laws address the new situation. In addition to a new emphasis on individual workers' rights to enter into contracts, the reconstructed legal system in Antigua and Barbuda after 1834 redefined individual rights, it established new conditions of labour (written and oral contracts, general hiring and seasonal hiring), and constructed new functions of kinship that related solely to the labouring population. This aberration of laws was not new in post emancipation Antigua and Barbuda. The laws of Antigua and Barbuda had always reflected a peculiarity in that while they were based on English laws and traditions, they were in the language of Mindie Lazarus-Black, '*imagined different*.'[18] The colonists loosely interpreted English laws in the colonies which defined relations within their society broadly and distinctly. After 1834, they used the law to define labour, class, and race relations in Antigua and Barbuda. They constructed a social pyramid that looked a lot like the plantation slave society. Until 1951 when universal adult suffrage shifted the balance of power politically from the top of the pyramid to the bottom, labour laws were the cornerstone of the hegemony by the colonial elite. This hegemony, political and social, was established and maintained at the expense of the majority. Where English law in Antigua and Barbuda was different, the difference was in part the result of the racial and ethnic distinctiveness of the majority peoples of colonial societies. In Antigua and Barbuda where white men (predominantly but coloured men could also enjoy this privilege) owned the land, laws allowed for land owners to control labourers and govern the entire non-white majority. Labour codes defined work relations in urban and rural Antigua and Barbuda, they fixed personal relations between individuals, not just employer-employee but also

18 Mindie Lazarus-Black, *Legitimate Acts*, 14.

all class and racial segments in the society.[19] This hegemony of the white minority was one to which the non-white population capitulated, co-opted and resisted in a myriad of ways into the first half of the twentieth century.

The ability of the white minority to constitute the society of their choosing was largely the result of the local system of government in nineteenth-century Antigua and Barbuda. The system of Colonial Assembly put local government in the hands of propertied and literate males, who were primarily white and coloured. In Antigua and Barbuda, where the colonists and not the British parliament established the boundaries of post-emancipation society the challenges to maintain control of the labouring population were exposed quite early. The colonial administration supported the planter-sponsored legislation that sought to maintain pre-emancipation conditions. Their first labour act made no provisions for establishing wages. It did not delineate responsibilities, nor was an oversight committee created to mediate contracts with the illiterate labouring population.

The decision to bypass apprenticeship had been made by the planters for economic rather than moral reasons. Post-emancipation society looked very much like pre-emancipation society, especially where work, class and other personal and work relations were concerned. The laws of the island colony did change, but the change sought to tighten the control of the planters and other colonial whites over the rest of the society. Physical punishment and imprisonment remained a defining feature of the work relationship between those who worked the land and those who employed and/or supervised the workers. Post-1834 colonial codes were not only far-reaching in scope of intervention in the lives of labourers, but were quite lasting, as described by Sammy Smith and V. C. Bird in twentieth-century Antigua and Barbuda.[20]

19 Smith and Smith, *To Shoot Hard Labour*. See discussion by Sammy Smith of the ways in which estate owners were able to meter out punishment, to imprison, and even murder blacks who worked their estate. Most demonstrative is the murder witnessed by Smith as a teenager of a female estate worker Harty Bab in 1890. In Antigua and Barbuda, some of these ideas have their origin in colonial laws, laws which have become part of the social structure of the society.

20 Ibid. See also criticism by V. C. Bird of racism and segregation in twentieth-century Antigua in his Minority report in the Soulsbury Report. Issues are also addressed

The System of Colonial Assemblies

The period from emancipation through the late nineteenth century was a very busy period for the Colonial Office. They were forced to address a number of industrial concerns throughout the region. Explosive conditions in Jamaica had resulted in the 1860s in a labour rebellion which cost the lives of hundreds of Jamaican peasants, as well as some members of the black and coloured middle class. The economic decline following the fall in sugar production was beginning to raise concerns in England. These concerns were too heavily focused on sugar however as they missed the dynamic of the increasing economic contributions of a new peasantry both in Jamaica and in Trinidad. The discourse around the economic viability of Caribbean societies remained narrowly focused on sugar despite its declining production as a result of natural disasters as well as the shrinking market for it in the United Kingdom. Local governments and estate owners in the Caribbean embraced a number of schemes including labour contracts and immigration; all in an effort to revive the sugar industry and boost their profits. Through 1895 however many of these monoculture societies including Antigua and Barbuda remained trapped in economic crisis. Estate owners blamed workers and the failure of government for their financial losses. The Colonial Office on the other hand quickly returned blame to the colonies, believing that the economic crisis in the sugar industry was the result of mismanagement by local governments.[21]

Joseph Chamberlain, the Secretary of State for the colonies (1895–1903), was among the most expressive of metropolitan politicians of the problem of Caribbean economies. He saw the problem as a structural one tied to the existing system of colonial assemblies. The assemblies were

---

by Mindie Lazarus-Black in 'Introduction: Life and Law in the Common Order', in *Legitimate Acts*.

21 Brian Dyde, *A History of Antigua*, 204; Cross and Heuman, *Labour in the Caribbean*; O. Nigel Bolland, *The Politics of Labour*, 63–77; David Anderson and David Killingray, *Policing the Empire: Government Authority and Control, 1830–1040* (New York: St. Martin's Press, 1991).

comprised primarily of estate owners, merchants and other local business owners who assumed responsibility for making business decisions for the colony. Chamberlain criticized the assemblies for pursuing economic and political interests that were to their own personal and immediate interests only. For Chamberlain the assemblies hindered attempts to modernize or improve the economic situation.

The inability of Caribbean colonies such as Antigua and Barbuda to attract new investors was blamed on the system of local government. Convinced that foreign capital was shy of the colonies because of the system of local government which posed a threat to their interest the Imperial government worked to remove local government and revive the failing economies of the Caribbean.[22] Chamberlain committed himself to bringing an end to local government in the Caribbean colonies.

In Antigua and Barbuda the failure to attract new investors and to modernize is seen in the abysmal conditions and other problems of the majority that were beginning to appear in colonial administrative reports. The 1878 Report of the Registrar-General, for example, recorded the highest death rate of any other colony for which statistical returns had been received. The high death rate was easily enough understood from a survey of the conditions in which the island's working majority lived. Most resided in cramped cottages either in free-villages, or in estate cottages. Irrespective of location housing was inadequate, small, poorly constructed and maintained, and without any form of sanitation or clean water, when water was at all available.[23]

While conditions were bad in both the early free village housing and the estate housing, the estate housing and their occupants were among the worst of conditions. These estates or 'nega-house' as they were referred to by labourers, were the site of the more desperate of conditions. In the only written account of life on the Antiguan estates in the twentieth century, a former Antiguan labourer Sammy Smith, describes. 'The normal size house was about sixty feet long by forty feet wide.' He described the

22 Ibid.

23 Brian Dyde, *A History of Antigua*, 204–206.

creative attempts of plantation peasants who constructed their housing of whatever resources available to them. 'The cellars was the pillars of the houses and was made up of stones fastened together with white lime. The window side would be covered by board and shingles. The other sides would be of board only. The roofs too was covered with shingles and sometimes felt would be used. The houses were also strengthened by several upright posts but there were no partitions.' Poorly structured it was not a surprise to learn from him that 'Most of the Houses would leak. The smaller holes [...] whistle when the wind would blow. After a time we would generally get wet when it rain.'[24]

The housing conditions and the overall quality of life for the rural peasants were abysmal. Poor quality structures were often overcrowded, not simply because of the large size of a family but because in some cases more than one family were assigned to the small houses. These houses provided little privacy, as there were no divisions or separations within the household and the absence of screens in the houses meant that adults and children and even families were all thrown together in the small rooms. Smith's description of housing brings to mind the overcrowded barracks of slavery.

> We used to live together like a flock of cattle, like goats or sheep in a pen. There were little repairs done to them houses. When the floor start to rotten, the people living there would pluck up the floor – the whole thing – to keep themselves from falling into the cellar. When the floor get pluck up, the bottom of the cellar would be the floor of the house. The bottom was earth.[25]

Colonial medical reports tended to blame illness on the masses. Like other aspects of their needs they were on their own where their healthcare was concerned. This exposure to bare earth and the high cost of clothing and shoes meant that most peasants went barefooted both inside and outside their houses. In rural areas these peasants were subject to *jiggers* and suffered greatly when this mite larva became attached to the skin. This infestation was particularly acute on the estates and greatly increased the suffering of estate workers. Smith describes estate housing infested with

24 Smith and Smith, *To Shoot Hard Labour*, 41.

25 Ibid., 42.

larvae and a peasant population suffering from jiggers. Because the larvae lived in the soil and the bare feet were constantly exposed to the soil many peasants and workers experienced difficulty walking and suffered the pain and discomfort of jigger infestation. But jiggers, he argued, were only one form of infestation estate populations suffered: in addition estates were infested with rats, mice, spiders, centipedes, scorpions and other creatures that resided on the islands. In addition to poor housing he complained bitterly about the lack of sanitation, 'there was no sanitation to speak of. There was no soap, nor disinfectants of any kind.' The shortage of water accessible to estate workers and villagers meant that 'most nega-house people hardly had regular baths'.[26]

While aware of these terrible conditions and flooded with suggestions about how to improve them, the Imperial government, the Colonial Office and governors (where they admitted to this awareness as was the case for Edwin Barnes, Colonial Secretary in 1863, and Governor Hill as well as Governor Sir Henry Irving in 1873/4) found the system of local government limited the ability of the Imperial government to do anything more than recommend the local legislatures address the problem.[27]

The problem of clean water accessible to the people both in the city of St. Johns and in rural areas remained a pressing one throughout the nineteenth century. Attempts to solve the water problem were made by the local Assembly which in 1864 authorized a loan for building a water storage unit in St. Johns City. But this project was not the result of their recognition of the need for clean water as much as a result of their desire to lower insurance charges in a city where fires remained a pressing problem into the twentieth century. The need for water for the extinction of fires to private property in the city was deemed more crucial than the need for clean water for the urban masses. The resulting water project, completed in 1867, directed water from north-east side of the island into a cistern outside of the city. From this cistern the water was fed directly into the city's fire hydrants, and public buildings as well as to several residents.

26 Ibid.

27 Brian Dyde, *A History of Antigua*, 182; O. Nigel Bolland, *The Politics of Labour*, 127; Susan Lowes, 'The Peculiar Class', 89.

Labourers and workers did not gain access to this water. As this example demonstrates, local politicians acted only when their personal and business interests would benefit.

Throughout much of the post-emancipation period local politicians continually refused to fund or support social and economic programs that directly benefited the common order or the workers. Other examples of this included the refusal to build upon schemes for providing healthcare to reduce the mortality rate and to prevent epidemics. In the 1870s when the mortality rate in Antigua and Barbuda was extremely high with nearly one-third of all death that of children under one year of age, local politicians continually rejected proposals for village clinics, water projects and for improved housing for the urban and rural population.[28]

The Norman Commission of 1896 served as the springboard to Joseph Chamberlain's aim to eliminate local assemblies in the Caribbean. The Commission's mandate, to examine the condition of the sugar industry and recommend solutions, resulted in their recommendation that local governments be abolished and that the Imperial government assume such responsibilities. The Commission thus provided in its recommendations the opportunity for the Imperial government to increase pressure on local governments to vote for their own emancipation. This almost unimaginable act was achieved in Antigua in 1896 when the local assembly voted itself out of existence. But the vote was not out of character for this assembly for as Caribbean labour scholar O. Nigel Bolland argues, Antigua and Barbudan politicians and estate owners voted to protect their personal interests and to ensure their survival as a racially exclusive class. Local government in Antigua in 1896 surrendered local rule for the Crown Colony system largely to ensure their self-preservation. The Antiguan assembly was beginning to be invaded by middle class coloured men particularly after 1870. The surrender by local whites was greatly influenced by their concerns that the coloured middle class was beginning to take over the political systems in the island. Their surrender to the Crown Colony system would successfully eliminate black and coloured men from the political arena until the mid-twentieth century.[29]

28 O. Nigel Bolland, *The Politics of Labour*, 127; Susan Lowes, 'The Peculiar Class', 89.

29 Ibid. See additionally O. Nigel Bolland, *The Politics of Labour*, 12.

The Transfer to Crown Colony

Crown Colony government came to Antigua and Barbuda in 1898 when the Antiguan legislature surrendered its power to the Imperial government ending local rule. The system of Crown Colony rule shifted decision making on economic and social issues back to London and the Colonial Office. This transfer was a significant one for the colony for it shifted the balance of political power to the Colonial Office and the process of implementing changes, long ignored or rejected by the local legislature was sped up. Crown Colony legislature comprised of colonial governor, administrator, attorney general, treasurer and colonial secretary, a group known as the executive council. In addition to these officials there was also an unofficial group which included planters, bankers, merchants and other bureaucrats.

Legislative power in crown colonies lay with the governor as the representative of the Imperial government. Crown Colony governors nominated men from among the eligible local population and these men were responsible for appointments such as that of administrator. Because there was no suffrage the process was one controlled both by the governor and the white oligarchy which was comprised of the estate owners, merchants and shippers and other businessmen on the colony. Before and after the introduction of Crown Colony the same families and groups dominated this body until universal adult suffrage in 1951 when the majority elected black and coloured union leaders.[30]

After 1898 the nominated and appointed members of the legislature were the same class of men (as well as the same men) who had comprised the locally governed assembly. The transfer to Crown Colony government had no dramatic impact on workers of the island, although the shift

30 I recommend to the reader the following sources for discussions of the peculiarities of political systems in the British isle. Kenneth David Fieldhouse, *The Colonial Empires: A Comparative Survey from the 18th Century* (New York: Delacorte Press, 1967); and *Colonialism in Africa 1870–1945* (New York: Cornell University Press, 1973); Sir Charles Jeffries, *The Colonial Empire and its Civil Service* (Cambridge: Cambridge University Press, 1938).

to Crown Colony did contribute to ending economic stagnancy on the island, by infusing much needed money into the sugar economy in the form of grants and loans from the Imperial government and private investors. The new legislature remained as committed as the old assembly to keeping workers in their place of complete dependency.

Throughout the first three decades of the twentieth century, Antigua and Barbudan working people experienced little improvements in wages and in their quality of life.[31] The primary preoccupation of the Crown Colony government in Antigua and Barbuda remained focused on securing the export economy of Antigua. Sugar remained the primary product for export in the new century with some growing interest in cotton, a product which grew in value with the start of World War I. After the war cotton would lose the short market share which the war created. Other than generating a demand for cotton World War I had a tremendous impact on the economies and societies of the Caribbean. The war intensified the suffering of the most vulnerable groups and rural and urban workers faced wage cuts and loss of jobs as a result of the economic contraction of the war. Workers responded with organized protests, spontaneous demonstrations and cases of sabotage were also reported by estate owners The war contributed both to increasing labour unrest and the growth of black nationalism among the British subjects both at home in the colonies and abroad including active servicemen and those Caribbean immigrants in the US and elsewhere.[32]

31 Discussions across the board from these sources are similar. Recommend review of O. O. Nigel Bolland, *The Politics of Labour*; Marjorie Nicholson, *The TUC Overseas*; Malcolm Cross and Gad Heuman, *Labour in the Caribbean*.

32 O. Nigel Bolland, *The Politics of Labour*, 195–203.

Conclusion

The surrender of the old representative assembly system in the late nineteenth century was an important turning point in the political order in Antigua and Barbuda. The transfer primarily served the interests of both the white oligarchy and the British Crown. The white oligarchies gave their support for Crown Colony in order to arrest the growing presence of coloured men in local government. Their action delayed the participation of significant numbers of black and coloured middle class Antiguans and Barbudans until the mid-twentieth century. Antigua and Barbuda represented the first example of the manipulation of laws and legal codes in the post-emancipation Caribbean. As the only Caribbean island to opt out of full emancipation in 1834, both the labour codes of the island and other laws and legal statutes implemented to control the free labour force; were models that were emulated by other Caribbean authorities. The Danes for example were among the first to look to Antigua as a model, sending an official observer in 1845 to report on the impact of emancipation both on sugar production and on social relations on the island. The reporter Louis Rothe found much to commend on the social conditions and on production. Other islands too were closely watched by the Danes for the impact of immediate emancipation on the economy and society, in particular they closely watched to see results of the labour acts introduced by the local legislature.[33]

Despite the change in form of government in crown colonies, the interests of the colonial elite remained closely aligned with that of the Imperial government. The transfer had shifted power from elected assemblies to colonial governors and the Colonial Office, yet this was less dramatic a

33 For historiography of Post-Emancipation Leeward Islands and the institution of laws including contract acts see B. W. Higman, 'Post emancipation of the Leeward Islands', in Karen Fog Olwig, ed., *Small Islands Large Questions: Society, Culture and Resistance in the Post-Emancipation Caribbean* (London: Frank Cass, 1995); Mindie Lazarus-Black, *Legitimate Acts*, 111; Susan Lowes, 'The Peculiar Class', 37–47.

change for the black and coloured masses; a population which remained excluded from the political process. Even the coloured wealthy and middle classes, who had in some colonies been included in the old system, were excluded from the Crown Colony system. It was more of the same with Crown Colony government. By the end of the nineteenth century, neither emancipation nor the change to Crown Colony government had produced any fundamental changes in the Caribbean social order and the economies of the region remained firmly tied to sugar production, despite the efforts of a small peasantry at diversification of food and export items such as cotton.[34]

Family laws and relations of power between workers and employers were based upon nineteenth century controls which were imposed and maintained by the small white male oligarchy of estate and factory owners and other business interests. They in alliance with the colonial administration stringently imposed their control over the island's majority. In the area involving the nineteenth century political systems, the discussion focuses on the problem of the system of colonial assemblies. This system of assemblies had been supported initially by the colonial government, but by the latter part of the nineteen century it came increasingly under attack as the cause of economic decline in the region. This discussion allows me to link the deteriorating social conditions and economic conditions of working people to economic and political stagnation in the island colony.[35]

Antigua and Barbudan planters stood alone in their decision to embrace full and immediate emancipation, but along with Antigua and Barbuda, the other British Colonies which chose the Apprenticeship System, imposed a new set of legal statutes governing labour and social relations. These legal changes were encoded in the laws governing the system of Apprenticeship. The system, imposed by the British Parliament, was instituted primarily to allay slave owner's fears of massive labour shortages and bankruptcy. While it was masqueraded as a system to help ex-slaves

34 Susan Lowes, 'The Peculiar Class'.

35 This argument is made by all contemporary writers of Caribbean societies referenced in this chapter including Brian Dyde, *A History of Antigua*; Douglas Hall, *Five of the Leewards*; O. Nigel Bolland, *The Politics of Labour*; and Franklyn Knight, *The Caribbean*.

ease into freedom, neither side were satisfied with the system and it was doomed to failure by its many contradictions. The system sought to establish a balance between freedom for ex-slaves, and access to labour for estate owners; it offered gradual freedom to a population which was demanding immediate freedom, low cost labour to a population, which had become very accustomed to exacted labour at no cost in wages.[36]

36 Ibid. See in particular Douglas Hall, *Five of the Leewards*, 23–24, 32–58.

CHAPTER 2

Sugar Monoculture in Decline

> Colonialism, slavery, plantation system have been crucial in shaping the social, political and economic institutions of the West Indies in addition to interclass and political relations.[1]

In this chapter I examine the role of sugar cane production in the economy and society of Antigua and Barbuda. The British Caribbean sugar economies experienced some disruptions in sugar production in the post-emancipation nineteenth century. For most of the islands sugar cane became one of many exports in the twentieth century. This was not the case for Antigua where sugar monoculture dominated into the mid-twentieth century. Because Antigua remained an island primarily focused on sugar cane, its society and economy reflected the peculiarities of sugar producers, a small peasant class, and economic dependence on one crop, a heavily coerced labour population, and insecure work conditions (sugar cane labour was largely seasonal and primarily manual). The primary social peculiarity of sugar monoculture was the dominance of the minority planter and merchant class over the economy and society.

In addition to the political economy of nineteenth- and twentieth-century Antigua and Barbuda this chapter focuses on social conditions, examining the relationship between the Colonial Office and the white oligarchy in Antigua and the Leeward Islands especially after the election of Crown Colony government in 1898. The Leeward Islands, despite their shrinking economic value in the larger global economy, remained central

1 Lawrence Nurse, *Trade Unionism and Industrial Relations*, 307.

sites of British investment through the first half of the twentieth century. This is also another peculiarity in relation to other sugar colonies in the region. In post emancipation Jamaica where sugar production plummeted from 1838 to the last decade of the century, peasant producers came to claim a crucial role in rebuilding the island's export economy, shifting that economy from sugar cane to banana and other fruit. This peasantry would be later captured by investors from the United States, as the United States from mid-nineteenth century replaced Britain as the central investor and a major market for the island's exports.[2] The relationship between colony and the imperial authorities was not fixed. The flexibility of this relationship is exposed in periods of economic and political crisis such as during the wars. Both World Wars had a dramatic impact on the nature of British imperialism and they changed dramatically some of the social and political structures in the British Caribbean colonies. Yet despite structural changes to labour and social relations (such as the emancipation of slavery, apprenticeship and full freedom) from 1834, the Antigua and Barbudan economy and society remained structurally similar to that of pre-1834 with the sugar plantation remaining the central economic unit and the owners and merchants maintaining their social dominance as a result. This post-emancipation economic history is quite different from that of the history of most of the British Caribbean sugar colonies in the nineteenth century. This issue is discussed further in this chapter where the particular case of Jamaica is singled out for further examination and comparison. While the economy of most of the Caribbean region from the 1880s to the 1930s, experienced some expansion, the result of new capital infusion, a few islands, Antigua and St. Kitts in the Leeward Islands and Barbados in the east, missed this process of modernization with its capital infusion, export diversification, and the concomitant social transformations.[3]

2 O. Nigel Bolland, *The Politics of Labour*, 115.

3 Roberto Cassá, 'The Economic Development of the Caribbean from 1880 to 1930', in Bridget Brereton, ed., *General History of the Caribbean. Volume V: The Caribbean in the Twentieth Century* (UNESCO Publishing and Macmillan Publishers Ltd. 2004), 7–41.

This process of modernization in the late nineteenth century in the rest of the region had a direct impact on the social and economic conditions of the ex-slave and ex-indentured populations, by contributing to the strengthening of a peasant class. On larger islands of the British Caribbean this process had begun with emancipation in 1834 and had further increased after the end of Apprenticeship in 1838. Where the late nineteenth century process contributed differently was that capital infusion and export diversification provided opportunities for peasants to participate directly in the export economy thereby engaging in more than subsistence agriculture.[4]

Even in the Spanish sugar colony of Cuba the peasant class gained strength in the late nineteenth century. The Cuban case was an exception in the region, as the tendency in sugar colonies throughout the region was the stagnancy of economic development of the peasantry. Peasant contributions ought not to be overstated however because where the peasantry gained ground in the export economy they were often not the only contributor to the export sector and what existed therefore was combined production from peasant producers as well as from plantations. Peasant producers did contribute significantly to the export sector and were crucial to reinvigorating some Caribbean economies, allowing these colonies to be able to reassert themselves in the world market.[5]

Politically Antigua and Barbuda experienced a dramatic change with the shift from local rule to Crown Colony government in 1898. Yet Crown Colony government did not bring the expected economic stimulus from foreign investors nor did it much improve the social conditions for the masses. Despite their loss of full control over local government, the planter class in Antigua and Barbuda maintained their hegemony through the class and race solidarity they were able to build with the colonial office and local colonial administrators. For example when the elected council became the nominated council in 1898, the governor who then acquired full power to nominate members to this political body, nominated only one non-white member. This council had had a non-white majority in 1897.[6]

4 Ibid., 10–15.

5 Ibid.

6 Susan Lowes, 'The Peculiar Class', 89.

By the early twentieth century Antiguan society had become a more hostile environment for middle class non-whites and enterprising blacks, and the shrinking population documented in the census exposes the response of these groups to local conditions. World War I further contributed to the shrinking population in the colony both from departures and death as record mortality rates expose the immense suffering among the island's majority. Interestingly, it was also the period in which the desperate conditions allowed for the creation of a peasant class, a group with access to land to work independently of estates, although many were encouraged to produce sugar cane to sell to the sugar factories. This peasant class would play an important role in social developments through the 1940s.

World War I also contributed to the rise in national and racial identity and solidarity among non-whites in the colonies. Recruited from both large and small colonies, thousands of non-white men were a part of the British West India Regiment. The discrimination experienced by the troops abroad would contribute to growing anti-imperial rhetoric and to radicalizing both recruits and those they came to influence in the Caribbean. The racial consciousness triggered by the war experience is demonstrated in Caribbean societies including Antigua and Barbuda despite the very small numbers of Leeward Islands men who joined the West India Regiment formed in 1915.

Racial consciousness and growing militancy and class solidarity were not the only changes affecting Antigua and Barbudan society in the postwar period. A great number of British citizens began to demonstrate interest in Caribbean societies. This interest was manifest in a desire to re-establish connections with the region and to influence conditions (improvement was the goal) in the Colonies. Among the greatest influence to be seen in the 1920s was that directed by the church and colonial administrators in imposing a particular European gender ideology upon Caribbean societies. Not surprisingly this ideology maintained (and perhaps expanded) the hegemony of the planter class in Caribbean societies. Gender ideology sought to further segregate and exclude women from the economy and limit their contributions to the society.

The Problem of Wage Labour

The post-emancipation history of the Caribbean is, like the physical region, fragmented.[7] Although the categories of West Indian colonies, Hispanic colonies and French colonies denote a particular political history in relation to Europe, they tell almost nothing about the internal history of these colonies. How similar were the experiences of labourers throughout the West Indian colonies? For those labouring in plantation economies through the nineteenth century, their experience of work conditions and social exclusion may have been more similar to say those of labourers in the plantation economy of nineteenth-century Cuba. But then again, the experience of plantation labourers in Barbados in the nineteenth century may have been more similar than say those of plantation labourers in the West Indian island of Trinidad. My point is that location and economy sometimes mattered more than did the political history.

Throughout the region the post-emancipation nineteenth century was a period marked by struggle on the part of the region's masses to establish themselves within their island's economies as free persons. What this freedom meant clearly involved: independence from estate owners, access to land upon which to work, control over their lives and the lives of family members as well as the ability to engage in the local or global economy or at a minimum to engage in subsistence agriculture.

Such efforts are perhaps best documented for the island of Jamaica, in large part as a result of Thomas Holt's 1992 monograph *The Problem of Freedom*, in which Holt highlights the economic fluctuations of sugar cane in the Caribbean region. His primary focus is on the impact of reduced production in post-emancipation Jamaica.

His economic evaluation of nineteenth- and twentieth-century Jamaica also includes an analysis of the global factors which affected the rise and decline of the peasant economy in post-emancipation period in the largest

7 Term used by Franklyn Knight in the subtitle to his book *The Caribbean: History of a Fragmented Nationalism.*

of the British Caribbean colonies.[8] In nineteenth century Jamaica critics of emancipation blamed emancipation and the ex-slaves for the decline of the island's sugar industry. Other observers advocated alternative explanations for the decline of the British Caribbean's greatest sugar producer through the nineteenth century. Among the most convincing of these explanations is the imperial introduction of 'free trade' – ending preferential treatment for British West Indian sugar in the Sugar Duties Act of 1846.[9] Jamaica was not the only sugar colony affected by the market adjustment. Sugar production throughout the entire region was dramatically reduced as estate owners sold and abandoned estates, unable to compete in a competitive global market with new producers in places like Mauritius and Cuba. Holt highlights the report of Governor Barkly's and in particular the position of Jamaican Richard Hill, a contributor to Barkly's dispatch to the Colonial Office. Hill rejected the popular argument which blamed the decline in sugar production in Jamaica on the Emancipation Act of 1834. Quite correctly he pointed out that the decline in sugar production still evident in 1854 had begun prior to 1834. He further argued that emancipation alone ought not to be blamed for the crisis in sugar, as the economic decline of the island (and of the region during the nineteenth century) was exacerbated by other decisions made by the Imperial government, such as free trade. Hill pointed out that post emancipation conditions such as free labour and compensation money, were economic advantages which the planters in Jamaica and other islands should have used to modernize sugar production, and to increase their income and production levels after 1834.[10] Holt's own conclusion that the world market played a crucial role in the declining production of sugar cane in post emancipation Jamaica is a convincing one. The island's production drastically plunged from the number one spot producing almost 50 per cent of British Caribbean sugar in 1820 to less than 20 per cent of sugar produced in the British West Indies in

8 Thomas C. Holt, *The Problem of Freedom: Race, Labor, and Politics in Jamaica and Britain, 1832–1938* (Baltimore, Maryland: Johns Hopkins Press, 1992).

9 Ibid., 117.

10 Holt, 117–123.

1900. Globally Jamaica had been responsible for producing some 20 per cent of the world sugar in 1820. By mid-century its contributions had been reduced to a dismal 2 per cent of world sugar production.[11]

Further, what Holt's study has highlighted is not an overall reduction across the island but instead a reduction as a result of geography. Sugar estates in the more fertile areas of the island not only remained in production following emancipation, but several actually increased production during this period. Much of the decline was the result of smaller estates on less fertile lands which were abandoned by their owners. He further noted that this decline had begun prior to emancipation and that the combination of emancipation, free trade and global competition pushed additional estates out of production.[12]

The other story to this production decline in sugar cane in Jamaica is the story of the rise in the peasant producers, not just as subsistence producers but also as export producers. In post-emancipation Jamaican, farmers gained access to lands with the decline of sugar production on the island and began to engage in the production of a variety of tropical fruits including bananas, limes, coconuts and pineapple. This peasant enterprise initiated by small farmers in eastern Jamaica, would come to capture a significant share of the island's export earnings by 1903 when it contributed 56 per cent of the export earnings of the island. This shift was largely the result of new markets in the United States, which by the twentieth century had become the most important trading partner next to Britain for Jamaican exports.[13] But the twentieth century conclusion to the rise of the Jamaican peasantry as crucial participants in the export economy is less than a victorious celebration of the successful economic initiatives of independent labourers and entrepreneurs. As the value of fruit exports increased the American investors who monopolized the transportation of the produce, were able to monopolize the entire process through their access to capital, and their political relations within the colony. By the

11 Ibid., 119.

12 Ibid., 121–123.

13 Ibid., 348 and O. Nigel Bolland, *The Politics of Labour*, 115.

end of the nineteenth century one company, the United Fruit Company (UFC) controlled fruit production on the island. The emergence of the UFC marked the end of the enterprising peasant producers in Jamaica, many of whom were reduced to working for wages for the company or left rural areas for the cities.[14]

The economic decline documented by nineteenth-century scholars and eyewitnesses for Jamaica, was magnified in scope and impact on the small Leeward Island colonies. Unlike Jamaica which experienced economic rebound after the drop in sugar production, the falling sugar production in Antigua would have a direct impact on the lives of working people for over one century. Despite the constant complaints by sugar estate owners of economic hardship, scholars examining the Antiguan economy reject the complaints as exaggerated and instead argue that even despite reduction in production, these employers were able to enjoy more for less. Susan Lowes has emphasized the commitment of the oligarchy to keep the work force in line in Antigua and Barbuda. She noted that licensing laws and taxes were part of this effort and that additionally these were used to shift financial burden of administering the colony onto the workers. Additionally she noted contradictions in the claims of employers that reduced production caused them financial crisis, noting that estate owners were using fewer labourers to produce more sugar in some years. Additionally, the real crisis in sugar production was the result of natural disaster which had nothing to do with the labour force. Note for example her production numbers for the 1890s in Table 1.

14 This history is documented by Holt for Jamaica but other scholars including Aviva Chomsky has written a history of the United Fruit Company (UFC) in the Caribbean and Central America. This company controlled fruit production, both in Jamaica and throughout Central America. Aviva Chomsky, *West Indian Workers and the United Fruit Company in Costa Rica, 1870–1940* (Louisiana State University, 1995).

Table 1 Antigua Sugar Production in the Late Nineteenth Century

Antigua Sugar Production in the Late Nineteenth Century Sample of five years of Production				
1891	1895	1898	1899	1900
12,091	7,219	6,928	10,041	7,603
Source: Susan Lowes. 'The Peculiar Class'				

The impact of the economic decline of sugar production on Antiguan workers was unemployment, underemployment and shrinking wages. In the unstable wage economy of the nineteenth century, Antiguan workers suffered particularly because they had few options outside of estate work and many remained dependent upon the estate to maintain themselves and their children. Shifting wage rates in nineteenth century Antigua demonstrate the power of employers over workers.

An Island Suited Only to Sugar Cane?

At emancipation in 1834 estates offered wage of 6d to workers. This rate goes up to 9d as estate owners competed for skilled and stable labour force, with some estates paying as high as 1s through 1846 when wages fell back down to 6d.[15]

Colonial administrators insisted throughout the post-emancipation period that because of the 'uncertainty of rainfall' Antigua was suited only to sugar cane production.[16] This was a view they shared or adopted from

15 Susan Lowes, 'The Peculiar Class', 47.

16 'Antigua Plan for Development and Welfare: 1949' (hereafter HD 6595A). This report in the TUC Library, documents the islands economic history from the late nineteenth century.

local estate owners and it remained the justification for limiting agricultural diversification from sugar cane to other crops. Throughout the first half of the twentieth century sugar remained the dominant export crop and the principal source of employment and of revenue for the Antiguan economy. While sugar remained dominant, cotton production was slowly being introduced after World War I so that by the 1940s cotton had become a subsidiary crop primarily produced by peasant cultivators. The Antiguan labour force involved in cotton production was primarily women and children. These cotton farmers laboured on privately owned lands, including estates, and as Walter Citrine's inquiries would expose in 1938 these peasants played no role in the cotton market and were excluded from any representation on the local Cotton Growers Association, a largely white and male club.[17]

The title 'king' that had been applied to the monoculture production economy of the Caribbean – suggests that sugar was the sole economic engine that drove these economies – but more importantly, *king sugar* reflected not just an economic dominance but psychological one as well. In the West Indies sugar production had become so deeply ingrained in the society that even when it became clear that it was no longer economically viable those who controlled the society remained blindly committed to an unproductive monarchy. The halcyon days of sugar cane production in the eighteenth century blocked planters from accepting twentieth-century realities. Eighteenth century production figures become an important marker for all future years.

It is difficult to assess the economic condition of the island in the twentieth century, as all profits were compared to eighteenth century population and trade figures. The total exports of 1787 at 592,597 pounds of sugar would become the twentieth century albatross, keeping sugar estate owners committed to repeating the glory days of high sugar production. Because of this situation it is important to question many of the nineteenth and twentieth century reports of a sugar economy in crisis. How do the production levels actually match up relative to wages paid, and profits earned by

17 In Walter Citrine's 1938 interview with the Antiguan Cotton Growers Association.

estate and factory owners and their investors? After the eighteenth century no sugar or rum production and no population figures could match the expectation of a successful economy for estate owners in Antigua unless these numbers could meet or exceed that of 1787.[18]

While the 1787 production figure remained elusive there were some relatively good years for production through 1891 before drought and infestation dramatically impacted the 'Cinderella' environment of the island.[19] These natural disasters were followed by inflation abroad which increased the cost of imports especially food items to the island. This vulnerability to outside forces was another problem of a monoculture economy. The crisis in sugar production and inflation abroad impacted all segments of the society and the action of the local legislature in the 1890s economic crisis further heightened the crisis. The local governing body acting out of its own self-interest reduced financial support for services such as public dispensary, schools and civil service posts and salaries.[20]

There is much correlation between the global economy, the local economy and the suffering of the working people of the British Caribbean throughout the first half of the twentieth century. In this sugar economy little was given to workers over the basic wage and even in a good economy the peasants were barely able to feed, clothe and house their families. Whether the economy was good or bad little changed in the conditions of the working people. The estates did not pass on any of their profits to workers and as the 1938 Royal commission would uncover in 1938 the peasants and workers on the sugar and cotton estates of the region were completely excluded from any benefits of the economy. Peasants and workers on Antigua suffered during period when profits were high for estate owners and investors and they suffered miserably when there were no profits and when losses were experienced. In addition to the challenges posed by nature to the sugar economies of the West Indies, it is clear that imperial policies played a close second to weather and other natural disasters. This

18 HD 6595A.

19 Susan Lowes, 'The Peculiar Class', 66: the 'Cinderella' term borrowed from Lowes. See discussion of sugar production in the 1890s.

20 Ibid.

was largely the perception in the colonies, a perception supported by the region's economic history. The British Parliament greatly influenced the fate and fortunes of English Caribbean plantation owners and workers. But the Imperial government represented two faces on the same coin for it both supported and threatened the Caribbean oligarchy. This influence was not always positive to plantation owners and their allies as was the case of the Emancipation Act of 1834, which abolished British Caribbean slavery and the 1846 Sugar Duties Act which opened up West Indian planters to the competition of free trade. The perception of the masses of the Imperial government on the other hand, was more complicated. They saw the Imperial government as alternating roles between paternalism and indifference. To workers, many of whom were women and children in twentieth-century Antigua, the British Parliament and the Colonial Office were the only powers that could intercede in their behalf. It was in the power of the Imperial government to improve their work conditions, to provide them with better wages and to alleviate their suffering under an abusive legal system. They waited patiently for the Imperial government to intercede.

The social, political, and economic institutions of the colony remained into the third decade of the twentieth century focused on the needs of the island's small elite of landowners, business men and merchants. The interest of the island's majority was largely overlooked. True, Colonial administrators periodically called for money to be allocated for the improvement of education and morals of the majority but their real impact was in their ability to protect the interests of the minority population.

The political and financial needs of the colonial elite and of British investors were the primary preoccupation of the British Parliament and the Colonial Office, and remained so until the 1930s when numerous instances of worker unrest throughout the Caribbean forced metropolitan investigations that would eventually result in the legalization of trade unions in 1941.

The Trades Union Congress (TUC) played a crucial role in the legalization process for trade unions in the Caribbean, through its representative on the 1938 Royal Commission, Sir Walter Citrine.[21] Throughout the first

21 Sir Walter Citrine microfilm diary and notes (reels 8 & 9) hereafter MF 226–227.

half of the twentieth century the rural and urban work force of the region continued to play a crucial role in a global export market for sugar and cotton; but the labouring populations had neither global nor British metropolitan representatives to promote their interest. The British Parliament and local courts had traditionally held the role of labour regulator and this role had been primarily directed at protecting the interest of capital over labour. Not until the 1920s was the question of Caribbean labour raised by the British Parliament with the Colonial Office.

This was largely a result of pressure by the International Labour Organization (ILO), the British Labour Party and the TUC. The 1925 Labour Commonwealth Conference was the watershed event that helped develop the colonial policies of the British Labour Party.[22] These early efforts met limited success as they were focused on the few Caribbean colonies such as British Guiana and Trinidad, with a large industrial labour force and established trade unions. In the smaller Caribbean islands, organized labour could not legally exist until 1940 following the recommendations of the 1938 Royal Commission. Sir Walter Citrine, as a Commission member, would become an advocate for labour in the war years following the Commission investigations. Thanks in large part to the publicity generated by the Colonial Office in the *Gazette* and by local publications, Sir Walter Citrine's advocacy on the behalf of the Caribbean working people quickly spread throughout the British Caribbean, so much so that his reputation preceded him from one island to another. Given the oppressive work and social conditions in the colonies it is not surprising that Caribbean workers were quick to embrace Citrine and the TUC as instruments for change and as a powerful ally for mediating against the power of the plantation oligarchy.[23]

The British Caribbean plantation economies were by the twentieth century way past their political and economic prime. No longer the primary

22 O. Nigel Bolland, *The Politics of Labour*, 144–145. See also Chapter 3 of this work for discussion on labour and political economy.

23 Marjorie Nicholson, *The TUC Overseas*; MF 226–227; O. Nigel Bolland, *The Politics of Labour*.

site of British capital investment, the Caribbean colonies competed with other export economies for British capital as well as other foreign investment. US investments, particularly after the 1898 Spanish-American War, largely focused on the sugar economies of the former Spanish colonies of Puerto Rico and Cuba and on fruit production in Jamaica. The Leeward Islands sugar economies were a hard sell for investors, even those not interested in big returns on their investment.[24]

The decline of British Caribbean sugar economies into the twentieth century did not diminish local political and economic power of the sugar elite, nor did it lessen the commitment of the Colonial Office to support these economies and their underlying social systems. Through the twentieth century, the working people in Antigua and Barbuda struggled under conditions that had improved only slightly from slavery. It is therefore no surprise that local workers saw the relationship between the crown and the Creole elite not as much a partnership but clearly in terms of an alliance with shifting power systems. By the twentieth century workers in Antigua and Barbuda explained their terrible economic condition in terms of the overthrow of the Imperial government by local politicians, this despite the return of Crown Colony government in the late nineteenth century. Local peasants used terms such as 'planter kill king and rule country' to express what they saw as the overwhelming power of the planter elite.[25]

It is clear that the partnership between the British government and the plantation elite that had been established under slavery and lasted for some three centuries was still firmly in place in the twentieth century. It was not until the rise of Labour in the Metropole and the post World War I ideology of compassionate colonialism that social conditions, in particular the conditions of the common order, become the focus of the British Parliament and international labour organizations.[26]

24 Franklyn Knight, *The Caribbean*; Bonham Richardson, *The Caribbean in the Wider World: 1492–1992* (New York: Cambridge University Press, 1992).

25 Smith and Smith, *To Shoot Hard Labour*, 37.

26 Marjorie Nicholson, *The TUC Overseas*; Malcolm Cross and Gad Heuman, *Labour in the Caribbean*; 'The Soulbury Commission Report' (CO 152/520 4).

Antiguan Society from Crown Colony to World War I

By the end of the nineteenth century Antiguan society had undergone a series of dramatic changes as a result of the shift from slavery to free labour. The white oligarchy used their political power vis-à-vis local assemblies, to maintain control of the colony. The hegemony they established was achieved through laws, by labour contracts and by social practice. This hegemony was maintained into the twentieth century, despite workers' attempts to organize and resist in a myriad of ways. The Antiguan oligarchy's success in dominating Antiguan society is demonstrated not only by their control over estate labourers, but also in their destruction of the non-white middle class, a group which had gained in size and political power from emancipation through the 1890s. By the end of the nineteenth century with all earlier opportunities for their survival as a class eliminated, this group largely disappeared. Some of this class migrated from the island, while others lost class status. The construction of a racially exclusive ruling class is therefore re-established in Antigua by the end of the nineteenth century.[27]

The emergence of this racially exclusive class was facilitated by the political shift from local rule to Crown Colony government. Despite expectations that Crown Colony would improve the social conditions for the masses, and would stimulate the island's economy, the economic crisis continued, intensified in the twentieth century particularly during the two world wars, periods which greatly exposed the inequality and the desperate conditions of Antiguan workers.[28]

27 Susan Lowes, 'The Peculiar Class', 126. This subject is the focus of this 1994 dissertation. See her statement on the absence of connection between the nineteenth- and twentieth-century middle class. 'At some point in the mid nineteenth century something had happened to set back the progress of non-whites; indeed the setback had been so severe that the non-white middle class of the twentieth century appeared, at least to its members, to have been born anew'.

28 Herman Merivale, *Lectures on Colonization and Colonies* (New York, A. M. Kelley, 1967); and from observers who travelled through the territory: John Davy, who travelled the islands between 1845–1848; and Danish observer Louis Rothe.

Leeward Island societies were more than mere shadows of the colonial documents such as the Annual Reports, Blue Books and Census. These documents, numbered and ordered by administrators missed the lived lives, the ongoing resistance, and the oppressive social conditions which drove men off the island (hidden in census reports documenting the shrinking male population across race and classes). In addition to the shortages that exacerbated the poverty among the island's majority, the War created opportunities for some land redistribution, a tactic designed to quell the growing unrest among labourers. Land redistribution created a small peasant class which along with estate workers orchestrated the first demonstrations and riots in twentieth-century Antigua. In addition to class solidarity, the inklings of Black Nationalism also became evident in the region following the War. This chapter examines the relationship between the Empire and the colony and the nature of the impact of this relationship on the workers and peasants throughout the first three decades of the twentieth century.

The theoretical literature on British colonialism in the Caribbean context has been greatly advanced by the works of imperial studies scholars such as Frederick Cooper (1996) and David Kenneth Fieldhouse (1996). Regional scholars including Elsa Goveia, Mindie Lazarus-Black, Rhoda Reddock and Caroline Carmody examining women in slave society in Antigua, the law and labour conditions in the region; have shown the ways in which the colonial experience in this isolated region of the British Empire was crucial because of the larger impact which the island had on the Metropole and other parts of the Empire. Contract Acts and family laws, adopted first in Antigua and Barbuda, would be later adapted in other Caribbean colonies, in Africa as well as non-British colonies in the region. As far away as Africa, techniques of labour control similar to those used in the Caribbean would be applied. These connections show the links between the Caribbean colonies and the larger world. The exchange of commodities and people across the Atlantic and even the Indian Ocean facilitated these global links and exchanges which were very relevant for Antigua and Barbuda and the Leeward Islands throughout the twentieth century. From Asia, Africa and Britain administrators and travellers and a wide range of commodities flowed making a real link within the British Empire. Such movement also took place regionally as administrators and travellers, island-hopped from the southern tip of the archipelago to the most northern island of the Bahamas and to the Atlantic islands of Bermuda.

Throughout the twentieth century, the Colonial Office was kept apprised of conditions in the Caribbean, through reports of governors, administrators and unofficial sources including land and estate owners and others with business interests on the island. *The Annual Report* to the Colonial Office for the Leeward Islands was one of the reports prepared by regional administrators. The *Blue Books* were compilations of reports which addressed economic conditions, population (most recent census was included), as were crime and prison reports and other summaries of activities. While much of the information contained in the Blue Book reports were repeated from the censuses, the reports were more heavily focused on the political economy of the region, demonstrating that the economies of even the small island colonies, remained of primary concern to the Colonial Office and the British Government.[29]

As discussed in the first section of this chapter Antigua and Barbuda is unique in nineteenth-century British Caribbean history in that the island's economy remained a monoculture economy into the twentieth century. On Antigua sugar cane production fluctuated in the nineteenth century, but unlike Jamaica where the production declined continually through much of the century following emancipation and apprenticeship, in Antigua production went in both directions both up and down with some years experiencing tremendous increases even in cases exceeding some pre-emancipation periods.[30]

By the end of the nineteenth century, the island was clearly to remain a sugar monoculture colony. This fact further supports the argument that money was still being made by Antiguan sugar producers. To offset reductions in production and to boost the quality of sugar produced on the island, the colonial office agreed to finance the building of a factory on

29 Annual reports include specific dispatches on a range of topics. Letters on local acts and comprehensive reports known as the *Blue Books* were crucial to the Colonial Office administration.

30 O. Nigel Bolland, *The Politics of Labour*, 115.

the island. The Antigua Sugar Factory, LTD (ASF) established by local and foreign investors in 1903, would become the island's economic engine through most of the twentieth century.[31] As in the case of Jamaica where the company would reduce peasants to wage labourers; ASF by the 1940s controlled the processing of sugar cane on Antigua and had built up such a reputation in the colonial office that the office sought the advice of ASF management on the island's budget as well as other issues.[32]

With the establishment of the ASF the colonial office signalled its commitment to sugar monoculture into the twentieth century and even with suggestions from the Norman Commission, the same Commission that had recommended the establishment of the sugar factory, that peasant production and some alternatives to sugar cane be explored; the economy never wavered from sugar. This perhaps was one of the reasons why the export economy of Antigua and Barbuda survived intact. The unwavering commitment it received, as well as the focused target of the limited foreign investment.[33]

Because they refused to pursue alternative exports estate owners and merchants in Antigua embraced new technologies and investment strategies for the sugar export economy. In Antigua where land and in particular fertile land for sugar production were limited estate owners maintained control over land and the processing of sugar cane by syndication and by the establishment of a central sugar factory. The ASF and the Syndicate Estates were a corporate response to the challenges being experienced by

31 The two primary investors in the Antigua Sugar Factory (ASF) were sugar moguls Thomas DuBuisson and George Moody Stuart. DuBoisson owned and operated estates in Guyana while Moody Stuart owned and managed estates in Antigua in addition to the management of the ASF.

32 Communications from colonial office with Moody Stuart 3 June 1919 CO 152/368. Additionally see discussion on ASF by Susan Lowes, 89–117.

33 Colonial Office reports on sugar industry and on Caribbean economies include the Wood Report of 1922 (Wood Report); Report of the Sugar industry of the West Indies 1930 (Lord Oliver and D. M. Semple Report). Additionally this issue has been discussed in length in sources such as Bonham C. Richardson, *The Caribbean in the Wider World*, 38; O. Nigel Bolland, *The Politics of Labour*; Smith and Smith. *To Shoot Hard Labour*; Susan Lowes, 'The Peculiar Class'.

the plantation economies in the Caribbean. In the larger plantation economies such as Jamaica and Guyana similar entities emerged. The United Fruit Company in the case of Jamaica and Bookers in Guyana were able to dominate the economies of these islands subverting the efforts of peasant producers by their wealth, size and by their ability to gain the backing of colonial administrators.[34] At the start of World War I Caribbean workers already facing high unemployment and under-employment rates experienced enormous deprivations. Accounts of starvation, suicide and tremendous suffering abound in the few oral and written accounts left by early twentieth-century workers in the region. Most describe a desperate population of men, women and children trapped in dilapidated estate housing or inadequate private housing with little alternative to subsistence agriculture or estate work. Estate owners and colonial administrators wrote and spoke of the absence of profits from the estates and other enterprises, and the hardship of having to pay wages to workers. Workers on the 'quiet isle' suffered immensely; children and adults weakened by lack of food were vulnerable to diseases resulting from malnutrition.[35]

Shrinking populations, like shrinking profits was a major preoccupation of twentieth-century administrators and investors. In post-emancipation Leeward Islands growing numbers of estate owners sold or abandoned their estates and left the colonies for Europe or Canada. Workers on the other hand had few options and the opportunity to leave the island for work elsewhere was rare and for many was the very last option taken. It was mostly the whites and middle class coloured men who left the island, the latter group departing in greater numbers in the late nineteenth century. The cause and consequence of their departure will be discussed elsewhere in this book. The census reports prepared every ten years document the

34 O. Nigel Bolland, *The Politics of Labour*, 119.

35 Primary account of the twentieth-century challenges faced in Antigua documented by Smith and Smith, *To Shoot Hard Labour*; O. Nigel Bolland, *The Politics of Labour* highlights the fact that Antigua was a quiet island and that the labour disturbances occurred in other islands. Malcolm Cross and Gad Heuman, *Labour in the Caribbean*. Even V. C. Bird addressed the issue of the quiet labour force by his reference to the island as a graveyard in his Minority Report to the Soulsbury Report.

falling population, a phenomenon which was frequently commented on by colonial administrators and visiting Commissioners.

By the end of World War I Antigua and Barbuda held the record among British Caribbean colonies for both high mortality rates and falling population rates. The rate of population decrease in Antigua and Barbuda was not necessarily tied to mortality as many left the island in search of work or better opportunities. As documented by the administrators in the 1911 census the decrease of the population of the island since 1901 was of great concern. This decrease since 1901 was 2,784. Since 1891 he insisted it was no less than 4,725. 'This is very regrettable, and what makes the features of the case worse, is that decrease is to be found principally in the male population, this having decreased by 3,266 while the female population has decreased by only 1,459 during the same twenty year period.'[36] In Table 2, created from the population information of the 1911 Census, I highlight the island wide gap between the male and female population by distinguishing between population and gender in St. Philips parish where many of my informants were born and raised, and St. John, the island capital and a destination for many of these informants who eventually migrated as adults to this urban area.[37]

The population was distinguished by urban and rural location but the distribution and sex distinctions in the urban and rural areas greatly reflected the overall population. For example a comparison of the population by gender of rural St. Philips to St. John Parish show those women were in both cases the majority sex both in the white and in the black and coloured populations. St. Philips parish was home to a number of sugar estates including Lavington, Lyons, Montpelier and Gaynors. Many white administrators and employers of the island colony resided in St. John which had the largest white population as the capital of the colony.

36 *Report on the Census of Antigua and its Dependencies of Barbuda and Redonda 1911*: 4. (Hereafter Census of 1911).

37 Ibid.

Table 2 Race and Gender in the Census of 1911

<table>
<tr><th></th><th>St. Philips Male</th><th>St. Philips Female</th><th>St. John Parish Male</th><th>St. John Parish Female</th><th>St. John City Male</th><th>St. John City Female</th></tr>
<tr><td>Whites</td><td>8</td><td>23</td><td>57</td><td>54</td><td>281</td><td>331</td></tr>
<tr><td>Black & coloured</td><td>395</td><td>1,628</td><td>2,768</td><td>3,386</td><td>2,814</td><td>4,484</td></tr>
<tr><td colspan="7">Census total for Antigua 31,394 and for Barbuda 871</td></tr>
<tr><td colspan="7">Population by race for the islands of Antigua and Barbuda 1911</td></tr>
<tr><td colspan="3">White</td><td colspan="4">1,015</td></tr>
<tr><td colspan="3">Coloured</td><td colspan="4">4,932</td></tr>
<tr><td colspan="3">Black</td><td colspan="4">27,224</td></tr>
<tr><td colspan="7">Source: Census of Antigua, 1911</td></tr>
</table>

As the population information shows the larger white presence on the island, both the male and female white population was urban, located in the city and parish of St. John. It is also important to note that the white female population outnumbers the white male population in St. John city and white males in St. John parish barely outnumber white females. The female majority of the island was in both the white as well as the black and coloured population.

World War I had an enormous impact on the society and contributed to raising race and social class awareness among Caribbean peoples. In Antigua where *the enemy* and the workers figured prominently in the concerns of white Creoles and colonial administrators, the efforts to maintain control over workers during the war, served to heighten workers' solidarity and activism. The efforts to control the workers was reflected in proclamations and restrictions imposed upon the working people. The Leeward Islands Gazette for 7 March 1918 posted the anxieties of administrators and estate owners. 'A Proclamation' signed by the Acting Colonial Secretary and the Provost Marshall of the region Thomas Alexander Best, outlined the problems facing the presidency and his administration's position on the issue.[38]

> Whereas I am deeply concerned for the welfare of the labourers of Antigua and the prosperity of the Island and am desirous of composing the differences which have lately arisen between the labourers and their employers. I have determined to appoint an impartial Commission to enquire and advise what shall be a fair settlement of these differences.
>
> PENDING THE REPORT of the said Commission, I call upon all loyal and law abiding subjects of his Majesty the King to return to their daily work and to refrain from all conduct likely to disturb the Peace and add to the distress occasioned by the War.[39]

In addition the colonial administration posted new regulations in the *Gazette* concerning labourers, regulations directed at those seeking to organize workers. These regulations were greatly aided by the existence of the war and fell quite conveniently under the 'provisions of the Defense of the Presidency Ordinance' of 1917.

> 1. Any person who shall by means of threats intimidation or otherwise, induce or attempt to induce any agricultural labourer to refrain from performing his work as such labourer or shall cause or attempt to cause any such labourer to abandon his work shall be guilty of an offence under this Regulation and shall be liable on conviction thereof to be imprisoned for a period not exceeding one year.
>
> 2. Any person who
>   a. By word of mouth or in writing or in any newspaper, circular or other printed publication causes or attempts to cause dissatisfaction or unrest amongst the agricultural labourers of this Presidency or any of them, or
>   b. By means whatsoever interferes with, delays or prevents the reaping of any crop shall be guilty of an offence under this Regulation and shall be liable on conviction thereof to be imprisoned for any period not exceeding one year.[40]

38 *Leeward Islands Gazette*, 7 March 1918.

39 Ibid.

40 Ibid.

It was a thorough regulation that sought to end any attempt of workers to organize. Those workers who defied the regulations were imprisoned as were workers who engaged in strike action and or other punitive action against employers. A period of one year imprisonment was promised for those who 'interferes with, delays or prevents the reaping of any crop', for those who 'trespass on property and root-up, cut, break or in any other manner cause to be severed from the soil, any plant or root used for the food of man or beast.' Workers and their leaders faced immediate arrest and trial by a Court Martial for such offences.[41]

When World War I began Antigua was already suffering grave economic hardships. The war exacerbated the shortages and heightened social tensions on the island. The economic crisis which began in the late nineteenth century and which had triggered labour disturbances in the region had been the result of a drop in the price for sugar on the world market. Leeward Islands employers had responded in characteristic fashion by reducing wages and the size of the workforce. Antiguan workers already faced unemployment, underemployment and low wages, the shortages and further reduction of wages caused by the War would push their situation past crisis into desperation.

By 1917 they resorted to uncharacteristically bold action in order to protest the depressed wages and their unfair work conditions. Organized protests in Antigua and Barbuda, St. Kitts and elsewhere in the Caribbean was as much a sign of the desperate economic situation for workers as it was an expression of working class solidarity. On the island of St. Kitts in 1896 and 1917, cane workers revolted against unfair wage and working conditions. In a collective show of protest they deserted their workplaces and gathered in large groups to demonstrate. Several cane fields were burned and when police and militia moved to stop them the demonstrators threw stones and bottles at them. These incidents are referred to in several sources including Cross and Heuman (1988), Bolland (2000) and Lewis (1974).[42] This

41 Ibid.

42 Malcolm Cross and Gad Heuman, *Labour in the Caribbean*; O. Nigel Bolland. *The Politics of Labour*; Patrick Lewis, *A Historical Analysis of the Development of the*

labour revolt was put down brutally by the combined forces of the colonial administration and employers. While the revolt had been a response to desperate wage and working conditions, the state refused to deal with the cause of the actions, and no attempt was made to address the demand for increased wages which had put workers on the streets. Instead the state in St. Kitts, as it would elsewhere in the Leeward Islands presidency, dealt with the workers' actions as a case of civil disorder, and severely punished 'ringleaders' and others involved in organizing the protests. Throughout the first four decades of the twentieth-century workers in the Leeward Island presidency could expect no relief from their depressed condition and the state response to their demands continued to be brutal and punitive especially at their attempts to organize for collective action against employers.[43]

St. Kitts was only the beginning and over the next nineteen years the labouring people of the British Caribbean were provoked to revolt against unfair wages, and work conditions. In the year following attempts by St. Kitts estate workers, to form a Union in 1917, estate workers on Antigua organized a march and strike. This action mentioned above was in response to the decision made by estate owners with sanction of the state to change the method of paying cane cutters. State militia and police violently broke up the march killing and injuring several people.[44]

The World War I West India Regiment

Military service during the war further exposed the problem of race and colonialism. Many works on twentieth-century labour protests in the Caribbean have insisted on a central role for demobilized West Indian

---

Union Party System in the Commonwealth Caribbean, 1935–1965 (Thesis: University of Cincinnati, 1974).

43 O. Nigel Bolland, *The Politics of Labour*: Malcolm Cross and Gad Heuman, *Labour in the Caribbean*; CO 152/520/4.

44 Ibid.

soldiers in the 1930s labour activism without making any direct connection between leaders of the labour protests and World War I military service. It is clear however that the war experience was an eye-opener for Caribbean soldiers and for the Caribbean population. Through letters, reports and local papers, the Caribbean population learned of the discrimination being experienced by their volunteers. This further increased the unrest among local populations whether they had relations involved in the war efforts or not.[45]

The British West India Regiment had been mobilized to serve in World War I in 1915. Of the over fifteen thousand recruits from the Caribbean the Leeward Islands contributed the smallest number, two hundred twenty nine. The small size of the Leeward Island contingent was no doubt the result of the desperate conditions in the region. Low wages, high unemployment and high cost of food items made it difficult for the state to recruit qualified volunteers, for many able bodied men were unwilling to leave their families without support from their wages while they went off fighting in unknown lands.

The Leeward Island recruits, who numbered some two hundred and twenty-nine were for the most part experiencing life outside of the region for the first time when they joined British forces in Europe and Africa. According to a letter quoted in Fraser, one group of soldiers from the Leeward Islands wrote complaining about their treatment stating 'We had all along imagined ourselves to be Imperial troops'. Disillusioned by their experience of discrimination from British soldiers with whom they served they returned to the West Indies as different persons. In addition to the changes wrought by the trauma of the war their exposure to racial discrimination and to European political and labour ideology, such as communism, radicalized this group.[46] Racism and segregation marred the experience for the West Indian soldiers who served with imperial forces. In Europe, Africa and the Mediterranean where they were stationed, West

45 Peter Fraser, 'Some Effects of the First World War on the British West Indies', *Caribbean Societies* (1:29, 1982): 26.

46 W. F. Eklins, 'A Source of Black Nationalism in the Caribbean: The Revolt of the British West Indies Regiment at Taranto, Italy', *Science and Society*, 35:1 (1970): 99–103; Peter Fraser. 'Some Effects of the First World War'.

Indian volunteers were constantly reminded by white British soldiers that they were not their equals. They suffered verbal abuse and rejection, and were segregated by housing, and assignment of duties. West Indian volunteers who had expected their military service to be against the enemies of the Empire found instead that rather than combat duties they were assigned service duties to British soldiers. In addition to the indignity of service duties they were further appalled by the decision to pay them less than British soldiers for their service. The discriminatory pay was to be one of the most contentious issues among both volunteers and the large black and coloured population in the colonies who followed very closely the experience of their volunteers in the war.

By the end of the War those volunteers who returned to the Caribbean were overwhelmingly radicalized by their experience. For many their experience served to expand the gap between them and their Creole and white counterparts as British subjects or citizens. Back in the Caribbean these men sought ways to change the nature of their dependence and subordination to whites in their home colonies.[47]

Table 3 Leeward Island Volunteers and World War I West India Regiment of 1915

WORLD WAR I WEST INDIA REGIMENT OF 1915	
Caribbean volunteers	15,601
Leeward Islands volunteers	229
Deaths	1,256
Volunteers wounded	697
Service rank of volunteers	
Officers	397
Other ranks	15,204
Source: Eklins (1970)	

47 W. F. Eklins, 'A Source of Black Nationalism in the Caribbean'.

The fact that fifteen thousand men, many of whom had never travelled to Europe and had no investment in European politics volunteered to put their lives on the line was a factor of the feelings of patriotism and the propaganda targeting the region. Many signed up hopeful and optimistic about the impact of their service to the Empire, yet, despite the hope and optimism it quickly became apparent to the black and coloured volunteers that their military experience was to reflect their marginalized and exploited status at home. The assignments of the West India regiment were largely non-combatant. Many including the soldiers themselves felt their assignments reflected British concern that they not fight against white troops. Most served as labour battalions under direction of white officers. In addition to non-combatant service in the war the West India regiment faced wage discrimination. When in 1918, a 50 per cent wage increase was approved in the British Parliament for British soldiers, the raise excluded the 'native soldiers' a category to which West Indian soldiers was assigned. The exclusion from the wage increase offered to white soldiers and their ongoing experience of racism, the assignment of humiliating duties, cleaning up after white soldiers, and the absence of black officers from the officer corps of the British army, fuelled resentment and anger on the part of black soldiers.

Responses varied and the most extreme involved the 9th Battalion stationed in Taranto, southern Italy – which in December 1918 attacked their officers and penned a petition to the Secretary of State for the colonies. Some one hundred eighty Sergeants are said to have signed the petition. The group received no response from the Secretary of state for the colonies, instead their unit was disbanded and many were returned to the Caribbean.[48] In 1919 other members of the West India regiment formed the 'Caribbean League'. This was a radical group which sought a collective response to their grievances and which is reputed to have advocated the use of force to gain their objectives. The members of the Caribbean League struck for better wages; and demanded the assignment of black officers. When news of their organization reached the military some of its members were charged and convicted of mutiny and given prison sentences

48 Ibid.

ranging from three to twenty years. One member was executed by firing squad.[49] The agitations and protests by these volunteers led to concern by colonial administrators about their return to the West Indies. In the Leeward Islands and elsewhere Governors warned that returning men were likely to create a great deal of discontent among the local population. These concerns raised by local officials with the Colonial Office led to the granting of equal pay to West Indian volunteers. This pay raise was secured by the Colonial Office which hoped that the money would stem the belligerent nature of the returning volunteers. In addition some West Indian governors had their police and militia on alert for returning soldiers. In Jamaica a war ship was made available to local authorities and there was even discussion by the local legislature of arming police with machine-guns in ready for returning soldiers. The tensions surrounding the demobilized soldiers heightened racial and anti-colonial feelings in the colonies in the post war era. Following the war many joined Black Nationalist organizations including the UNIA and Black Cross Nurses organizations. Others became labour activists and political leaders. While there are no direct links to the Caribbean League volunteers and the Leeward Islands that I have been able to uncover. These events affected the entire region, even the Leeward Islands where volunteers comprised only 2 per cent of the entire regiment which served during the war.[50]

Conclusion

The uniqueness of Antigua and Barbuda in the Leeward Islands and the British West Indies, through the nineteenth century was not just the result of its size (Antigua is one of the smallest though by no means the smallest

49 Ibid.

50 Malcolm Cross and Gad Heuman, *Labour in the Caribbean*; Caroline Carmody, 'The Peculiar Class'; O. Nigel Bolland, *The Politics of Labour*; Marjorie Nicholson, *The TUC Overseas*.

of the British colonies in the Caribbean), or the act of immediate emancipation in 1834. The island's history and economy was further influenced differently by the maintenance of its sugar monoculture into the twentieth century. Despite the periodic decline in sugar cane production after 1838, no real sugar crisis can be claimed for the small island nation which despite its size and lack of outside investments and agricultural diversification maintained the ability to generate profits for investors from sugar cane production into the twentieth century. The economy clearly influences the society and in the society of the small Leeward Island a tiny elite of sugar estate owners and sugar factory managers, merchants and investors maintained social dominance with the support of the colonial office and colonial administrators well into the first half of the twentieth century. Despite this racially exclusive and class-based alliance between the Colonial Office and business interests; a small peasant class would emerge after World War I and would ally itself with working class and middle class non-whites on the island. World War I participation by Caribbean volunteers contributed to heightened class and racial consciousness in the region. These further contributed to the emergence of class awareness and solidarity among working people on the island.

Even before the arrival of the 1938 Royal Commission to the Caribbean, workers in Antigua as well as other islands of the British Caribbean had begun to form union type organizations, to advocate for their interests as a working class. Additionally they had begun to advocate for adult suffrage and for the right to participate in their society. Despite the gender ideology which advocated a limited place for women in the society and economy of the island colony in the twentieth century, the island's female majority played a significant role in both. The diminishing economy in the twentieth century resulted in shrinking populations. Men of all races left the island colony leaving the economy and society dependent on the labour of women of all classes.

Women participated in the island's formal and informal economy as estate workers, domestics and urban vendors. They participated in local organizations, community groups and in churches. They taught local children and worked with local merchants. On the cotton estates it was women and children who engaged in cotton production. Working class activism on the island was evident from the World War I period as the economic conditions deteriorated through 1918 and employers sought to protect their interests by lowering wages and changing pay conditions. Workers and peasants responded with protest and vandalism. The colonial administration sought to protect the peace and employers' interests by use of local militia to break up strikes and marches. In addition a series of regulations including the *Defense of the Presidency Ordinance* threatened imprisonment to workers who refused to work and to anyone who encouraged such behaviour.[51]

Yet the threats and growing vigilance of employers and state militia to suppress organized protest failed to stop revolts both in Antigua and St. Kitts in 1917 and 1918. In addition to labour protest over lowering wages, limited opportunities for work and shifting pay conditions, Caribbean workers were also provoked to protest the treatment and conditions experienced by mobilized soldiers in the West India Regiment, a regiment mobilized in 1915 and which comprised over fifteen thousand volunteers from the British Caribbean colonies. Only two hundred and twenty nine of these volunteers were from the Leeward Islands, but as elsewhere in the region, some of these volunteer soldiers who returned following the war would become active labour leaders and advocates of Black Nationalist ideology. Movements such as that led or inspired by Marcus Garvey calling for fuller participation for black and coloured men in their societies had large support from these World War I volunteers, and from others whom their activism inspired.[52]

The problems of the Antigua and Barbudan economy and society were clearly the product of the dependence on one product – sugar. Yet throughout the twentieth century, land owners resisted agricultural diversification because of a loyalty to sugar cane and its legendary eighteenth-century profits.

Yet while the eighteenth century sugar economies remained elusive throughout the twentieth century, estate and factory owners continue to enjoy profits. Underemployment, lowering wages paid and hiring large

51 Posted in the *Leeward Islands Gazette*, 7 March 1918.

52 W. F. Eklins, 'A Source of Black Nationalism in the Caribbean'.

numbers of women and children who earned less than men, allowed profit earnings often in the most difficult of world economic conditions. Despite the social and economic challenges they faced many Caribbean people maintained a fierce loyalty to the 'Mother Country' and their volunteering for service during the World Wars demonstrates this overwhelming loyalty and patriotism. Clearly many people in the colonies, the masses included identified with Britain despite their distance and the absence of real benefits of British nation identity. The connections between Britain and the British Caribbean societies have remained tangible despite the difference in the histories and institutions that have marked the history of both regions. These connections have long eluded historians and other scholars who have looked elsewhere, but not the Caribbean, to explain British history. Catherine Hall's declaration in 2002 resonates with me in the construction of this narrative.[53] To understand Caribbean national formation, in particular that of the Leeward Island colony of Antigua after 1951, requires understanding the outside influences not just British colonial influence but that of the United States as well on the islands of the region.

53 'I have become a historian of Britain who is convinced that, in order to understand the specificity of the national formation, we have to look outside it.' Catherine Hall, *Civilizing Subjects: Metropole and Colony in the English Imagination 1830–1867* (New York: Routledge, 1992).

PART II

Labour, Demography, and Gender

CHAPTER 3

Women in a Modern Colony

This chapter highlights the historical role of women in Antigua and Barbuda from the nineteenth century to the mid-twentieth century, using primarily colonial administration reports, interviews and oral history. These resources document the role of women in the island's economy and society. It is clear from the evidence that free non-white women in Antigua and Barbuda have played crucial social roles, despite their marginalized social status. Coloured women formed and financed the self-help efforts of the Female Orphan Society in the nineteenth century. They continued into the twentieth century to support and finance social and educational institutions to improve the lives of members of the black and coloured population. When locked out of wage labour, they became involved in small scale peasant production and service industries in the urban areas.

The history of women in Antigua and Barbuda has been greatly influenced by the political economy of the islands. Through the mid-twentieth century the island remained a sugar plantation economy. In the sugar plantation economy of Antigua women, as the island's majority population, were greatly influenced by and greatly influenced the society. In addition to the impact of their size in the population women were impacted also by the social and political structures of the island colony. The low marriage rates indicate the low social and economic status of the island's female population. In a society where respectability meant everything, black and coloured women and their children were excluded from access to education, from equal access in churches, especially the Methodist and Anglican churches. Respectability even limited access to non-agricultural work. This was clearly another means by which the small white elite maintained itself as a distinct racial and social group in Antiguan society.

Yet while it might have maintained a monopoly on respectability, the white elite did not succeed in denying the black and coloured population the opportunities it needed to construct itself as a distinct social class, creating institutions to protect its self-interest. Additionally, despite their failure to meet the respectability requirements established by the elite, Antiguan black and coloured women of the working class and middle class created the foundations upon which the early trade unions and political parties were built. They stubbornly struggled to feed, to educate and to advance the interests of their children and their social class. They rejected the limitations of respectability, and created their own institutions and value systems which allowed for illegitimate children to be educated. It was Antiguan women whose contributions in education created the working class and lower middle class men and women who organized the island's first trade union and political party.

Census and prison reports and bluebooks are used in this chapter to evaluate Antiguan society and analyze the impact and meaning of colonial policies on people's everyday lives. The 1911 and 1921 censuses expose a small island with a lot of women. Not only does the census report this black female majority, it also exposes the fact that very few of this majority were married. In fact the census figures show that the number of married women on the island had gone in the wrong direction, down, since the last census of 1891. This female majority was engaged in occupations in only 8 of the 18 occupations on the island. In essence, the island's majority faced professional exclusion as well as a gendered wage structure that limited their ability to provide for their families.[1]

Through the use of family laws the small white oligarchy exerted control over the social reality of the Antiguan masses, yet the while oligarchy continually violated their own respectability rules. Both white and black men in Antigua maintained multiple unions influenced by colour, social class, and by location. In slavery sexual unions and blood ties with whites could and did change the daily lives of some slaves, and for some altered the

1 Patriarchy is clearly at work in that the low numbers of unmarried women is considered abnormal while the low number of female professionals is normal.

course of their future relationships and status in the society. Concubinage emerged as a prevalent practice in both urban and rural Antigua, and this practice produced both a coloured and middle class population, largely female, which contributed to the building of institutions which served the social and economic needs of the coloured and black population. Legal scholars Lazarus-Black and Elsa Goveia, the late West Indian historian have written important monographs outlining the experience of this population in nineteenth- and twentieth-century Antigua. I expose the challenges faced and overcome by black and coloured women and their role in aiding the re-emergence of a non-white middle class in twentieth-century Antigua.

In addition to colonial documents I use interviews, and oral histories to insert women's experiences into the records. The informants who provided information included in this chapter were born and raised in Antigua to several generations of Antiguans dating back to pre-emancipation nineteenth century. These stories of the island make an important connection with the colonial documents and colonial policies. While the documents expose administrative attempts to manufacture an image of a successful colony, a critical reading of the documents occasioned by the interviews and oral histories, exposes a colony whose economy was based upon the labour of men, women and children, but primarily women, who comprised the island's majority and upon whose backs the sugar and cotton economy of Antigua operated.

Census Reports from 1911 and 1921

Throughout the twentieth century the island's female population remained the majority. In addition, the Antiguan black and coloured population continued to avoid the institution of marriage, or it continued to elude them. The *Census* and *Blue Books*, the reports of colonial administrators that were sent to the Imperial government, documented both numbers of the population, distinguishing gender, civil condition, and professions.

Table 4 provides a sample of the 1911 documents on the demographics of Antiguan society in the first decade of the century. Women were engaged in some eight of the eighteen occupations listed in the census. They had no place as police, legal profession, ministers of religion, civil engineers and surveyors, managers of plantations, mechanics and handicraft men. Here no separate column was created and left blank as in the case of merchants, agents and dealers. In the category of hotel keepers only a column for 'Females' was included, a notation that suggests that hotel keeper was an all female occupation. In the 1921 census report 'notes in summary of sections' the population of Agricultural labourers generated the following commentary from census administrator H. L. Humphrys. 'As would be expected, this class claims a number far in excess of any of the other groups of occupations, and numbers at 10,009.' The number includes both the labourers and others employed in agriculture. Included in this class but not counted as agricultural labourers were the sugar estate proprietors, attorneys and agents, managers, overseers, sugar boilers, petty proprietors and cultivators. The next highest category is that of domestic servants. In this census this group is part of a class called domestic and includes laundresses, housekeepers, and chauffeurs. This group constitutes a largely urban population, the majority of which resided in St. Johns City and St. Johns Town. Further this was a class predominantly female, with significant coloured men and women numbering among its members. Of interest is the absence of a breakdown of male and female in occupations/professions. This breakdown is to be found in the 1911 census. While a breakdown in occupations is absent in this category it continued to existed in other categories such as degree of education, infirmity and nationality. In the category *degree of education* the total number of women listed as able to read and write was 11,263 to male 7,991.[2]

2 *Census of 1911.*

Table 4 The Female Majority in Antigua and Barbuda 1911

Excerpt from Report on the Census of Antigua and Barbuda 1911 Population 32,269	
Females 18,280 White females 528 Coloured females 2,395 Black females 15,357	Males 13,989
Civil Condition of 1911	
Married females 3,078 (1891 – 3,514)	Unmarried females 13,836 (1891 – 14,406)
Professions in which women appear in Census of 1911 by Gender	
Public Officers 51 (males 137)	
Medical profession 2 (males 7)	
Clerks and shop assistants 56 (males 176)	
Shopkeepers and Hucksters 618 (111)	
Agricultural Labourers 5,555 (4267)	
Domestic Servants 1,488 (362)	
Source: Census of 1911	

The annual report on the central prison of the Leeward Islands documents the ongoing resistance as well as the challenges faced by the region's masses. The 1926–1927 year was clearly a difficult one for Antigua and Barbudans who overwhelmingly were incarcerated over all other groups in the region. Of the one hundred seventy-one persons incarcerated through 31 March 1927 only thirteen were not from Antigua. Dominica was next in line to Antigua for the highest number of people incarcerated with six persons. Interesting also is the fact that the administrator noted that the total number for that year was in fact the lowest number of annual admissions or incarceration on record. The highest number, during the previous twenty-one years (1896–1927), was 327. This is not surprising in 1918, a year of labour unrest in the region. That year, the sugar cane cutters in Antigua attempted to strike to express their dissatisfaction with the change of pay, the state militia broke up the strike killing, wounding and arresting workers.[3]

3 Annual Report of the Central Prison of the Leeward Islands, 1927.

Table 5 No Small Group: The Unmarried Females of Antigua and Barbuda

Excerpt from Report on the Census of 1921	
Population 29,767	
Females 17,225	Males 12,542
Civil Condition of 1921	
Married total 5,373 Unmarried total 22,743 Married females 2,956	Married persons representing 18.71 per cent of the population Unmarried females 13,087
Profession	
Public Officers 159 Medical profession 8 Clerks and shop assistants 258	Shopkeepers and Hucksters/Hucksters and Pedlars 344 Hotel Keepers/Hotel and Boarding House Keepers 3 Agricultural Labourers 9,338
Source: Census of 1921	

In the list of offences for which the prisoners were convicted; females were committed for: wounding (4) assault (17/higher than men). larceny (6) praedial larceny (7) and damage to property (1). Significant numbers of women were incarcerated for bad language, the report documented 18 women, while only four men. In addition women outnumbered men for their incarceration for disorderly conduct. While men were employed in a variety of tasks both inside and outside of the prison, women were employed solely within the walls of the prison as laundresses, seamstresses and stone-breakers.[4]

4 Ibid.

British Genealogy and Gender Ideology

The interests of British subjects in Caribbean genealogy and British gender ideology influenced policies of the colonial administration through the first two decades of the twentieth century. The impact resulted in limiting women's access and role in the labour market and professions. The census documents expose the challenges women in Antiguan society faced. As the island's majority they were also its most economically vulnerable population (they were largely unmarried and excluded from the professions). Because women earned less money and most households were headed by unmarried women the majority of Antiguan households were significantly impoverished.

The list of the professions and occupations in the census distinguishes Antiguan society as a patriarchy where very few women were engaged in professional occupations and where a limited space within these professions were made available for coloured women. Black women and their children occupied the agricultural and domestic workplaces, spaces that had been constructed for them in Antiguan society since the seventeenth century. While Black women and children were confined to domestic and agricultural workplace into the twentieth century, their white and coloured counterparts both in Antigua and Barbuda and in Britain were beginning to experience some access to the professions.

The occupations for the island in 1911 and 1921 included four classes: professional, commercial, agricultural, and industrial and domestic. The professional class, the smallest in size of the three classes included colonial bureaucrats/administrators, public officers, local police, ministers of religion, lawyers, medical doctors, engineers, surveyors and teachers. The second smallest class was the commercial class, a group which included merchant, business and bank managers, shopkeepers, clerks and salesmen. In addition hucksters, pedlars, hotel and boarding house keepers, and a number of minor bureaucratic positions as well as ship's employees were numbered in this group.[5]

5 *Census of 1911*: Report of the Census of Antigua and its Dependencies 1921 (hereafter Census of 1921).

The remaining two classes comprised the island majority. Agriculture was by far the larger of the two and the largest of all four classes. This class included agricultural labourers, as well as managers and owners of estates. Of the more than ten thousand persons counted in agriculture for 1911 planters and managers comprised only 211 persons.

The industrial and domestic classes included the island's working trade such as mechanics and handicraftsmen and seamstresses. Mariners, fishermen and boatmen also comprised a significant group, the general labourers within this category covered dock workers who loaded and unloaded cargo on the St. Johns' docks. Domestics, including servants and laundresses, easily outnumbered all other groups in this class except for the fact that colonial administrators further divided this population into two categories: 'Unoccupied' and 'those living on private means.' These sub-categories within this class allowed colonial administrators to indirectly acknowledge the overwhelming use of female and child labour in the colony. Of the persons living on private means more than 80 per cent were women. Because this class was largely urban and female my assumption is that these women were prostitutes and the mistresses and children of white and coloured men. Even the administrators were confused about this category and particularly its size. The Registrar General's scepticism of this group is clear in his notes in his report 'the women have been put in this classification owing to the want of a more appropriate one. There are certainly not 299 persons who can strictly be considered as living on private means.'[6]

It was a society in which many people found themselves barely able to make ends meet and where many depended upon the kindness of the state, private individuals and some churches for basic necessities such as food and shelter. Medical care and social services were provided on quite limited scale and the more desperate persons were to be found languishing in the Hospitals and other public institutions. Of the one hundred ninety six persons in the hospital and poor house more than half were female. Women were also a large population of those persons confined to the lunatic asylum; their number was just below half of this population. They were however the majority in the leper asylum and for 1917 and there was

6 *Leeward Islands Bluebook 1917.*

a small number of women in the central prison, although their numbers would increase in the 1920s.

The island's only publicly funded training school provided training only for men and its student body in 1917 was quite an insignificant number to the overall male population on the island. Only 53 men were receiving training in this institution. There was no comparable institution for women although since the nineteenth century private individuals had taken responsibility for educating and training coloured women for domestic service. Clearly the female majority of Antigua remained confined in domestic work and agriculture and judging from the unclear categories of the registrar general some women sought other means of support in the Antigua and Barbudan economy. With some of the lowest marriage rates in the region Antigua and Barbudan women struggled to survive in a limited economy. Their struggles are evident in the colonial documents such as the census records and the bluebooks, although the colonial administrators who documented their struggles and creative responses were often themselves confused about what was going on among the local population.

Despite their flexibility and creativity throughout the early decades of the twentieth century the poorest of the population in the colony often waged a losing battle with time and fate. As the colonial documents show, significant numbers of this black and poor population succumbed to poverty and illness. Particularly vulnerable were the elderly, and the infirm, men and women broken by years of manual labour for low wages who succumbed to devastating illness because of poor diets, the lack of potable water and no medical care. The lucky ones, concubines of white men and middle class coloured men, lived by private means; the unlucky ones, died in the hospital, the asylum or the poor house, their bodies confined to pauper's graves. The stories of these common people – the economic victims of twentieth-century colonialism – went untold despite the annual reports, the census, the blue books and other documents of the colonial administration.[7] The administrators efficiently counted the bodies and recorded the

7 Smith and Smith, *To Shoot Hard Labour*; Caroline Carmody, 'The Peculiar Class'; Neville Cleofoster Brown, *The Emergence of a Bishop*; Census of 1921; Leeward Islands Bluebooks, 1917.

households, very concerned with establishing in these records a particular kind of society. The colonial records themselves were fictional in that they told the story that the Colonial Office sought to hear. These were stories of contained colonies with employers providing work opportunities and labourers contributing if they were good and not contributing because they were bad. It was a simple fairy tale where the lines were clearly drawn, except for times when the actions of the population caused social disruption which spilled over from the pages of the colonial report and showed the Colonial Office and the larger Empire a different story of colonial life.[8] On their own the colonial documents are often misleading in their depiction of the dynamic within the societies themselves. The Census of 1911, for example, was no doubt reviewed and promptly filed by the Colonial Office administrators. It reflected much of the same to administrators accustomed to recording numbers of populations and noting any changes that would affect the ways in which the colonial society was financed or overseen. Could it be for example that a colonial administrator would have seen a society where economic change or at least diversity was sorely needed? The Colonial Office played a passive role in the administration of the British colonies and not until the order was disturbed by revolts, class conspiracies or riots by working people did the British government through the Colonial Office pause in its incessant documenting in order to investigate and introduce changes designed to restore calm and order to the Empire.

Used as instruments of colonial control and administration the census and the maps depicted only part of the society they recorded. While administrators counted, organized, named and filed, the peasants and workers lived their lives, encumbered by the colonial project that sought to control, to name and to order them. The colonial project influenced life in the common order but the common order had its own rhythms of daily life, working, loving, caring for spouses and children and engaging in a variety of forms of resistance individually or collectively.

8 Accounts for Antigua include Smith and Smith, *To Shoot Hard Labour*; Keithlyn Smith, *No Easy-Pushover: A History of The Working People of Antigua and Barbuda 1834–1994* (Scarborough, Ontario: Edan's Publishers, 1994); CO 152/520/4 within the Soulsbury report is 'Minority Report', in which V. C. Bird documents the history of labour abuse, racism and segregation in post-emancipation Antigua.

History of Women and their Associations on Antigua

In her discussion of household forms in Antigua, Lazarus-Black noted that 'Those who spent all of their lives in the fields differed in their mating and reproductive patterns from those who lived in towns or belonged to masters with small estates.'[9] But irrespective of location and work experience both white and black men in Antigua maintained multiple unions. Colour, class and location influenced these unions. In slavery sexual unions and blood ties with whites could and did change the daily lives of some slaves and for some altered the course of their future relationships and status in the society. Control of Antiguan society however in slavery and in freedom was held or dominated by the colonial oligarchy. The institution of marriage and the family was greatly controlled by this group, as was no other institution in the colonies. Family laws allowed this oligarchy to exert some control over the social reality of the Antiguan masses. In one of the earliest studies of Antiguan society the late West Indian historian Elsa Goveia asserted that free women of colour in Antigua preferred liaisons with whites to marriage with men of their own class because of the status and economic advantages that their liaisons with white men offered them. These liaisons existed despite laws banning them and the social stigma attached to them.[10]

In the past free men of colour were often forced to form relations with enslaved women, a relationship that produced enslaved children. The English law pertaining to children acquiring the status of their fathers did not apply to the enslaved population where children instead acquired the status of their mothers. This ensured a self-generating slave population for slave owners in slave societies of the Americas from the seventeenth century until nineteenth century emancipation. The marriage and inheritance laws of the island had has been assigned some of the responsibility for concubinage in Antigua. Some black and coloured women chose to remain

9 Mindie Lazarus-Black, Legitimate Acts and Illegal Encounters: Law and Society in Antigua and Barbuda (Washington, DC: Smithsonian Institution Press, 1994) (hereafter Legitimate Acts), *Legitimate Acts*, 87.

10 Elsa V. Goveia, *Slave Society in The British Leeward Islands at the end of the Eighteenth Century* (Connecticut: Greenwood Press, 1980, c1965).

unmarried in order to build a legacy for their children, and because of the freedom which their unmarried status afforded them. Married women not only lost status but marriage ensured that husbands controlled them, their children and any property, even property which they had owned prior to marriage.[11]

While black and coloured women sought concubinage with whites as the better alternative to marriage with black or coloured men, most white men involved in these unions were not interested in forming legal relations with coloured women. Local codes discouraged unions across race and the white population was extremely reluctant to break the colour barrier. Rare, was the situation when white men were willing to put it all on the line. Antiguan society was one where property and position made the man, but nationality, religion, family connections, office and colour were all crucial to his standing and the standing of his family.

To marry out of class and caste was not only illegal but it carried social stigma and the real loss of social standing for whites.[12] Whites were forbidden to marry free coloureds and servants and slaves were also forbidden from marrying. While the eighteenth century fine for ministers who married persons outside of their class and caste may not seem much of a restriction, the social punishment and the fine worked in tandem to ensure compliance on the part of most members of the society. Additional restrictions included the refusal of the state to recognize as legitimate those marriages not performed by an Anglican minister or to recognize common law unions. The prevalence of concubinage was further exacerbated by the imbalance in the sex ratio. In the free coloured population, as in the larger population, the sex ratio favoured women. In addition a decline in the

11 This is clearly the position of Mindie Lazarus Black and Susan Lowes who have both written about Antiguan society in the nineteenth and twentieth century. The twentieth century census reports of women and children living on private means in St. Johns reflect the longevity of this practice. Women in Antigua continue to overwhelmingly reject marriage, opting for multiple relationships and single parent households.

12 The most well known violation of the legal and social bar was the marriage of the coloured abolitionist Anne Hart, to Methodist minister John Gilbert.

number of white women in the early nineteenth century served to increase the number of white men in sexual relationships with coloured women. This decline in the white female population not surprisingly coincided with the increase in the number of the urban coloured population. The urban centre of the island saw both a dramatic increase in people of colour and the emergence of a black middle class that was largely coloured. This increase in number stimulated class formation and the coloured middle class of Antigua both peaked and declined in the nineteenth century, both in relation to numbers and access to resources.[13]

Whereas in the early nineteenth century specific social organizations were formed and supported by this group, including schools, and social help organizations, in the post World War I period this group had seen a drastic reversal in its fortunes. After 1896 it was a numerically and financially reduced population that had to be re-constituted in the twentieth century. It was this fact that accounted for the almost absence of middle class coloured participation in the labour and political struggles in Antigua and Barbuda. By the 1940s it was the working class and peasant population which formed the local organizations including the first trade union and political party in Antigua and Barbuda.[14]

It is clear that uplift and elevation were primary goals of the free non-white population in Antigua to emancipation in 1834. In post-emancipation Antigua and Barbuda this group's targeted goals were for political and social inclusion. These would be defeated by the end of the nineteenth century by a combination of nature, global events and the actions of the white elite. The non-white middle class in Antigua demonstrated similar

13 The challenges of this class are well documented by Susan Lowes, 'The Peculiar Class'.

14 Ibid. The free coloured population of Antigua began to embrace the institution of marriage in the first quarter of the nineteenth century. Between 1814 and 1826 marriages among the free coloured were a high percentage of all marriages in the Anglican Church in St. Johns. These marriages were a sign of Christianity and of status, as well as a way to protect property. There is suggestion from these growing marriage rates that the population of coloured people had experienced growth, such that increased marriages and the creation of separate social organization began to appear in St. Johns City.

characteristics to their North American counterparts in terms of their commitment to raising the level of morality and improving the standard of living for the poorest of their community. The emergence of The Destitute Females Friend Society in 1815 (renamed the Female Orphan Society), is one example of the hands-on response to social conditions that impacted them directly. The coloured middle class women of St. Johns who founded this society and who single-handedly financed it throughout the century sought to take charge of directing the future of young girls of colour. A female society, whose primary objective was self help, the organization targeted the female off-spring of interracial concubinage relationships.

Like the white elite the middle class coloured women in the early nineteenth century saw these girls as the product of 'religious and moral degradation'.[15] Unlike the white elite, they sought to help these girls to find 'respectability'. No doubt motivated as much by the interest in improving the quality of life of young non-whites, as by the fact that these girls looked very much like them and their own daughters, the female society committed its financial and social resources towards intervening in the lives of these young women. Clearly the organizers of the society were also motivated by self-interest in this endeavor to protect their own status and overall reputations in Antiguan society. It remains unclear whether the girls who were wards of the society were removed from their mothers by force and put into the care of the society or whether they were willingly given up for care by their mothers.

While the society identified itself with the care of orphans, sources insist that most of these orphans had parents who were alive but who because of their concubinage relationships were deemed to be improper guides to their young.[16] The female coloured orphans under the care of the society were given basic education in reading, writing and arithmetic

15 Mrs Lanaghan, *Antigua and Antiguans: A Full Account of the Colony and its Inhabitants* (London: Saunders and Ottley, 1844) two volumes: 285–289. The group charter quoted by Mrs Lanaghan uses this language to describe the population of coloured girls who were targeted for relief.

16 Ibid.

but the majority of their training was in the 'arts of female plain-work'.[17] In essence they were trained to provide domestic service. Their labours helped to support the society which housed, fed and clothed them until their release into the employ of white and coloured families or until they were of age and situation to set up their own households. Not surprisingly many of these girls returned to situations very similar to what they were saved from by the society. Some, seduced by their male employers or other white and coloured men, were forced to leave the place of employment when they became pregnant. The system of placing coloured girls in white and coloured homes, both formally through organizations and informally, through family contacts and others networks, continued to exist into the mid-twentieth century.[18] These girls were not only the product of urban liaisons and concubinage relationships but were also the product of liaisons between rural whites, estate owners, factory supervisors and colonial administrators and black and coloured women. Often the coloured offspring were removed to St. Johns City and Town for education and other self-improvement opportunities.

Middle class ideologies for the first and second groups of coloured middle class reflected the influence of the respectability bar by which the white elite had sought to separate themselves from non-whites. For the middle classes legal marriage was an important marker of status, but as the records of the Female Orphan Society show, many coloured women remained unable or uninterested in accessing the higher status, social mobility and purported advantages which marriage provided for them.[19]

Many of these women rejected the judgments against their moral character and sought to prove that they too (despite their unmarried status) could raise respectful children and live according to the dictates of their middle class counterparts. They sought to distance themselves from the class

17 Ibid. 259.

18 Examples abound in oral accounts of twentieth-century Antiguans who had been sent to St. Johns, from rural areas. These persons rarely knew both parents, and some knew neither. Informants also referred to this in particular Mrs Edris Bird interview with author June 2003.

19 Mrs Lanaghan, *Antigua and Antiguans*, 259.

of vagabonds, a term used to cover the large, poor urban population. While middle class respectability eluded this group they constructed their own ideals of family and respectability. They isolated themselves from some of their neighbors and families, especially those who constantly drank, cursed and fought publicly, who did not attend church and or who engaged in prostitution. This was the image of the vagabond in Antigua and for many Antiguans even today the term vagabond continues to define and divide the masses. In St. Johns and in other towns throughout Antigua coloured and black women insisted on separating themselves and their children from the chaotic and rowdy elements of their community by insisting that they were *in* but not *of* the communities where they lived. I heard this phrase uttered time again by a group of twentieth-century witnesses who spoke of their childhood either with single mothers or with both parents, but who were black and coloured members of St. Johns City.[20]

Rural families were differently constituted than urban families in Antigua, despite the small size of the island. Throughout the first half of the twentieth century location greatly influenced the type of unions formed by men and women. In rural areas most black and coloured men maintained multiple unions, and these relations were accepted in rural communities and produced male and female headed households with children who sometimes lived with both parents and sometimes did not.

Despite the size of the island the population reflected a surprising diversity among black and coloured population in particular. This diversity was to be found both in slavery and freedom, and was reflected in social classes, the types of families, the nature of communities and in the boundaries of acceptable and unacceptable behaviour. This makes it extremely difficult to impose upon one group the patterns and experiences of another. In the towns of the small island black and coloured persons practiced a different conjugal pattern to those in rural areas. The range of patterns which could be seen in the island even into the early twentieth century reflected a growing influence of the churches in the society. In the nineteenth century church authorities depended upon the generosity

20 Mrs Edris Bird interview with author June 2003.

of the local white population and their followers in England and Europe and were therefore unwilling to tamper overtly with the racial and social structures of these societies. By the twentieth century too the black and coloured masses had come to perceive the Salvation Army and the Moravian Church as institutions more supportive of them. But while the black and coloured did not suffer the exclusion and judgments in these institutions as they did in the Anglican and Methodist churches, the Salvation Army and Moravian workers were as committed as the Anglican and Methodists to imposing European patriarchal values upon them[21]

Prior to emancipation black and coloured women were important allies of missionaries spreading Christianity among the enslaved population. The relationship between these women and the missionaries was a complicated one despite the partnership dating back to slavery.[22] Severely criticized by the church as a main source of sin in the society, many single black and coloured women were barred from congregations and were refused services including baptism for their children. In addition to its severe punitive attitude towards unmarried women, the church also buttressed the extremely patriarchal structure of English and West Indian society. Church teachings accentuated male supremacy and maintained a double standard of morality. Women who refused to marry were often excluded from congregations and sometimes from church schools. While the churches were less successful in changing familial and conjugal patterns of rural plantation workers, they were successful by the twentieth century in convincing most people that Christian marriage was the most ideal form of union.[23] After emancipation,

21 'Periodical Accounts: 2nd Century', vols. 9–10 (1914–1920). Annual accounts for Moravian Church from various Caribbean islands where the church had established missions. The collection of letters, reports and other narratives which constitute the accounts provide crucial insight from the perspective of both local insiders and outsiders on Caribbean societies. Accounts for the island of Antigua stress education of young women as one of the primary goals of the mission, next of course to its recruitment mission.

22 Mindie Lazarus Black, *Legitimate Acts*, 86. Lazarus-Black observed that the missionaries did not demonstrate much support for women in general, and were particularly critical of coloured and black women in concubinage relationships.

23 Ibid.

women continued to play a central role in the missions of the churches. This female participation would become an important factor in the evolution of family and gender ideology in Antiguan society, especially urban society where women were among the majority of the churches' devoted converts and tended to a host of church functions. Women continue to be the more active gender among church followers.[24]

The personal lives and especially the matrimonial status of black and coloured women, especially those living outside the 'respectable' boundaries was (especially after the 1920s) a favourite target for churches and self-help societies. They particularly targeted female headed households as an aberration among black and coloured members of the society. But as scholars of nineteenth-century Antiguan society have noted, the church had not been so vigorous in its attack on white female-headed households which were the norm among the free white population. As Lazarus-Black, Elsa Goveia and Tim Hector have shown, free white women were the head of households in many English speaking colonies in the Caribbean into the nineteenth century. In eighteenth century St. Johns a high percentage of white settler households were headed by white females.[25] It is clear that race played a tremendous role in these societies and that it is likely that the colour of the female-headed households, more than changing times, was a primary reason Caribbean societies would normalize this family form among one race and stigmatized it among the other. There is also the likelihood, because race and racism are central factors in these societies, that the attempt to change the households of the black and coloured population was less about enforcing the elite social value of respectability than it was about exerting white control over the black and coloured population.

24 Female informants interviewed in Antigua in 2003 mentioned their church affiliations and active participation. This role of women in churches is also highlighted by Caroline Carmody, 'First Among Equals'; 287. In her discussion of village leadership patterns and women she noted that the church and church related activities were central in the lives of her informants.

25 Mindie Lazarus-Black, *Legitimate Acts*; Elsa Goveia, *Slave Society in the British Leeward Islands*; Tim Hector 'Women in Antigua: A Historical overview', *CLR James Journal*, 8:1 (2000/2001).

Women and Education

Colonial ideology regarding gender changed dramatically in the post World War I period. The 1920s saw economic boom for the island but by the late 1920s into the 1930s was a period of major depression following this boom. This decline resulted in serious changes in the organization of production (rise of peasantry) and major transformations in the sexual division of labour, not only in Antigua and Barbuda but all the British colonies in the Caribbean.

Sexual Division of Labour (SDL) had long been practiced in these sugar plantation societies with clear assignments of tasks to black, white and Indian indentured women. In the 1920s social scientists were caught up with new ideas for modernizing Caribbean societies. A new domestic ideology, one which separated women from wage-labour and defined them as 'housewives' irrespective of race or social class, was a clear attempt to reconstitute the lower order.

Education was an important means for remaking the colonized and disseminating colonial ideologies in the twentieth century. For the British Caribbean colonies, government-assisted denominational schools played a central role in this.[26] While religious proselytizing was a central activity of these religious organizations, they also played an important role in the spread of literacy on the island. Most of the religious organizations ran state-supported and privately funded schools. Not unlike the institutions in Europe, the curriculum of these religious schools included the inculcation of Christian patriarchal values. By the 1920s the curriculum of these institutions reflect a clear sexist demarcation between boys and

26 Rhoda Reddock, *Women, Labour and Politics*, 66–60. Religious institutions in the region cited in the censuses of 1911 and 1921 include the Church of England, Moravian, Wesleyan, Roman Catholic, Christian Mission, Seventh Day Adventist and the Salvation Army. Interesting to note that the 1911 census had included Non-Christian section which included Hindoos [sic], Mohamedans, Parsees and others; Census of 1911.

girls education.[27] For example, military drill and agricultural education was provided primarily to boys, despite the fact that Caribbean women had extensive knowledge and experience in agriculture and in islands such as in Antigua they were the majority of agricultural workers.

It was through education that European groups, church and colonial administrators made the greatest in-road in affecting local culture and imposing middle class values among the labouring population. In 1891 education was made compulsory by the legislature of the Leeward Islands colony. Yet despite the implementation of compulsory education between 1911 and 1921 the number of people able to read decreased from 44 per cent to 38 per cent. In addition to making education compulsory the legislature had also taken over education from the various religious denominations. By the 1920s the island had three Secondary Schools and a Female Training College – to prepare girls to become certificated teachers. The training college was maintained by the Moravians and received a grant from the government. The male counterpart institution the Rawle Training Institute was located not in the Leeward Islands, but at Codrington College in Barbados. Young men from the entire region were transported to Barbados for training to become certified teachers. These training institutions were available to a limited number of students and admission was based on placement in school exams.

Six students were selected annually three (3) boys and three (3) girls for education training at Rawle and the Training College.[28] Women's labour was still very important in agriculture, manual labour and petty production and trade throughout much of the first half of the twentieth century. Prior to World War I sex differentiation in the school curricula was slight. In the period following the war, the Caribbean economies declined and as employment was drastically reduced, women especially experienced a dramatic decline in the availability of jobs. In addition school curriculums in the colonies began to offer housewife oriented courses to female students. By the 1930s differentiations between male and female place in the society became more rigid.[29]

27 Susan Lowes, 'The Peculiar Class'.

28 Census of 1921.

29 Rhoda Reddock, *Women Labour and Politics.*

European patriarchy and British colonialism sought to change the culture and gender ideology of the colonial majority. The black and coloured poor were encouraged to embrace attitudes and patterns of relations that were acceptable among the middle and upper classes for both whites and coloured. Unlike the middle and upper classes of white and coloured people in the British Caribbean the region's majority had long demonstrated the following characteristics: Absence of legal registration; income earning women and multiple/consecutive relationships. Colonial education and religious systems imposed heavy sanctions on these families. Children whose parents were not married were denied access to education. These individuals were denied 'respectability' but respectability was denied to all non-whites, most non-British and to non-Christians as well. By the 1920s there emerged a more concerted effort to enforce the standard of the upper classes on the entire population. As Rhoda Reddock argued in *Women, Labour & Politics in Trinidad & Tobago* this enforcement was codified by the *Education Code of 1935*. The code, government policy in the British Caribbean colonies forbade the employment of married women as teachers. Of course the exceptions in these cases were made when unmarried women were not available to provide the service.

Because social reordering, or social reconstruction like all matters of the colonial administration, had been introduced to promote the best interest of the colonial administration, these laws were often un-enforced.[30] The economic needs of the colonial economy often took a back seat to the desire of the state to encourage the masses to 'right living'. In essence, despite the talk of the middle class respectability, women's labour was central to the economies both during slavery and continued after slavery in the wage labour colonial systems in the Caribbean. Both in the nineteenth century and twentieth century women's labour in petty-commodity production and trade filled the additional need of the colonies until light manufacturing and other production and services could take over. For Antigua and Barbuda, factory production and service never eliminated the central role of female labour in the economy of the island.[31]

30 Ibid.

31 Ibid. Edie Labadie interview by author April 2003.

The ideal family life promoted by the Colonial administration and which was the model for 'respectable' persons and those seeking respectability involved: marriage by Anglican minister; a white church wedding with a big reception; a non-wage-earning wife; a respectable house, one where the woman did not work and that was clean and presentable; and church attendance in the Anglican church in particular. For the vast majority of the black and coloured population of the region and specifically Antigua such a household was not economically viable. While it is true that some among the lower classes embraced it as an ideal to strive for, others realized the disadvantage such a household implied for women. Other women in the society had developed their own philosophy of male-female relationships based on their own or others' experience.[32] The early twentieth century ideal of the dependent, non-wage earning housewife was influential in shaping education and labour policy in the colonies. Yet while respectability restricted women's labour to certain occupations and levels of occupations the boundaries often were much more flexible as far as white women and middle-class coloured women's labour was concerned. Exceptions were easily made to accommodate these groups. Another side to limiting women's labour to the sphere of domestic service was that the designation of women to the responsibilities of housewives allowed for their greater exploitation as the labour of housewives was largely unpaid labour. In the case of domestic servants these jobs offered low pay and lack of recognition and visibility by organized labour.[33] As scholars Elsa Chaney and Mary Garcia Castro have shown in the cases of Trinidad and Latin America, domestics, because they were an isolated group of workers, had no recourse to collectively struggle or to organize.

The emergence of trade unionism in Antigua and Barbuda did allow for domestic workers to become unionized and emerge from the shadows. However, it is important to note that recruitment was not as aggressively directed at this population in Antigua by trade union activists, as much

32 Rhoda Reddock, *Women Labour and Politics.*

33 Elsa Chaney and Mary Garcia Castro, eds. *Muchachas No More : Household Workers in Latin America and the Caribbean* (Philadelphia: Temple University Press, 1989).

as agricultural workers, dock-workers and factory workers. In Antigua the success of the process of 'housewifization' of women, is evident by attitudes prevalent in the 1970s when most people expressed ignorance of the historical role of women in the labour force of the island.[34]

On the sugar estates throughout the twentieth century women were hired in weeding, forking, cane-cutting and heading cane into trucks. Men monopolized the skilled jobs and were paid higher wages even when they completed the same tasks as women. Wages paid to agricultural workers had barely increased before World War I and were reduced afterwards. As a result of the shrinking market for agricultural products and the disruption of markets caused by the war, employers reduced their labour force and reduced the wages paid to workers. Women in 1915 found themselves being pushed out of the labour market as estate owners faced with shrinking need in a large labour market increased the size of jobs in order to make these jobs available to men. The increased work made it impossible for many women to complete them and successfully allowed the shift from women's tasks to men. Both ideology and the shrinking labour market served to reduce the demand for the labour of peasant and working class women during the war and in the immediate post-war period. Yet it is crucial to realize that the needs of many Caribbean families remained great, and women who headed households had to find other means of supporting themselves and their families.

When women were excluded from permanent wage-labour they became involved in small-scale peasant production. In small plots they produced sugar cane, food crops and domestic animals. Others in urban areas took in laundry and were involved in other service. This kind of change is not always reflected in the colonial documents as government officials went looking for the 'norm' and those operating outside of this norm were not anxious to share the truth with the authorities. I was initially surprised by the drop in census figures for hucksters and pedlars between 1911 and 1921. Whereas the 1911 census lists 618 shopkeepers and hucksters of which 111 were women, the modified 1921 census, lists a total of 344 Hucksters

34 Rhoda Reddock, *Women Labour and Politics.*

and pedlars without distinguishing gender. As the numbers demonstrate the categories of shopkeepers and hucksters were reduced in size to almost half what they were in the 1911 census.

Life in Rural Antigua: Stories of Informants

The British Caribbean colonies were like much of the world in the 1930s experiencing great economic crisis. As export economies dependent upon the world market, the global depression would have its most immediate and most devastating impact on export economies including those in the Caribbean. As grave as conditions were for the agricultural and domestic workers of the region prior to the depression, conditions would become even grimmer and more severe in the 1930s. There had been little room for social and economic advancement among the common order despite emancipation in the nineteenth century. Work and living condition had become more restrictive for workers as the colonial administration and employers sought to tighten their control and create clear distinction between the classes after emancipation had abolished their most important barrier.

For many workers especially those still living and working on estates (bound to plantations) the planter class had indeed 'killed king and ruled country.'[35] There was no aspect of life in the colonies that the planters did not dominate. Where work was concerned they set the work day, the work assignment and the pace and amount of work which each labourer was to complete. Witnesses such as Sammy Smith recalled over fifty years later that some planters ran private prisons in which they incarcerated workers for failing to meet their weekly labour quota, and for other petty violations.[36]

Planters took advantage of British history, nineteenth-century British laws, and the chronic land shortage in Antigua to limit workers mobility and

35 Smith and Smith, *To Shoot Hard Labor*, 74.
36 Ibid.

collective action. The control of the twentieth century Caribbean labour force was greater where laws against sedition were in place. Sedition laws crafted during World War I (which remained in effect until the 1938 Royal Commission arrived in the Caribbean in 1938), were used to punish workers who spoke out against existing work conditions and who attempted to garner support of other workers in these efforts. Smith also recalled a threat that kept many estate workers humble, the threat of eviction from the estate where they lived and worked. The shortage of land on these small islands reduced the former slaves' ability to establish themselves in independent communities and their continued dependence upon estate owners for housing as well as jobs would secure the domination of the landowning elite in these societies.[37] Estate owners sought to exercise complete control over the lives of their workers. Their mechanisms for control included not only their control of the land, and their common alliance against workers but also their control of state mechanisms such as police and militia as well as the courts. In Antigua of the twentieth century, workers, estate workers in particular, lived in a world that resembled that of medieval England of serfs and lords. In medieval society the serfs were bound to the land and evacuation from such land by lords spelled certain death, for no other lord would accommodate or employ such a serf.

The threat of eviction and its implication of starvation for a worker created a servile workforce on the estates.[38] 'Me poor muma [...] she died poor [...] lived poor and died poor'.[39] Selma Brodie was born 4 January 1916 in rural Antigua, the village of New Field in St. Philip's Parish. St. Philips was one of four Parishes that divided the small island colony and it was home to the largest number of sugar estates and mills. Selma, like generations before her (including her father who had been born in Freetown, the first of the free villages formed by ex-slaves) grew up around sugar cane fields in the culture of a plantation economy. Like her father and mother before

37 Caroline Carmody, 'First Among Equals'; Smith and Smith, *To Shoot Hard Labour*; O. Nigel Bolland. *The Politics of Labour*; 'Sedition and Undesirable Act of 1938' (hereafter JL 648).

38 Novelle Richards, *Struggle and the Conquest*, 5.

39 Selma Brodie interview with author March 2003.

her Selma's childhood was one of work in the sugar cane and cotton fields, interspersed by school. Childhood was difficult among the common order as adults earned wages which barely kept them and their dependents fed and covered. Like most children on Antigua, Selma and her siblings were raised by one parent, a mother, who struggled to support eight children on her own. Selma's story and the story of her mother Adelaide Charles are common to the experience of the Antiguan peasants and workers in the first half of the twentieth century. The stories of their struggles to survive under difficult economic circumstances constitute the history of the struggles between the old order (plantocracy) and the new (trade unionists). The struggles between the old order for continuance of the political and economic supremacy of the elite and the demands for change from among the common order and from metropolitan allies can be seen in the life stories of two generations of Antiguan men and women.

'My mother was from Sea View Farm.'[40] Selma's attempt to recall her childhood and to assist me in the documentation of her mother's life was a project she engaged in with enthusiasm laced with much sadness. Her mother's life had been a difficult one, a fact that Selma and her siblings all recalled. Asked what kind of work her mother did, Selma describes a variety of work on estates and her various stints as an entrepreneur selling food to cane field workers at Long Lane and Gainers, the two main estates in the village of St. Philips. She worked at the mill in Montpelier estate making molasses and her daughter Selma recalled that she would bring home corn and molasses. She worked in the cane fields, weeding, cutting, planting and any other tasks assigned by overseers. As Selma recalled her mother's struggle to support a large number of children on her own, with little aid from the three men with whom she had her children and her many jobs to do so, she spoke of her own life at 84, and the leisure time that she enjoyed now. 'I didn't have no leisure time when I was a girl. All my leisure time is now'.[41] Selma attended school at Freetown until eighteen. She lived for much of her teenage years with her godmother Alberta Hamilton

40 Ibid.
41 Ibid.

(Botee) who was an estate worker. As part of the systems for survival used in Antiguan society, children, in particular those, whose parents struggled to support them, were taken in by relatives and family friends. Many times the surrogate family was no better equipped financially to support the child and the child's labour would become central to the family income.

Alberta Hamilton worked for Long Lane estate hoeing weeds from the cane fields and both Selma and Alberta's daughter Vic worked for the estate cutting and tying sugar cane. Because they were children workers Alberta collected their wage. Work on the estates took place around their school attendance and both Vic and Selma worked in the estate in the morning before school. Before work they made roast dumplings, a flour dough which they rounded and flattened and roasted over a fire. After school they went straight to Long Lane where they continued the tasks they had begun in the morning before attending school.

Alberta Hamilton had one child of her own and while one might expect that with less of a burden hers would be an easier life, Selma recalled how hard it was for Alberta to make ends meet, 'even my godmother had it hard' recalls Selma, a statement which resembles that made by her sister Evelyn regarding their mother's challenges to feed them. 'She took me in order to help Ade.'[42] Selma and Evelyn's mother's name was Adelaide Charles. Evelyn told also of the difficult time their mother had finding food for so many children. She described mealtimes when her mother laid out the calabash bowls and often there was barely enough food for all of the bowls.[43]

At Alberta Hamilton meals were just as sparse. Alberta Hamilton's poor cooking skills were the least of the problems for Selma and Alberta's own daughter Vic. The problem was the low wages that made it difficult to buy vegetables much less meat and despite their rural locale they had no access to gardens and were required to purchase their food at the markets. Dinner, the biggest meal, consisted – when they could get it – of roast salt-fish (codfish), fat pork and fungi or cooked cornmeal paste.

42 Ibid.

43 Evelyn Edwards, interview with author, April 2003.

While the law defended the interests of the planter elite the workers found ways to express their frustration at unfair work conditions. Cane burning was a common response for workers and it was rare that the firebug was caught, for workers did not make a habit of telling management on each other. But all cane fires were not directly set by workers and Selma recalled one cane fire inadvertently set by a worker who had taken a cigarette break in the field. The fire occurred at Lion estate around 1936. 'I was walking in the field and I saw fire and yelled out Fire! Dali was smoking cigarette and had dropped a lit cigarette which caught trash and burned down the field.'[44] She kept the source of the fire to herself, refusing to answer questions by the estate manager and overseer about what or who she saw prior to the fire and her call for help.

I was surprised by the response to the term 'peasantry' from Selma's children, especially her older son Clement, who declared it a term used by the plantation owners to describe them. He resented it as a term meaning dependent and poor, and insisted that they were not peasants.[45] But the resentment of the term and their condition as agricultural workers which spurred resentment in the next generation had been one hard fought for by generations of agricultural workers who through the third decade of the twentieth century lacked access to land of their own and the freedom, independence, and self-respect that land ownership brings. In fact the lack of access to land especially for farming was a major cause of hunger for those of the common order particularly during the World Wars and the 1930s economic depression.

Born in 1921, Enid Brodie insists that she remembers much of her life from nine years old. Five years younger than her sister Selma, Enid spent more time than her older sister Selma, away from her mother and siblings. At age 9 she was taken in by family friends, a couple from the village of Parham. She lived and worked for them doing farming, messenger and as the family's domestic servant. It was a life of endless work and little opportunity for school. It was a hard life despite the fact that her mother had been

44 Ibid.

45 Clement Joseph, in conversation in summer 2003 in New York City.

promised that she would be taken care of and sent to school. Little concern was paid to her schooling or to her health and when she came down with typhus fever as a teenager she was sent back to her mother in New Field. Upon recovery Enid did not return to Parham but was sent instead to live with her father in Freetown. She remained in Freetown until one of her siblings (her father's children) beat her and her mother asked for her to be returned home. She was back with her mother for a short while before being returned to the family in Parham.

Back in Parham, Enid was once again responsible for the household and farm work, her work load increased because the woman of the house was sickly, although Enid could not recall what illness she suffered. In addition, Enid recalled the physical abuse suffered by this woman at her husband's hand. She recalled that he would beat his wife and often would lock her outside of the gate of their home. When Enid finally left this family and returned home her mother and other family members in New Field were angry at the family who had taken her in for not maintaining their responsibilities to see that she got an education. Enid had only one dress when she was returned to her family.[46]

Evelyn, the younger of Adelaide Charles's daughters also recalled the challenges of childhood. She too had been farmed out to live with family members and with friends of the family because her mother could not afford to feed them all. Evelyn too worked on the estates and recalled to me in 2003 'I began to work at Longlane estate when I was about twelve. I would go to school half day because my mother was alone with all of us and we had to help out.' The children worked in the little gang, child labourers who on estates were responsible for collecting trash that was put in the mill to make food for the animals. 'We pick up weed after the men dig up the grass. We used to distribute manure to cane bunch and even distribute the cane treatment called "salty moron" to the cane bunch. All the work done on the estate little gang did their share. We work hard in dem days.'[47]As both the census reports and the story of my informants

46 Mrs Enid Brodie interview with author May 2001.

47 Mos. Evelyn Thomas interview with author April 2003.

indicate, women and girls played a tremendous role in the island colony of Antigua (as did men and boys), they were its majority population and as the economy was focused on agriculture so too was the work experience of many women and girls.

Conclusion

As both the census reports and the personal histories of my informants indicate, women and girls played a tremendous role in the island colony of Antigua (as did men and boys), they were its majority population and as the economy was focused on agriculture so too was the work experience of many women and girls. Yet nineteenth- and twentieth-century Antiguan society was a patriarchal one and women's exclusion and limitation was extensive, especially the non-white female population.

The efforts of the white elite to distinguish themselves from the black and coloured population resulted in the creation of a number of barriers. The most effective barrier was that of respectability, a condition that involved legal marriage, a male head of household, religious affiliation with Anglican church, education and pedigree. This was a tall order that most black and coloured people were unable to meet. Despite the exclusion which they faced for not meeting the respectability bar, the black and coloured middle class built institutions to support their self-interest and maintained value systems that created healthy social and economic environments for themselves and their children. It is clear that they were hurt economically and politically from the exclusion and discrimination they faced in their society. But the exclusion and discrimination also forced them to create their own institutions and these institutions such as the lodges and church committees would serve as important environments for leadership training.

In rural Antigua throughout the third decade of the twentieth century, black and coloured women and their children comprised a significant segment of the labour force on sugar plantations and cotton farms. Many children, especially the children of estate labourers, only gained partial schooling as they were forced to cut their school day short to work in the fields. In this chapter, my informants recollected their rural childhoods and the nature of the challenges they faced in female-headed households.

Limited education or partial education greatly affected upward mobility of many Antiguans. But the greatest threat to any mobility for the Antiguan masses was the respectability barrier imposed by the elite and by the churches. Most rural children were born handicapped by their illegitimacy, and lacking respectability, as children born out of wedlock, they were denied access, not already denied by their social class. Baptized before church service began on Sundays, denied access to education and therefore limited to manual labour on the plantations and farms of rural areas, the challenges to rural and urban working class and peasants in Antigua were enormous, where social and political access was concerned. Yet, despite the challenges faced by peasant and working class Antiguans, and in the absence of a strong middle class, it was the lower middle and working class groups in Antigua who founded trade unionism, using the networks of lodges and village organizations as the basis for organizing and for leadership. The TUC influence is central in the story of trade unionism, but local foundations was the basis upon which this European institution was built.

CHAPTER 4

The Foundations of Trade Unionism

> Everywhere I go in these islands I find it difficult to see who the future leaders of the workers are to be. None the less, I am always on the lookout for a young and reliable man.[1]

This chapter highlights the role of the Trades Union Congress, hereafter TUC, in union organization since 1940. The actions of Vere Cornwall Bird (hereafter V. C.) and Walter Citrine (hereafter Citrine) were crucial to the history of labour in Antigua and Barbuda. V. C. was a founding member of the Antigua Trades and Labour Union (hereafter ATLU), and Citrine, was the TUC representative on the 1938 Royal Commission. These men loom large in the archival resources and secondary sources as well as the oral reports and interviews. They are, and V. C. in particular, the primary actors in labour and political formation in the last thirty years of this book.

Despite the recommendations of the 1897 West Indian Sugar Commission that peasant development should be encouraged in the British Caribbean, only a very small peasantry existed in Antigua in 1938.[2] The recommendations of the 1897 Commission chaired by Henry Norman had strongly supported the creation and support of a peasantry and less dependence on sugar cane for the Caribbean colonies. These recommendations

1 MF 226–227 Walter Citrine Letter from Barbados.

2 West Indian Department Report (1938) CO 950/1. The Norman Commission members included in addition to Henry Norman, Sir Edward Grey, Sir David Barbour and Mr Olivier, of the Colonial Office, as secretary.

were completely ignored by the Colonial Office no doubt because of the dramatic social changes that they would have brought to these colonies.[3]

The failure to implement changes to Colonial society at the end of the nineteenth century created terrible social conditions for labourers especially during the war when eyewitness Sammy Smith recalled the suffering. 'During and after the war people nearly eat one another. There seemed to be no end to the hunger and starvation [...] the people all around was dying from all manner of diseases. Every week, small as our village was, somebody dead. Ever so often you would find dead bodies in the guts and ponds around the place. Plenty people rather dead than go on suffering every day.'[4]

Antigua and Barbudan society already in crisis at the turn of the twentieth century, was pushed beyond its limits by the war. The suffering was greatest among the masses that were the last to be paid and to be fed. Extreme shortages of food and foodstuff including oil for lamps and for cooking what food could be had greatly increased the mortality rates among the most vulnerable. Many died from diseases and malnutrition and others committed suicide so great was their despair. It was this despair that Sammy Smith insists was the reason why land access was allowed during World War I.[5] Access to land no matter its size or its quality offered a chance for

3 Ibid., 127. The Commission's recommendations included some dramatic changes in Antiguan society and it is no surprise that recommendations such as that calling for support of the Antiguan peasantry with crown lands and private lands as well as the development of infrastructure to support this peasantry were largely overlooked. This would have destroyed the economic and political power of the small sugar elite. O. Nigel Bolland, *The Politics of Labour*, 143. Crown Colony system had been established in the late nineteenth century to strengthen imperial control over the Colony. It proved to be a detrimental to the coloured middle class and reinvigorated the white elite. The second commission in the 1920s to re-examine political organizations in the colonies was the Woods Commission. This commission report of 1922 recommended political changes designed to shore up give coloured middle class more access in their societies. The distinct group to be targeted for inclusion were described by Commission as the 'educated and largely light skinned members of the colonies'.

4 Smith and Smith, *To Shoot Hard Labor*, 124.

5 Ibid.

independence from land owners and for subsistence production to end the dependency on estate owners, low wages, and the high cost of imported food. The war pushed these economies over the brink, but despite their suffering the colonial population demonstrated an unwavering support and loyalty to the Empire. This support in the form of volunteer soldiers and other acts of loyalty, as well as the impact of the war experience itself, in forcing the British to critically examine their role as colonizer, led to investigations of the political and social bases of Caribbean colonial societies. In the first two decades following World War I, the British parliament authorized three investigative bodies. The Wood Commission 1921–1922, chaired by E. F. L Wood was established to investigate the political and social conditions in the colonies and recommended the opening up of the political system in the colonies to the black and coloured middle class.[6] Less than a decade later the Olivier Commission was sent to investigate agricultural conditions, particular the state of West Indian sugar. The 1938 Royal Commission was established as an investigative body to witness and investigate conditions in the Caribbean colonies and recommend remedies to the any problems they uncovered.

Antigua and Barbudan society was still suffering from the hardships caused by the first war when the global economic depression hit in the 1930s. Surviving the shortages of World War I was not easy for the masses and despite the access to land granted to the rural work force in Antigua during the war by landowners, it was not until 1930 that development schemes, including a land settlement operation, were begun by the Colonial Government. Colonial Development and Welfare Grants managed by the Colonial Office were awarded to the colony at £14,000 annually from 1930 to 1938. The use of the funds (or lack thereof) would become one of the issues of contention between labour and colonial administrators by 1940.[7] On Antigua, where land had remained a scarce commodity, land settlement schemes designed to give the masses access to land for agricultural devel-

6 O. Nigel Bolland. *The Politics of Labour*,142.

7 Colonial Office report Development and Welfare in the West Indies (1942) HD6595A.

opment were adopted in 1930 with less than 20 settlers. Seven years later some 284 peasants had been settled on lands for agricultural development. These settlers working on state and private land supplied the sugar factory with 67,000 tons of cane in 1937. The success of earlier schemes and the growing economic crisis throughout the 1930s allowed for the continuation of this scheme which by 1943 involved 1,345 such settlements on over 12,000 acres of land.[8]

Travelling to the Caribbean in October 1938 as a member of the Royal Commission of 1938, Walter Citrine, Commission member and secretary of the Trades Union Congress makes an observation of the two images of the West Indies that he had uncovered. He wrote that in twelve guidebooks the islands were depicted as a 'western paradise', but that other sources revealed another kind of place that 'was composed of rude and squalid huts. I learned of natives earning 1/– a day on the plantations, of the lack of proper nutrition, the prevalence of venereal disease and there soon grew on me the impression that whatever else Great Britain had done she had not looked after the natives too well.'[9]

This was an observation quickly confirmed by experience for Citrine's tour of the Caribbean islands; both small and large would expose conditions that challenged his long held sense of British colonialism as a benign and supportive system where the 'native' populations of the colonies were concerned. In Nevis on Christmas Day in 1938 Citrine encounters an old woman whom he interrogates about her work and life. She described for him her labour on her land where she grows food and makes coal for use in cooking. In addition to this labour the sixty two year old woman worked for the Nevis public works where women earned 6 pence per day and men earned 1 shilling for the same work. Citrine is struck by the familiarity in demeanour of the Caribbean working people to that of the English working class, and it is perhaps this familiarity that contributed to Citrine's solidarity with them. He committed himself and the resources of the TUC in the cause of changing the very social and political nature of Caribbean society.

8 Ibid.
9 MF 226–227.

To complete the change in the Caribbean social fabric required the creation of trade unions run by competent men. This would become his primary concern during his investigative visit through 1938, to find men capable of trade union leadership. The 1938 Royal Commission marked an important turning point in the administration of the British Caribbean colonies. Not only did the members of the Commission become increasingly aware of the failures of the Empire and its colonial administrators, they were also less inclined as earlier Commissions had been, to overlook the many problems of the Empire. Conditions at home in England and the global labour situation favoured improvements in the Colonies and the Commission members, despite their disagreements on some issues, agreed unanimously to the report's recommendations for change.

It is clear that the labour and social unrest in colonial in Africa and Asia would play a role in influencing the British public in regards to colonialism. The language and attitude of Citrine and other members of the Commission reflected this African and Asian colonial influence. The language of the report and the language of awareness used by Citrine and other members speak to this influence: 'I will never again talk about our "trusteeship" for the coloured peoples of the Empire without a feeling of shame.'[10]

Uncovering Caribbean Conditions

The Royal Commission of 1938 was perhaps the most far reaching and effective of the last three of such Commissions. Earlier Commissions had been convened in 1897 and in 1929 to look into economic and social issues affecting the Caribbean colonies some of which were similar to the issues of the 1938 Royal Commission. A great part of the effectiveness of the Commission was no doubt tied to the personalities of the Commissioners themselves. Many of them had prior experiences in the colonies. The nine

10 Ibid.

member Commission chaired by Lord Moyne, comprised of Professor F. Engledow, Sir Percy Graham MacKinnon, Mr. Hubert Henderson, Dame Rachael Crowdy, Dr. Mary Blacklock, and Sir Edward Stubbs, who was Vice Chairman of the Commission.[11]

Sir Walter Citrine's presence on the 1938 Royal Commission was a surprise not only to Caribbean workers and labour organizers but also to scholars of the TUC. Of equal shock was the presence of Morgan Jones, Labour Party MP Until the 1920s, neither the Labour Party nor the TUC had shown much interest in assisting workers in the Empire, although the TUC's first representative to arrive in the West Indies, Hon. F. O. Roberts MP, had arrived in Trinidad in 1926.[12] The staff and accompanying spouses of the 1938 Royal Commission included Commission secretary Mr. T. I. K. Lloyd, and C. Y. Carstairs, secretaries of the Commission were staff of the Colonial Office. Mr. Rolph Assheton subsequently resigned from the Commission after the visit to the Caribbean to take the position of Parliamentary Secretary to the Ministry of Labour and National Service. MP Morgan Jones died shortly after returning from the Caribbean from an illness contracted in British Guiana.[13]

While colonial experience might have played some role in the effectiveness of this particular Commission, its most effective Commissioner (where labour issues and the Caribbean masses were concerned) was not the experienced Commissioners but instead the inexperienced Sir Walter Citrine, General Secretary of the TUC and the organization's representative on the Commission.[14] Citrine had little colonial experience, yet he more than any of the other Commissioners was most effective in connecting with the working people of the region and he became their symbol of the possibility for change in the colonies.

11 West India Royal Commission Report; HD 6571.

12 This surprise is registered by TUC scholar, Marjorie Nicholson, *The TUC Overseas: The Roots of Policy* (London: Allen & Unwin, 1986): 51–53.

13 HD 6571 Specific information on death of commission member was contained in Citrine's letters and reports.

14 HD 226–227. See Citrine's letters and the commission report for discussion of the role the members sought to play in the lives of Caribbean people. Citrine exposes in his reports and diary his familiarity with the Caribbean working people and their plight.

It was the poor condition of the Caribbean economy and the seeming deterioration of social order that provided the impetus for the British Government's decision to authorize the 1938 Royal Commission. Throughout the Caribbean region beginning in 1934 a series of labour riots shattered the uneasy calm that had followed earlier labour discontent of the Post World War I period. These latest riots were the result of workers' demands for living wages and for better working conditions. The riots resulted when their often reasonable demands and peaceful demonstrations were met with force from local militia, police and private forces. These incidents were not confined to a few islands but seemed to spread from island to island for the four year period between 1934–1938. There were a few incidents during and after the Commission visit through 1938.

The decision to send a royal Commission according to sociologist O. Nigel Bolland, was the result of the particular attitude of the Colonial Office to treat the Caribbean colonies as a region in terms of response. In effect, trouble in a few warranted an investigation of the total. The Commission arrived in Antigua not because of problems on the island, for as Bolland and others scholars have pointed out, Antigua had come to be perceived as a quiet isle where labour unrest was rare.[15] The Royal Warrant dated 5 August 1938 was 'to investigate social and economic conditions in Barbados, British Guiana, British Honduras, Jamaica, the Leeward Islands, Trinidad and Tobago, and the Windward Islands, and matters connected therewith, and to make recommendations.'[16]

A Role for the TUC

Until the assignment of Sir Walter Citrine to the Royal Commission in 1938 the TUC had paid very little attention to labour in the British Caribbean islands, and the Leeward Islands in particular were much ignored. The

15 O. Nigel Bolland, *The Politics of Labour*, 212–368; see also discussion on 333–335.
16 HD 6571.

TUC records on the British Caribbean at the TUC Library in London, UK provide evidence of this. TUC scholar Marjorie Nicholson states the obvious of TUC limited interest in labour issues prior to the late 1930s labour unrest.[17] This is not lost on other scholars of the Caribbean, including Caribbean social scientists, historians and labour activists in particular whose tendency it is to ignore the TUC altogether in discussions of Caribbean labour history even in the late 1930s.

Thus the tendencies are two-fold. The TUC's contributions to the rise of trade unions in the British Caribbean colonies became overlooked entirely or the centrality of the role of the TUC in the creation of trade unions and the fostering of labour parties is downplayed. In the case of Antigua and Barbuda many labour historians mention the role of Walter Citrine in encouraging the formation of trade unions in the region, when he arrived there in 1938. This is as far as most of this literature goes in acknowledging a role for the TUC in Leeward Island's labour history. As a graduate student conducting research on labour and trade unions in London in 2002, I was surprised to encounter the Leeward Island files at the TUC library in London. The array of notes, articles, reports on the Windward and Leeward Islands, exposed a history of TUC support that dated to 1938.[18] My research and documents of the ATLU indicate that Walter Citrine and the TUC were extremely involved in the early organizing of workers in the Leeward Islands and that on Antigua and Barbuda after 1938 they provided extensive support for Leeward Islands trade unions. This involvement included providing literature and training union personnel.

The exclusion of the TUC from the history of labour in the Caribbean is a clear indication of Caribbean nationalism that seeks to downplay the

17 Marjorie Nicholson, *The TUC Overseas*, 51–53. The first TUC representative to arrive in the West Indies did so in 1926 and the focus was largely in the Southern Caribbean and Guiana.

18 Prior to reading these documents I had read and reviewed text and bibliography of a number of secondary sources including Novelle Richards, Caroline M. Carmody and Malcolm Cross and Gad Heuman. The role of the TUC in Leeward Islands labour was certainly mentioned but the level of involvement had escaped me until my foray into the archives.

role of outside forces, particularly colonial institutions, even labour institutions in the larger labour movement in the Colonies. For its part the motives of the TUC also bears examining. Throughout much of the twentieth century the organization had shown almost no interest in the Caribbean labour force. In the late 1930s the TUC inserted itself into the Caribbean labour situation using the Royal Commission as its outlet for changing dramatically its relationship with the British Caribbean labour. Colonial paternalism was the charge directed at the TUC by critics in the region, and their surprising presence in 1938 certainly begs the question about why the sudden interest. For scholars such as Nicholson, the role of the TUC in the Caribbean region after World War I was clearly part of the larger political process of decolonization.[19]

Marjorie Nicholson: The TUC Overseas

To the degree that Walter Citrine is absent from Caribbean labour literature, he is central in any TUC literature of the period. TUC librarians insist that to understand the organization and its policies in the twentieth century requires reading the works of TUC scholar Marjorie Nicholson. Nicholson's work includes an examination of the TUC's efforts to assist the development of trade unionism in the British-dependent Empire. She notes that it was not until after World War II that the TUC's policies and methods were 'substantially charted' yet the Commission of 1938 shows a TUC presence prior to the outbreak of the war. The question of TUC motives is not a clear one for her to answer and the two possible answers are wrapped into a question – 'Was the effort based upon trade union fraternity or colonial paternalism?'[20] The TUC it seems has been accused of both, both in the Caribbean and in Britain.

19 Marjorie Nicholson. *The TUC Overseas*, 1–5, 82–83.

20 Ibid., 1–3.

TUC policies in the region was clearly a combination of both efforts, and Nicholson, has identified the organizations's General Secretary, Sir Vincent Tewson as crucial to the new role the organization would play in the dependent Empire in the post-war periods. During both pre and post war periods TUC leaders were tapped by the British government to help assist in creating colonial organizations that would assist in moving the program of decolonization forward. They were also responsible for leadership training for future state leaders in the colonies. Recognizing this TUC role certainly explains the actions and concerns of TUC leadership in the Caribbean and elsewhere in the colonial Empire. Tewson's questions 'How will they be able to run a country, if they can't run a trade union branch?'[21] a concern he expressed long before any TUC presence in the Caribbean mirrors the concern expressed by Walter Citrine in the Caribbean where he constantly lamented the shortage of men with the capacity to lead trade union branches.

In many ways what the TUC was trying to do in the Caribbean was understandable. It was an organization that responded to requests or demands for action and one which made decisions in specific situations in response to individual or group requests. Its action policy response largely grew of the demands made upon the organization by other organizations including International Labour Organization (ILO) and the British Government as well as trade unionists in the United States and the Caribbean. These actions would eventually be developed into a coherent policy for the Caribbean colonies.

Where the Caribbean policies were concerned the TUC involvement grew after 1938. This growth seems to have been largely guided by Citrine who sought to maintain his connections with Caribbean workers after his return to the UK It became clear for Citrine and the TUC that the Caribbean labour force, alienated from the labour movements in Britain despite the rhetoric of solidarity that accompanied emancipation a century before, had been underserved by the TUC and that their needs were dire.

British trade unionism according to Nicholson had been built on the first simple assertion of the right of working men in combination to have a

21 Ibid.

say in determining their wages and conditions of employment. At its inception the movement called for reconstructing relations between workers and employers. In the Caribbean colonies not unlike the early movement in Britain such changes required changes in British law and required a new commitment by government. The British government had been forced by trade unionism to take on new responsibilities for labour conditions, for intervention in disputes between labour and capital, as well as regulating social and political life of the working people.

Nicholson notes that from very early British trade union organizers realized that trade unionism was inseparable from the development of political ideas and institutions. Where the Caribbean situation was concerned in the post World War II period in particular, the example of British trade unions had peculiar weight in Empire dependencies. Labour was one element in the relation between the Empire and its various instruments of populations controlled. The British trade union experience was quite relevant (thought far from equal) to the problems of colonial workers where British firms, British laws and British-controlled governments were dominant. Certainly race, slavery and the differences of law distinguished the experiences for both groups of labourers.

In both Britain and the Caribbean trade unions were formed before working people had political rights. In the struggle for the vote and for seats in Parliament and legislature trade unionists had to be willing to adjust themselves to new social and political realities. These adjustments including developing new awareness and embracing various ideas and partnerships. For the ATLU the evolution took two decades to the 1960s; and the challenges encountered by its leadership and the leadership throughout the region, greatly mirrored those encountered by the British movement.

The TUC and the Colonial Trade Unions

From the 1930s the TUC's colonial advisory committee sought to find ways to extend trade unionism outside of Great Britain. The colonies became a focus both because groups and individuals sought help from

Great Britain and because within Britain there were trade unionists who saw the colonies as natural extension sites for the TUC. The invitation to Citrine by MacDonald, the Secretary of the Labour Party in 1938 to serve on the Royal Commission provided a perfect opportunity for the TUC to pursue its goals of extending trade unionism to the Caribbean region. Sir Walter Citrine was accompanied on the Commission by Labour MP Ralph Asheton, and Morgan Jones. Despite the concerns that they alone were not enough to inspire confidence among Caribbean populations that would result in the trans-Atlantic labour partnership; the Commission's mission of building confidence among the labouring population and in building trade unions in colonies where no such organizations had existed prior to 1938 – was a tremendous success. By 1941, even the smallest British colonies in the West Indies could boast of the presence of unions. In Trinidad where unions already existed there were demands that the Commission investigation include demands for constitutional changes in 1938. The arrival of the Commission was met by a guarded population. The departure of the Commission was more emotional, as the population in Trinidad realized that some Commission members were on their side and supported their demands for better working and social conditions.

Prior to 1938 steps had already been made towards forming trade unions by Caribbean workers. In the larger colonies such as British Guiana, and Trinidad, some unions were already established and had already reached out to the TUC. In Guiana by 1938 some five unions as well as the British Guiana Workers' League, the Man-Power Citizens' Association and the Seamen's Union as well as Transport Workers' and Post Office Workers' Unions already existed. In Trinidad the Trinidad Workingman's Association (TWMA) and the Trinidad Labour Party were established affiliates with the TUC by 1935 and other unions sought affiliation not with existing TUC affiliates but with the TUC directly thereafter. In Jamaica as early as 1919, a Trade Union Ordinance had allowed for the beginning of trade unionism on that island.[22]

22 O. Nigel Bolland, *The Politics of Labour*, 359–368.

In the Leeward Islands the formation of unions and attempts at collective bargaining were discouraged by the laws in the presidencies. It was therefore not surprising that Commission staff member Orde Brown found 'no registered trade unions anywhere.'[23] In Antigua he expressed the opinion that existing organizations such as the Antigua Workingmen's Association and the Employers' and Employees' Association were possible sources for union formation. Citrine and Brown focused their attention throughout the smaller British colonies on placating leaders and members of friendly societies and workers clubs as well as teachers and other civil service groups. It is important to recognize that Caribbean workers, those in the smaller colonies in particular, had already put in place one of the key elements of trade unionism, that of collective action. The partnership with the TUC from 1938 was a crucial one because the TUC was the only British organization that could effectively represent the interests of Caribbean labour in the Colonial Office. Certainly, the close relationship between the TUC and the British Labour party provided a supportive environment for labour organizing and the Colonial Office consistently turned to the TUC for help where issues of labour and trade unions in the West Indies were concerned.

Walter Citrine and the British Labour Tradition

Prior to the 1938 Commission the TUC and Labour party had looked with growing interest at the Caribbean labour population, discussing ways to expand their organization's influence among the subject people. This interest had first been directed in 1918 and even during labour's brief period in government in 1924, and 1929, neither solidarity nor any real contact had been made with colonial labour populations. In the Leeward Islands throughout the first half of the 1930s neither the TUC nor the Labour party were known to the working people of the region. Caribbean workers

23 Orde Brown, *Labour Conditions in the West Indies* (hereafter HD 8191.5).

therefore through the late 1930s had no reason to look to British labour organizations for help in their struggles in the colonies.[24]

TUC interest in the Caribbean region in the late 1930s is clearly expressed in the correspondence of Walter Citrine during the Commission visit to the Caribbean 1938–1938's tour. Beginning with his first correspondence in December 1938 Citrine makes clear the objective of the TUC and the role which he was to play as a labour representative in the Caribbean, responsible for establishing a relationship and for building trade unions. His later correspondence exposed the fact that the challenges to union organizing were varied and were not always the result of local problems. The smaller islands of the eastern Caribbean proved to be a particularly difficult case because of the small wage-earning population and the absence or paucity of capable men. Clearly Citrine's own racial, class and gender biases limited his choice of leaders. Yet the challenges in the region went far beyond the limited view of who could be leaders. The letters which Citrine wrote during the Commission visit throughout 1938, reflect the varied concerns for him and other Commissioners. The Caribbean provided a range of experiences and challenges to the aims and objectives of the TUC.[25]

Both Commission members and their accompanying spouses documented their Caribbean experiences. Citrine's wife Doris accompanied him to the Caribbean in 1938. In a letter written to the TUC office and addressed to Ms. Macdonald, her husband's secretary, she shared her own experience of the journey and of the Caribbean environment. She states she is not writing a descriptive letter because Sir Walter has already done so but she states towards the end of the letter – 'I am writing this on a balcony overlooking the conference room and I can see when the session is finished as soon as there is several movement. It commences at 10 a.m.–5 p.m. quite a long day for this climate here. Most of the witnesses are very well informed and interesting people.'[26]

24 Marjorie Nicholson, *The TUC Overseas*, 82–83.

25 MF 226–227.

26 Ibid. Letter dated 8 November.

The impression of the Caribbean and of its people through the eyes of even the most progressive members of the Commission is an interesting one, and despite their progressive attitudes, even the Citrines are not quite clear on the equality and ability of Caribbean people, and they are clearly concerned about the social and political challenges existing in Caribbean societies that would make the kind of labour utopia envisioned by the TUC a difficult task. In Jamaica Citrine addressed the challenges of a society where trade unions already existed. In addition to Jamaica this included the island of Trinidad. Both islands had trade unions and trade union laws. In Jamaica trade union leaders Bustamante, Norman Manley and Coombs had to be reconciled and the relations with the Governor Sir Arthur Richards repaired. In addition, Citrine highlights an area of labour progress in Jamaica in the form of the Trade Union Bill introduced 2 December 1938. 'The Bill, as it now stands, is a far better one than our own Trade Union Act of 1927 from a trade union point of view.' He further described what made the Jamaica bill an improvement on the UK bill. 'It has dealt with the principal circumstances which I have brought out in Commission regarding the power to sue a union for tort and picketing which it places on the same basis as our English law. There is no mention of illegal strikes due again to my influence with the governor [...] I am going to use this Bill in other parts of the West Indies'.[27]

> I have still to see my fellow commissioners who have gone to Honduras but [...] I am satisfied that the work in Jamaica has made it worth while coming [...] I hope I shall get along all right with Moyne [...] I have no intention of allowing this mission to become a hush-hush inquiry.[28]

The Commissions would split up periodically and investigate other islands including Puerto Rico, Cuba, the Dominican Republic and the US Virgin islands. Members then compared their findings on these islands to those in the British Caribbean colonies. In Cuba, Citrine reports that things are not as bad particularly in regards to housing as in Jamaica. He makes reference

27 Ibid. Letter from Constant Spring Hotel, Jamaica.

28 Ibid. Source is letter from Havana (10 December 1938): 4.

to the education system of Cuba and to the problems for Jamaican immigrant workers after the Cuban sugar boom on that island had ended. He complains in his letter (M. Y. Rosaura. Saturday 17 December) 'the Cuban government now wishes to get rid of as quickly as they can'. He seemed almost shocked at his experience in Puerto Rico which he described as 'the most encouraging place I have visited'.[29] Elsewhere in Central America and particularly on Honduras where British settlers had carved out a sugar colony (Belize), he described as 'very pessimistic.' Belize is described by Morgan Jones as a swamp with 'no Trade Union or Labour leaders worth their salt.' He noted quite woefully that 'things are not very hopeful for labour there.'[30]

St. Croix visited by Citrine is described as 'so small we could learn very little from it.' As in Puerto Rico the federal government loans were the basis of ongoing construction, and Citrine noted that the government (this being the United States) was 'practically almost the only employer, running its sugar industries through a body called Island Company.' Citrine notes the surprise of local officials when he told them that their existing system was operating 'like socialism'. He is inspired by the existence of a labour union with some fourteen hundred members (1,400) members.

> As for Trade Unionism, the prospects in this island vary considerably. Sometimes as in Montserrat, Tortola, Anguilla and Dominica it seems hopeless to do anything. There are only a comparatively few who are real wage earners in the sense that we know it. There are many devices, such as the share system whereby the landlord accepts produce in lieu of rent and charges pretty highly in the process, I am certain. Other times there is a mutilated system of peasant proprietorship in operation. Thus in Dominica, the island we have just left, there are only about 1,000 labourers who earn wages out of 10,000 dependent on agriculture. It will not be easy to start a trade union under such circumstance.[31]

In this situation he suggested a federation of trade unions for the region to handle wage negotiations – its branches or separate unions would have full autonomy in local matters. Of additional concern he notes in his letter the

29 Ibid. Source is letter from M. Y. Rosaura (December 1938): 1–3.

30 Ibid.

31 Ibid. Source is letter from Guadeloupe (14 January 1938): 9.

existence in the Leeward Islands of a disturbing legal code. The Sedition Act of 1938 'There is one thing I want watched at home. That is the sedition act passed in the Leewards a few months ago. This, I think, is dangerous and some of its clauses might make it difficult to conduct trade union action.'[32] In addition in this letter Citrine calls for response at TUC Colonial Advisory Committee to protest clauses of the Act particularly the parts which defined what seditious intention was.

By January of 1938 Citrine had made his way to Barbados, where he continued to look for local leadership and investigate the labour conditions of the Eastern Caribbean. But while he may have been a labour progressive he was still a white British man, who was convinced that the local black population needed white male leadership in order to run their societies effectively. He wrote of his experience in St. Lucia where a mudslide had destroyed villages and killed 140 people. Citrine wrote that upon his arrival on the island he saw people attempting to repair a road that had been destroyed by the mudslide and his reaction to what he witnessed: 'when I saw the poor natives repairing the roadway without a single white man on the spot, as far as I could see, it seemed to me that they were doing it in such a fashion as to make it possible that there would be another landslide'.[33] In the southern Caribbean, his ongoing search for capable male leaders led him to comment on the situation in St. Vincent where 'all the progressive peoples who seemed to want to lead the people to better things in these Windward islands, seemed to be druggists'.[34] It is clear that Citrine had his own issues of racism and classism. These appear quite clearly to me from his letters and in his responses to the black and coloured population in the region. Not surprisingly, Citrine is unaware of his own prejudices. True, he is nothing like his West Indian contemporaries (white elite and colonial administrators), who he recognized as far more discriminatory in their relations with the local white and coloured population, and whose actions he complained about throughout his visit.

32 Ibid., 8.

33 Ibid. Source is letter from Barbados (January 1938).

34 Ibid. Source is letter from St. Vincent.

> Altogether, I cannot say with any truth that I feel sure of the impartiality of British administration here. It is singular that there was not a single black person present at the dinner last night I went to at Government House. I have heard that wherever there is sugar there is a colour bar. With bananas it is different and the intermingling of the races is far better. I am told people may be invited to a garden party who are coloured but not to a dinner. I know that is not true of the Leeward Islands because I distinctly remember seeing several Black men present at a dinner we had in government house.[35]

Citrine continuously expresses in his letters his unhappiness with the 'colour bar' in Barbados. 'The people are good people but (that) on the whole they are patronized and treated definitely as inferiors by the whites.'[36] But while the colour bar was one visible to Citrine and one which he rejected, he was not able to see his own 'gender bar' stating in his letter 'everywhere I go in these islands I find it difficult to see who the future leaders of the workers are to be. None the less, I am always on the lookout for a young and reliable man.'[37] If the TUC thought that what they would be able to achieve was a more manageable labour population for the British Empire, they clearly knew that the introduction of trade unionism in the Caribbean could go either way for the Empire, either it created the servile labour force from a trade unionism under imperial control and which has control of workers, or trade unionism could create the opposite political situation and construct nationalist political parties which severed all relations with the Empire, violently. The potential for political action through unionism was clearly among his concerns when he toured the region and he noted, in the Leeward Islands.

> I have addressed public meetings in addition in Antigua, St. Vincent, St. Kitts, and I am going to address one in Barbados on Wednesday evening. I am always careful to speak on Trade Unionism and I do not introduce politics, always conveying the impression that the Trade Unions can themselves put the case in the legislative field. I think it would hamper the trade union movement in these places if too much stress was placed on the political aspects and so I carefully keep away from it.[38]

35 Letter from Barbados (January 1938).
36 Ibid.
37 Ibid. Source is letter from Barbados (January 1938).
38 Ibid.

By the end of his tour of the West Indies, Citrine had achieved its aim of identifying the first batch of trade union leaders in the region. He identified this group in his letter from Georgetown Guiana, in which he recommended ways by which the TUC would maintain its influence over local trade unions. In this correspondence Citrine suggests the TUC to maintain its involvement in the region by subscribing to local daily papers. The papers were to serve as record of activities in the islands. In his letter introducing the first recruits, Citrine also instructed the TUC office to arrange for their training as well as provide to them crucial trade union materials. Each person on the list was to be sent a copy of the study course, and the book of the Tolpuddle Martyrs. The first group of recruits was all male.

CHAPTER 5

Local Level Leadership

> I might go as far as to say that the history of Antigua from 1938–1964 has been the history of the Trade Union.[1]
>
> — NOVELLE RICHARDS

The legalization and formation of trade unions in the Leeward Islands created the opportunity for much needed social change. This social change was not only in relation to improvements in conditions of work for labourers but also in creating opportunities for members of the working class and middle class to have an outlet for leadership. In many ways trade unionism was one of the most transformative institutions in Leeward Island history in the twentieth century. Not only did the trade union offer workers the opportunity for collective action, it also gave them their first real freedom to engage employers in discussions regarding pay rate and work conditions. In addition, unlike the rest of the region the leadership of trade unions was in the hands of working and lower middle class men in Antigua. The trade unions offered a unique opportunity for leadership for these men. The rise of trade unionism was aided by the existence of local social organizations such as lodges and friendly societies, organizations which had traditionally provided the outlet and opportunities for local men and women to organize socially and to act collectively. In the decade following the formation of the ATLU in Antigua and Barbuda, much of the local leadership shifted from the lodges, friendly societies and village organizations to unions. The TUC, whose institutional structure, laws and labour ideology was

1 Novelle Richards, 'Foreword', *The Struggle and the Conquest*.

imported into Antigua and Barbuda in 1940, had a gendered division of participation based in its history representing a primarily male industrial workforce in Britain.

The ATLU was born of two organizational influences. On the local level there were the local organizations, lodges, friendly societies and village organizations. While these organizations served both men and women, top leadership positions appear to have been reserved for men only. The foreign (and certainly more politically powerful) partner to the ATLU which came out of the British organized labour tradition was the Trades Union Congress (TUC). The TUC, an organization whose structure was also heavily patriarchal would pass on its history, traditions and institutions to trade union organizations in the Caribbean. The resulting product of these two influences was the ATLU, an organization whose membership and core constituency was heavily female but whose top leadership was exclusively male. This disparity in organizational power would become a tradition in both the union and in political parties formed by the union leadership over the next four decades. The ATLU inherited the double patriarchal patterns of its parent organizations, and while women's membership and active participation was crucial to the organization; women remained excluded from top leadership positions. This pattern of gender discrimination became a feature of the organization into the last decade of the twentieth century.

Gender Roles in the TUC and ATLU

In her book on trade union leadership in Antigua, the anthropologist Caroline Carmody (1978) describes this leadership pattern as one which was unique for the region.[2] This uniqueness, she argued, was the result of the connection between local organizations and the leadership core. This

2 Caroline Carmody, 'First among Equals', 1.

book provides an extremely useful outline of Antiguan organizational forms through the 1970s, as Carmody examines the relations between the patterns of leadership within local organizations prior to 1938 and the trade union leadership patterns that were formed thereafter. Her finding that both the leaders of local lodges and community leaders became active members in the union, many holding top leadership positions, demonstrates that the ATLU at its inception was influenced by local leadership tradition, and was not completely the instrument of the British trade union tradition. The TUC clearly influenced the overall structure of the organization and sought to control the philosophy and actions of the members and leadership of the organization. In the early stages, the organization's leaders willingly embraced the British labour movement philosophy and to this day continue to recite the 'Red Flag' to affirm its identification with the overall philosophy of the movement. Yet from very early on, as early as the 1950s, it also became clear that these two traditions produced great conflict within the organization and especially within the TUC.

Local organizations embraced the symbols, themes and imagery of the TUC but they also were clearly the products of the village and grassroots organizations such as the lodges and the labour and political organizations that emerged from 1940 onwards.[3] This position is confirmed by the local trade unionist, Novelle Richards whose monograph on trade union movement in Antigua confirms Carmody's analysis. In his work *The Struggle and the Conquest* Richards wrote 'The late 1930s was an influential period for the union, an organization that was born from the lodges and other grass roots organizations whose members and in particular, leadership came to comprise the membership and leadership for the trade unions.'[4] Novelle Richards is clear on the role of local initiative in the selection of union leaders 'in looking for leadership for the trade union it was to the lodges that all eyes were turned, for it was realized from early that the trade union had to be a people's organization and therefore could only draw its

3 Ibid., 1–3. Carmody concluded in her work 'that in Antigua, the organizational and leadership patterns are unique in relation to the rest of the British Caribbean'.

4 Novelle Richards, *The Struggle and the Conquest*, 1.

membership from the working class people who comprised the membership of the several lodges.'[5] The majority of the early trade unions' leaders were lodge men, and as the trade union became a crucial factor in the social and political life of the 'people' lodges and other local organizations that had been the focus of local organizing and leadership would decline to the point of extinction by the 1970s. Trade unions and political parties became the central focus for the training of leaders after universal adult suffrage was achieved in Antigua in 1951.

By the 1970s Carmody's female sources confirmed women's active role in the early union as members, union organizers, and secretary and zone leaders. Many of these sources had themselves been active in the unions. When asked directly about women's absence from top leadership (a position which would include the two most powerful union positions of president and vice president) most responded defensively that women's role in unions was to provide support to the union members and to 'stand behind the men.'[6] Clearly neither the role of organizer, nor that of secretary or zone leader was a 'stand behind the men' position. They clearly became seen as such and the leadership limitations on women were clearly positions supported by both men and women at all levels of the union. Despite the importance of organizers, and zone leaders, these became characterized as 'stand behind the men' positions because they were positions which women in the union could occupy.[7] From the beginning of trade union organizing in 1938 through the 1970s when Carmody conducted her research, the ideology of a limited role for women in union leadership was well entrenched. Carmody, however, documents that there existed also the perception among some that in time women could gain a stronger role in leadership in both unions and political parties. Such a gain has not been achieved fully two decades later.[8]

5 Ibid., 8.
6 Caroline Carmody, 'First Among Equals' source is female informant on Antigua.
7 Ibid.
8 Ibid.

Trade Union Organizing and History of Leadership

The formation of lodges preceded the creation of trade unions and first union leadership came from lodges of lower middle and working class. The two primary organizations for lower middle and working class Antiguans in the late 1930s were the Odd Fellows and Household of Ruth. In addition to these lodges friendly societies such as the Ulothrichan Friendly Society offered the people the opportunity to socialize, and to create some economic security for themselves.

It was within these organizations that many local orators would be born, individuals who used their speaking ability to capture leadership positions. Richards recalled that the office holders in the local lodges were often the most talkative men in the villages. The most important leadership position in the lodges was that of the Grand Master, a position which required leadership of both the membership and other officers of the lodge. This position required oratory and people skills. Even after their election to the position of grand masters persons wanting to maintain their leadership role, needed to continue to canvass members and to maintain a strong influence over the membership of the lodge.[9] These organizations placed a great deal of emphasis on pageantry or displays of membership and loyalty to the organization. These were important for recruiting new members, as well as to build a sense of pride among the members. Displays were particularly important to these organizations and these included events such as special banquets and thanksgiving services which included a parade with brass bands. Perhaps the most pageantry was reserved for the funeral of lodge members when the lodges organized 'turn-out'. In effect the funeral for lodge members was organized and funded completely by the lodge. This was one of the benefits of membership paid for by lodge dues. At the funeral the lodge lead the procession and directed the performance of rites in the cemetery.[10]

9 Novelle Richards, *The Struggle and the Conquest* 3–7.
10 Ibid.

These organizations played no political role in Antigua and Barbuda, largely because they were denied any role by law. Their function was purely social and their activities were purely ceremonial. While Grand Masters sometimes sought to mediate for lodge members in their communities or with state officials, because most of the membership were denied suffrage these organizations lacked any political power. Their mediation was solely that of individuals seeking the support of local officials, and was not recognized as leaders speaking for a collective with any power or say in labour or other state affairs.

Attempts at collective action by lodge members were often crushed by the state and organizations identified as engaging in these actions would be eliminated.[11] The colonial administration kept a close control on the population of the region and attempts at social, economic and political advancement by the local population was heavily censored by the small white elite. These controls contributed to stifling the growth of the middle class on the island, as well as stifling the emergence of 'men with the capacity to lead'. The lodges and other agricultural and community organizations remained the only outlet for the development of local leadership until the formation of the Antigua Trades and Labour Union in 1940.[12]

Trade unionism as introduced by the TUC to the Leeward Islands and the Caribbean in the late 1930s was designed to provide an answer to the labour problems the region faced. The support the TUC's actions got from the British government reflected its willingness to seek solutions to the intensifying labour problem facing the region in the 1930s. The introduction of trade unions would solve one problem for the British crown and another for the TUC, the need for a new membership base. After a whole century of ignoring the large Black and Indian labour force in the Caribbean, the TUC, motivated by a need to expand its membership base sought to ally itself with Caribbean labour. It was clear that the TUC did not seek to create political organizations. In fact it sought through the 1950s to discourage Caribbean trade unions from becoming too politicized.

11 Ibid.

12 Issues addressed by Novelle Richards and Caroline Carmody.

Yet, anyone who looked honestly at the conditions in the region would have recognized that the problems of labour were social, economic and particularly political problems.

Vere Cornwall and Trade Union Masculinity

On the twin island nations of Antigua and Barbuda in late June 1999 thousands of people gathered to mourn and to celebrate the life of Sir Vere Cornwall Bird (V. C.). Born in 1909 to Amanda Edgehill in a poor community outside St. Johns, the island's capital, he had worked as a clerk and assistant surveyor before joining the Salvation Army. By 1938 when the ATLU was formed, V. C., who had been involved with Caribbean labour activities in Trinidad and in Grenada while serving as a Salvation Army officer, was elected to the union Executive. He would eventually resign his post in the Salvation Army to join the trade union movement in Antigua and Barbuda full-time. For over fifty years V. C. dominated political life on the island, he was Antiguan politics – as Leonard Tim Hector, local journalist and politician wrote in 1999 'Bird was all politics. His was the single-minded pursuit of political ends. Politics was his only occupation and pre-occupation. Longevity in power was his reward.'[13]

Bird's ascendance to the pinnacle of political life on the small island nation followed closely the route of British attempts to withdraw from its Caribbean possessions. By the early 1980s when the island gained its independence from Great Britain its fate was left to be decided under V. C.'s leadership. Accorded the title 'Father of the Nation' and addressed by both his supporters and detractors alike as Papa Bird. V. C. had come to embody both the good and the bad in the Antigua and Barbuda political system in

13 Leonard Tim Hector 'Hail Bwana! Farewell Papa!', in the editorial section of Fan the Flame, *Outlet Newspaper*, 9 July 1999 reprinted at website *Fan the Flame* (1996–2002), accessed 15 June 2005 <http://www.candw.ag/~jardinea/ffhtm/ff990708.htm>.

the second half of the twentieth century. It is V. C. who has been credited with freeing the island from 'the yoke of colonialism'. V. C. had begun his political career as a trade unionist. He had been one of the founding members of the ATLU and in 1943, became president of the union, the second president in the unions' short history from 1940. In 1968 he became the first Premier of Antigua and Barbuda when the island received associated statehood with Britain and was the first Prime Minister of the island in 1981 when the island gained its independence from Britain. When V. C. retired from direct political participation in Antigua and Barbuda politics in 1994, he left firmly in place two sons Vere Junior and Lester to carry on his political legacy.

V. C. as Informant

One of the many roles that V. C. came to embrace on Antigua was that of griot. He travelled the island schools, graced podiums of Caribbean political and educational platforms telling the history of the Antiguan working people and the history of struggle in the Caribbean against British Colonialism. He never wrote, and the few books produced on his behalf were done without his endorsement. In addition much of the history of the Caribbean has been written excluding V. C. despite the central role he played in both Leeward Islands history and in the history of the Caribbean region in general. V. C. was a prominent player in early attempts at regional integration, and he was crucial to the emergence of the Caribbean Free Trade Agreement (CARIFTA), the forerunner organization to CARICOM, which in 1968 created the first truly regional organization.[14] It was V. C. who orchestrated the attack against land-monopoly by the small plantocracy and who directed the first land redistribution

14 <http://www.caricom.org/archives/agreement-carifta.pdf > and see also <http://www.caricom.org/>.

program in Antigua. It was also V. C. who successfully wrestled control of the island's economy from the local elite and from British and other foreign interests. One of his staunchest critics and his greatest admirers, the late Tim Hector, wrote a convincing explanation of the anomaly that was V. C. Hector argued that Bird contributed to his exclusion from the history books. V. C. Bird had no hobbies, no past-time. Writing was not his forte like Williams or Balaguer. V. C. himself boasted nationally, even vaingloriously, that he had not read a book since he left school at 18. His ideas, he felt, were all his own. It was a total misconception.[15]

As the griot, the story teller, he told the story of the labour and anti-colonial struggles of his generation to school children of all ages, rarely deviating from the script of the struggle of the people against the landed elite and a racist British colonial structure. These were recorded by the party-owned newspapers and broadcast media. In 1978 the Premier made his speech on 'The Development of Trade Unionism in Antigua'. He centred the Royal Commission of 1938 and Walter Citrine as important turning points for labour conditions on the island. Citrine himself recorded his experiences in the Caribbean between 1938 and 1938 as a member of the Royal Commission chaired by Lord Moyne.[16] V. C. reported that he witnessed, or at least followed closely the activities of the Commission on the island. Under what conditions Citrine reached out to suggest a meeting is unclear from his account, but he relates a requested meeting by Citrine, and that such a meeting was organized at the Cathedral Schoolroom in St. Johns where Citrine is reported to have said 'I wanted to speak at this meeting because I've seen the sufferings and the poverty. I will tell you what we did in England in order to rid ourselves of such conditions.'[17]

Citrine volunteered to share British labour techniques with the group and the result of this meeting was the calling of a second meeting by a

15 Tim Hector's online newspaper *Fan The Flame*, <http://www.candw.ag/~jardinea/fanflame.htm>.

16 Speech by the Hon.Premier V. C. Bird, 24 October 1978 at the State College. Printed in *Antigua Trade and Labour Union 40th Anniversary Magazine* (Antigua: Antigua printing and Publishing, 1980).

17 Ibid. Quoted from V. C. speech of 24 October 1978.

number of the men who had been invited by Citrine to his talk. This smaller private meeting V. C. reported was called at the home of Norris Allen who lived on Lower Bishopgate Street in St. Johns City. It was attended by a select group of men – Norris Allen, Reginald Stevens, F. O. Benjamin, S. A. Henry, V. C. Bird, Griffith Matthews, Randolph Lockhart, B. A. Richards, Thomas Martin, James Jarvis, Stanley Walter, C. A. Perry and Thomas Brooks. It was at this meeting that the decision to take Citrine's advice and form a union was made. The thirteen men gathered at the meeting became the provisional executive of the organization they named the Antigua Trades and Labour Union. President was Reginald Stevens; Secretary S. A. Henry and Treasurer F. O. Benjamin represented the first executive of the organization.

The ATLU, formed in a period of heightened expectations in the home of a working class Antiguan, marked a watershed in the history of the island. This same scenario repeated itself throughout the region, the creation of trade unions under the supervision of the TUC and with the support of the Colonial Office. This reflected a dramatic change in the British colonial labour policies in the twentieth century. It was the first time since emancipation in 1834 that the island's' black and coloured majority were protected in their efforts to create organizations to engage in collective action. This was an organization which was not forced to hide its objectives behind a purely social mission, but could openly state its mission to work for the collective good of the working people. The challenge of creating a union in a colony where the majority population was excluded from the political process would quickly make itself evident to organization leaders. The 1930s were difficult economic times globally but colonial people who seemed to suffer the most in periods of economic stagnation rose in rebellion four years after the centenary of immediate emancipation on the island V. C. described the labour situation in the region . 'The people were restless; they were tired of being ill-treated and fed-up with being oppressed, so they rebelled in Jamaica, Trinidad, St. Kitts and other countries.'[18] His recollection was that the British government's response to conditions in the Caribbean was the sending of a royal Commission to the region. The

18 Ibid.

members of this Commission saw the atrocious conditions under which Caribbean people lived and worked. On Antigua wages ranged from 4d a day for women and 10d for men; by workers 'toiled long and painful hours from six in the morning until six in the evening'. In addition to low wages housing conditions were desperate 'homes were built of wattle cut from the bush and trash from the field covered the roof. The floor very often was the earth.'[19]

The story of the 1938 Royal Commission is an important one for the region. This was the single most important Commission of the century, not because it was organized to investigate labour conditions in the region, but because it produced the greatest results for the people of the region, especially the Leeward Islands where the small size of the islands and the large agricultural labour force, made industrial organizing difficult. There was in twentieth-century Leeward Islands no 'aristocracy of labour', no industries and therefore no industrial labour force with power, size, and skills to negotiate with employers. The closest to industrial labour force that the island of Antigua had was the Sugar Factory, and the workers there were heavily restricted in their activities by the factory management. The urban working class in the region was divided between domestics, small business owners, druggists and newspaper editors, salesmen and women.

The black and coloured civil service was too small and too restricted by colonial laws to play a significant role in labour organizing even after trade unions were legalized in 1940, their participation was limited. The dockworkers, porters and jobbers, a steady flow of day labourers who loaded and unloaded the ships, were perhaps the most organized of workers on the island. These workers were represented by the Antigua Progressive Seamen's Friendly Society and the Antigua Workingmen's Association. Both of these organizations through 1940 had sought to protect their members' interests through petitioning the Governor and employers for increased wages and for shorter workdays for their members. They had no role as collective bargaining agents for their members and other than their social functions their actions were limited by law to petitions.

19 Ibid.

The Workingmen's Association, formed in 1933, had been inspired by a 1932 conference convened in Dominica by Caribbean leaders promoting both federation and adult franchise. Following the Dominica conference Harold Tobias Wilson, editor of the *Antigua Magnet* newspaper called a meeting with five other leaders in the Antigun middle class to discuss organizing a Union. Among the six founding members of the Association in 1933 were two women Miss Iris Barrow and Miss Lilian Henry. It was not until they began planning and seeking support for their union that they realized that the laws of Antigua made union organizing illegal. They were forced as a result to establish an association. According to Davis the early meetings of the association were held in the Odd Fellows Lodge in St. Johns.[20]

By 1938 the Workingmen's Association had become 'moribund'[21] as Davis described largely because of its inability to defend the interest of workers as a union and also because it 'was beset by spies.'[22] In the history of the Leeward Islands to 1951, the urban middle class and working class posed little threat to the existing labour and political system. Disfranchisement and laws of the colonies left workers vulnerable to employers and white Creole elites.[23]

In the more than four hundred years of British Colonialism, the recommendations of the 1938 Royal Commission had the single greatest impact on Caribbean labour history. Throughout the British Caribbean by 1938 the Commission had became the people's Commission. This was largely by virtue of the activities of Commission members Sir Walter Citrine, and Labour MP Orde Brown.

20 J. Oliver Davis, 'How Workers in Antigua were First Organized', in Ralph Prince ed., *Antigua and Barbuda: From Bondage to Freedom: 150th Anniversary of Emancipation* (Antigua: St. Johns Printery, 1984): 53.

21 Ibid.

22 Ibid.

23 Ibid. Davis recalled that the theme of the Dominica Conference in 1932 (a conference he did not attend) was 'No Federation without Representation and No Representation without Adult Franchise'.

The TUC and the Leeward Islands Trade Unions

The effort after the 1970s to return Caribbean labour history to Caribbean actors led to the cover-up of the relationship between the TUC and Caribbean trade unionism. Until the 1970s Walter Citrine figured prominently in the history of trade unionism in the Leeward Islands. V. C. had for many years acknowledged Citrine's initial role. He credited Citrine with having arranged a meeting at the Cathedral schoolroom of the Anglican Church. As V. C. recalled Citrine said 'A dozen Royal Commissions would make little difference to the appalling conditions in Antigua.'[24] In his view, the answer was the formation of a trade union through which the people could collectively end exploitation.[25] None of the thirteen men who met and formed the island's first trade union organization in 1938 were agricultural workers, the labour majority. At least one, V. C. had worked on an estate prior to 1938.[26] A provisional executive committee for the union was organized shortly after the first meeting with Walter Citrine. They embraced the name of a former friendly society, an organization that had

24 Ibid.

25 Speech 'The Development of Trade Unionism in Antigua', Speech made 24 October 1978 printed in *Antigua Trade and Labour Union: 40th Anniversary Magazine* (Antigua, Antigua Printing and Publishing, 1980).

26 J. Oliver Davis article 'How Workers in Antigua Were First Organized', in Ralph Prince ed., *Antigua and Barbuda: From Bondage to Freedom*, 53. Article provided additional details in his own recollection of early union activities. He recalled that Walter Citrine had been approached at the Agricultural Society's Office by Harold Tobias Wilson, the editor of the *Antigua Magnet* Newspaper and invited to address a public meeting at the Cathedral School Room. Davis himself as Secretary of the Workingman's association was responsible for extending invitation to all Friendly Societies, Lodges and other organizations that catered to the working classes. It is clear that local initiative played a major role according to Davis's accounts. If one takes into account the theme of the Dominica Conference, the early attempts to form a union in 1933 and the leadership role of the leadership of the Workingman's Association, then local initiative must take centre stage in the discussion of the formation of the first union on the island.

been registered with the Colonial Administration at the turn of the century. The formation of the ATLU in 1938 was one of the most liberating actions for the Antiguan masses. Yet on the other hand these founding members of the organization engaged in an act which threatened their own futures. As members of a small, black and coloured middle class, they owed their survival to the even smaller group of white Creoles who dominated political and economic life in the colony. The Union was immediately recognized by the ruling class of landowners and employers as a threat to their economic and social interests, and they responded to this perceived threat as they had historically, with the use of law and by their control of the labour market. Threatening job security and evacuations of employee/tenants on their estate lands, estate owners and sugar factory management made labour organizing an extremely challenging activity for the early trade union leaders.

On Antigua estate owners and other employers wrote and enforced the law. The administrators, employed by the Colonial Office were mostly white and coloured into the twentieth century and therefore traditionally aligned themselves with the interests of employers over that of Antiguan workers. In this environment where employers and state administrators were allied, the challenges to ATLU executive members were great. They had to overcome the power of employers and landowners by convincing a fearful class of workers and peasants to join the organization.

The first major victory of the ATLU was the registration of the union with the state in 1940, after one year of organizing. It was to be the first of many challenges which trade unionists would face and overcome in Antigua and Barbuda.[27] This registration followed a grueling period of recruitment in which volunteers travelled for miles, often by foot (as described by V. C. above), to convince workers to join the union. This was no small feat as workers were often resistant to union membership because of their fear

27 Ibid., V. C. Bird 1978 Speech at Antigua State College. Bird identified the leadership of early organization included Mr. Norris Allen, Mr. Reginald Stevens, President, F. O. Benjamin, Treasurer S. A. Henry, Secretary, V. C. Bird, Griffith Matthews, Randolph H. Lockhart, B. A. Richards, Thomas Martin, James Jarvis, Stanley Walter, C. A. Perry, Thomas Brooks.

of angering their employers.[28] Additionally, V. C. spoke of the scepticism harboured by this long victimized population who doubted the ability of the British government much less the local union leaders to make significant changes to the social structure on the island. These fears or doubts as V. C. called them 'stemmed from their lack of knowledge about unions, and their fear was the result of their certain knowledge of the ruthlessness of their employers.'[29]

The founding members and a number of recruits (a group which quickly became heavily female) engaged in the difficult process of convincing workers to join the union. Day after day, 'Sunday after Sunday, night after night',[30] he recalled, recruiters made the long walk from one end of the island to another, 'from Willikies and Comfort Hall to St. John's and from John Hughes to St. Johns.'[31] Despite the intimidation of employers and the fear of workers of loss of jobs and imprisonment, the trade union was successful in recruiting a significant numbers of workers in order to register itself with the colonial administration. At a union conference held on 26 February 1940 the union executive was ratified and on 3 March 1940 the Antigua Trades and Labour Union was registered on Antigua and Barbuda. The recruitment effort was enhanced by the successful registration of the union with the State. The survival of the union however required that most, if not all of the islands workers be registered union members. As union membership grew in the 1940s the union leaders came face to face with a larger and more pressing problem than fear and doubt.

28 Ibid., 53. J. Oliver Davis recounted that the first difficulty involved conflict among the urban middle class over the leadership and organization of the islands first union. He pointed to tensions between members of friendly societies and business associations. In the end it was mostly the members of the Small Traders Association who formed the first union on the island. According to Davis the first ATLU members were members of the Small Traders Association. This group rather than working with the existing organization established a new organization in 1938 the Antigua Trade and Labour Union (ATLU) with Stevens as President and V. C. Bird as Vice President.

29 Ibid.

30 Ibid.

31 Ibid.

The largely rural labour population had high illiteracy rates, and as V. C. recalled, while many were willing and able to lead as branch members for the union, illiteracy haunted the selection of leadership. 'When certain people were persuaded to accept leadership positions in the village, it was discovered that they could not read.'[32] It was imperative that leaders of the union branches be literate, and as the recruitment process continued the challenge of finding literate men to lead union chapters plagued the young organization.

Estate owners and other employers engaged in a massive resistance in response to the formation of the trade union in 1940. One response for estate owners was the creation of a syndicate, and later the formation of an Employers Union. So great was the resistance of some employers to the union that government intervention was regularly required from the 1940s and by the 1950s a labour advisory board was established to mediate disputes between the union and employers. Among the most resistant employers on Antigua were the Antigua Sugar Factory and the Waterfront. In the long run the board proved impotent and it was the union's emphasis on unity among its workers that broke the deadlock between the union and employers.[33]

In addition to dealing with resistant employers the ATLU leaders found their greatest challenge was to dismantle the system of social relations on the island. The trade union in 1940 proved to be the greatest instrument for breaking the relationship of dependency and subordination that had marked the relationship between labour and employers in the British Caribbean. V. C. outlined in 1978 a paternalistic system which lacked transparency in hiring. He provided examples of the ways in which the system of subordination was used against workers who had no recourse but to submit to the punitive fines, inconvenient pay schedule and secretive pay rates.[34]

Changing these conditions was the organization's first act in social reconstruction. The later segue into politics was no doubt the result of the

32 Ibid.

33 Ibid., Novelle Richards. *The Struggle and the Conquest.*

34 V. C. Bird 1978 Speech.

racial and class dynamics on the island colony, where black and coloured labourers and their union representatives alike were expected to subordinate themselves to white Creole employers. After 1940 the union took on employers demanding that workers know rate of pay prior to pay day and that the system of punitive punishment of workers, including punishment for counting their money when they collected it from the payroll clerk be ended. Much of the achievement of the early union against employers and the colonial administration was the result of their success in changing workers' attitudes, and the ability to build workers' unity. Both of these were crucial to the union's success. By 1951, the union theme 'The Unity of Labour is the Salvation of our Country',[35] had emerged, representing the recognition by union and its members of the importance of unity in labour and anti-colonial struggles. At a time when dismissal remained one of the strongest instruments which employers held, the unity of the working class proved a powerful tool for the union's success.

Wage Structure and Social Conditions

> I am always careful to speak on Trade Unionism and I do not introduce politics, always conveying the impression that the Trade Unions can themselves put the case in the legislative field.[36]

Citrine spoke of his care in his travels throughout the Caribbean not to offer too much hope to Caribbean populations that trade unionism would alter their social and political conditions. But it is clear throughout the 1950s that only British trade unionists failed to understand what local

35 Theme of ATLU graces every publication produced by union including Newspaper and Magazines its source of origin was unknown to union leaders asked in my interviews.

36 MF 226–227 Letter from Barbados: 4.

trade unions and their local populations recognized, that trade unionism was linked indelibly to political aspects of colonial life in the Caribbean. Citrine's care to avoid politics was not a situation that the Union leaders could follow. Living and working in colonial societies and acutely aware that the problems of labour were largely the result of their exclusion from political participation they aggressively began political organizing. The decision to stay away from politics was one that the TUC representatives could easily make but one which local labour activists could less easily make. For Antiguan labour activists, the primary issues were issues of land tenure, in particular the tenancy lands of the Syndicate Estates. These were lands owned privately by the agency Syndicate Estates, on which the majority of agricultural labourers on Antigua worked as peasant labourers. The Syndicate Estates therefore was the primary employer of agricultural workers, and a major source of resistance to labour changes on the island. Union leaders' struggles throughout the 1950s were primarily struggles with the Syndicate Estates as they sought constitutional changes giving rights and protections to workers, and a defined a role for the island's black and coloured majority. These were clearly trade union issues but more importantly they were political issues.[37]

Union activists also attacked the low wage structure on the island and attempted to negotiate for a shorter work day for agricultural workers. On many estates the workday lasted from 6 a.m. to 6 p.m. In rural areas many children of estate workers were also employed by the estates, mostly because their wages were essential to their families, but also because many estates held specific work assignments for small gangs of child labourers.[38] Wages were paid at midnight on Saturday which meant that workers did not have access to their pay or to the market for two days after pay as Sunday sales were illegal on the island.

37 Novelle Richards, *The Struggle and the Conquest*; CO 152/520/4.

38 Despite the fact that primary school education was free, there were few schools available for the majority of the islands children. There was on the island a high rate of truancy, the cause of which, as explained by Novelle Richards, children were bored by schools that did not speak to them.

Table 6 Wages on Sugar Estates in Antigua

Wages	Males	Females	Children
Large Estates	1s/1s 6d per day	7/8d per day	2/4d
Small Estates	10d	6d	
Source: Novelle Richards, The Struggle and the Conquest			

Table 7 Translating British Pounds into Local Currency

Pound £ = 4.80 Shillings = 24 cents Pence = 2 cents	Hapenny = 1 cent Bit = 2.6 Half bit = 1.3

The social condition on the island, especially the conditions of village life, was abysmal, as the Commission had exposed in 1938. Overall, whether in the village or in urban settings, most Antiguans lived in poor housing built of wattle and daub. Most still depended upon firewood for cooking and owned few cooking utensils. There was chronic scarcity of water and extremely high infant mortality. Primary education in the island was free, but schools were few and the conditions so hostile many students especially boys, refused to attend, choosing instead to hide away in sugar cane fields or find work at an early age. These were not surprisingly the main concerns of workers and trade union and political activists with the formation of the ATLU in 1940. These conditions would also propel the union's involvement into politics after 1951.

The issue of unity had been the central organizing principle of Caribbean workers even before the formation of trade unions after 1938, but it was not until the 1940s that they were able to legally incorporate the concept of unity or collective action with the legalization of trade unions. On Antigua where the female population was a majority, unity of labour was an even more valuable goal as the support of all labourers was needed in order to defeat the plantation oligarchy. 'The Unity of Labour is the

Salvation of Our Country'[39] signalled not only the need for class, race and colour solidarity but also for solidarity across gender lines as well. While by the 1970s women's contributions became overlooked, it is clear from witnesses that the role of men and women was crucial to the organization, and the success of the union and the Labour party. While the goals of the ATLU were defined in terms of improving the conditions for workers, it became very clear to early union activists that political participation by the working people was crucial to these improvements not only in work but also in their daily lives. Interviewed in the summer of 2002 and 2003 these informants, from the working class and peasant class shared their personal perspectives on the labour and political activities in which they were personally involved.

Conclusion

The key events analyzed in this book, the 1938 Royal Commission, the origin and legalization of trade unions; the removal of the punitive labour laws that allowed labour leaders to organize workers; and the opening up of Antiguan society to local participation by the colonial government, are all outlined in this book as crucial events in the emergence of a modern labour society in Antigua. The ATLU was able to mount a successful challenge to the landed oligarchy with the support of the TUC and British Parliament. The new institution, the ATLU, born of the social influence of the British TUC and local level organizations, emerged as male centred in its leadership. While women participated heavily in the organizing, recruiting and in the membership of the organization and remained deeply loyal to the organization, the gendered system of leadership limited them from participating at the highest levels. In addition to evaluating the role of British and local leaders in Antigua and Barbuda, this chapter documents the

39 ATLU Motto appeared on masthead of union newsletter through the 1950s.

social and political changes resulting from the formation of the ATLU. The organization provided the first real opportunity for the masses to challenge the small white oligarchy. The union, a legitimate organization with powerful friends and allies in the form of the TUC, succeeded in overcoming the oligarchy's massive resistance to organized labour. The overall success of trade unionism is seen in the size of union membership, in the overall solidarity among workers, and the decision of the British government to offer universal adult suffrage laws in 1951. It was the efforts of union leaders as political activists that pushed the colonial office to move ahead with plans for fuller political and social participation in Antigua and Barbuda. These issues are discussed in greater detail in the following two chapters.

PART III

Politics and Exclusion

CHAPTER 6

Gender Exclusions

This chapter examines male dominance and female exclusion in trade unions in Antigua and Barbuda. In addition, I have introduced the discussion of women and their roles in the economy of Antigua and in the union and the Antigua Labour Party (ALP) through the 1970s. In the late nineteenth century, from Great Britain to the United States, trade unions were male centred institutions, hostile to the influx of women workers in the labour market and in unions. Throughout much of the first half of the twentieth century, prior to World War II, the union movement showed little interest in working women and their concerns.[1] British Trade Unions and the TUC, like their counterparts in other developed societies such as the United States and Canada, reflected traditional attitudes toward women and the workplace. From the late nineteenth century when women's presence in the workplace was increasing in industrialized nations to the start of World War I, when the numbers of working women dramatically increased, unions, as largely male organizations, were challenged in their organizational structure to deal with the demands of working women, for membership and for recognition of their particular needs as union members. While trade unions and the TUC fought for the interest of working families throughout the twentieth century, they were through the first half

1 Maureen Baker and Mary-Ann Robeson. 'Trade Union Reactions to Women Workers and Their Concerns', *Canadian Journal of Sociology*, 6:1 (1981):19–31. This article analyzed a body of writings on trade unions and their reactions to women workers. Baker and Robeson recognized what the growing literature on women workers and trade unions advocate that these male organizations were largely apathetic to the demands or needs of women workers and that most male union showed negative reactions to working women, even those that gained membership in Trade Union organizations.

of the century, clearly more concerned with men as workers than they were with women's work. This fact is well documented by other scholars for the British TUC, and is evident in the interactions of TUC representatives in the Caribbean in the 1930s. While workers in Antigua were primarily agricultural, and women were significant in this agricultural workforce, the traditional attitudes of British trade union representatives of focusing on male members and excluding female union members from leadership, occurred and became deeply entrenched in the organizations despite the large female membership of the union and Labour party throughout the 1970s. This reflects what some labour scholars have identified as 'male world view' whereby union policies and priorities remained focused on the interests of the male membership.[2]

Scholars note that in the United States and Great Britain women workers who sought to organize received little aid from male unions and were barred from membership in some unions. Women's attempts to organize across the divide in Great Britain failed in the late nineteenth century because of narrow-minded attitudes towards women outside of the home. One such example in British Labour was the failure of women to be included in decision-making within the TUC despite their presence at every meeting since 1876. Women's exclusion remained in place through the 1930s. In addition to the denial of equal access and participation in unions because of traditional views of women's place being in the household rather than the workplace. Women's workplace and union participation was also denied because of the stereotype of the sex's 'emotional instability.'[3]

The British TUC mirrored traditional stereotypes in Britain about a woman's role. This role was primarily a domestic one within the home

2 Noted in Baker and Robeson's 'Trade Union Reactions to Women Workers and their Concerns'. Term was coined by female labour writers Constantina Safilios-Rothschild, *Women and Social Policy* (Englewood Cliffs, NJ: Prentice-Hall, 1974); Grace Hartman, 'Women and the Unions', in *Women in the Canadian Mosaic*; Peter Martin and Louise Kapp Howe, *Pink Collar Workers* (New York: Avon Books, 1977).

3 Rosemary Auchmuty, 'Spinsters and Trade Unions in Victorian Britain', in Ann Curthoys et al., eds, *Women at Work* (Canberra, Australia: Australian Society for the Study of Labour History, 1975): 109–122.

as caretaker for the family. This role was complementary to the man's role as family breadwinner. Support for these traditional roles for men and women, in Caribbean unions and in the Labour party is reflected by Walter Citrine's actions during the 1938 Royal Commission investigation and in organizational alliances with Caribbean labour leaders through the 1970s. The interests of women workers both in the UK and in the Caribbean were served only through the creation by women of separate women's organizations. In Antigua and Barbuda, the ATLU women formed a Women's Auxiliary, an organization whose purpose served Antiguan women the same way in which British women workers were served by the Women's Protective and Provident League or Women's Trade Union League.

The influence of TUC's traditional roles for men and women in unions and in the Labour party was transferred to the Caribbean largely unchanged because of existing patriarchal structures in Caribbean societies. In addition these traditional roles were practiced in the Caribbean through the 1930s, although primarily among the black and coloured middle class and the white elite. The ATLU reflected the traditional roles of the TUC, such as the practice of excluding women from organizational leadership and of ignoring of women's need for equal pay to that of men for their work. The ATLU expanded traditional values into the peasant and working classes in ways that the church and the colonial administration had failed to achieve in the 1920s. The spread of traditional roles in Antiguan society after 1940 was clearly the result of the success of the ATLU in becoming the organization of the Antiguan working people. The early leaders of the union succeeded despite planter intimidation and the limited resources at their disposal to build membership and to stand up to the white employers as they advocated for the largely working class membership. The ATLU was from its early beginnings a male organization, despite the crucial role of women in the preceding organization, and in the early union organization. By the 1950s the organization leaders had adopted super masculine imagery and with the formation of the Antigua Labour Party (ALP), the male centred leadership was cemented. Yet this male centred leadership existed alongside the reality of the central role that women played in the organization.

V. C. played a crucial role in mentoring two generations of male leaders and while he had both daughters and sons, only his sons inherited his trade union and Labour party legacy. Yet while V. C. and masculinity dominated the two most important institutions in twentieth-century Antigua, the role of women in the institution's success is hard to overlook, despite the success of trade union ideology in convincing many in the society that the struggle for rights and for better working conditions, had been waged by men only. Despite this mis-information I sensed little tensions between men and women both during my interview of informants and in the records of the union from the 1940s.

Working class men and women created a unified front against imperialism and the abusive and exploitive labour system. Informants, even those women who are excluded from the history, remain fully supportive of the goals and are proud of the achievements of the male leaders of the union and Labour party. Any strict translation of nationalism and nationalist concepts would exclude the Antigua story as it fails to fall into the strict category or conceptualized version of this 'ism' – best defined by Mallon as an 'already defined integrated community within a territory, language and accepted set of historical traditions.'[4] Locked out of this definition Caribbean labour leaders along with all other twentieth-century social groups in Latin America and the Caribbean could only find inclusion in the redefinition of nationalism constructed by Mallon. This definition identifies 'A broad version for organizing society, a project for collective identity based on the premise of citizenship – available to all.'[5]

In 1998, one year prior to his death, V. C. had received the Caribbean region's highest award the Order of the Caribbean Community (OCC), at the meeting of the Conference of Heads of Government of the Caribbean Community in Castries, Saint Lucia. It has been said that V. C. had refused earlier offers of knighthood by the Queen of England, a refusal which some saw as a political statement of his assertion of regional loyalty and refusal to be co-opted by the former colonial power. His death in June 1999 at the age of 90 triggered renewed focus both on Antigua and Barbuda and the wider

4 Mallon, 3.
5 Ibid., 4.

Caribbean region on the role of trade unions in the struggle for workers rights and for political self determination in the post World War II period.

Trade unionism and politics are the most male-predominant professions on the island nation. Not surprisingly, the popular image of trade unionism and of political leadership is that of a man: large and strong both physically and politically, brave enough to face overwhelming forces (such as British colonialism) and win. Committed to working for the 'common man and woman',[6] a deliverer, a Moses-like figure, who 'leads his people.'[7] These are images that have been ascribed to V. C. Bird, a man whose great statue lent itself to the popular imagery. On his death in June 1999 a national funeral and memorial celebrating his life and contributions provided an opportunity for trade unionists and politicians to reflect, and to reconstruct the history of labour and politics on the island. V. C. Bird's death in 1999, provided a new context within which state historians, regional and local politicians and trade unionists could retell the history of trade unionism and act out black manhood in the context of earlier labour struggles.

The events which marked V. C.'s passing included a state funeral and several memorials. These events in addition to interviews with people on the street were recorded and later produced by the government of Antigua and Barbuda in the form of two videotapes.[8] The *State Funeral* tapes are an important source of trade union imagery and tradition on the island. They offer crucial evidence of the images of trade unionism as produced by trade unionists themselves. Most importantly they provide very significant insight of how male trade unionists remember the union's history (for those who had been involved in the founding of the ATLU) and what current male members see to be the legacy that they have been left by the founding members. Today both trade union masculinity and masculinity of political leadership in Antigua and Barbuda are one and the same. This masculinity is distinct however from the masculinity of the 'common

6 The State Funeral of the Right Honourable Sir Vere Cornwall Bird, KNO, ON, OCC. 9 December 1909–28 June 1999 (Antigua: Government of Antigua and Barbuda 1999), 2 videocassettes (hereafter State Funeral tape A and B).

7 Ibid.

8 Ibid.

man' or of the mainstream masculinities of the white business elite, landowners and British administrators. It is also distinct from that of the coloured middle class. Shaped largely in relation to mainstream masculinities trade union masculinity has emerged as extremely heroic.[9]

Trade union membership has been an important avenue for advancing the political careers of Antigua and Barbuda males. It was from within the trade and labour union that the Labour party operated throughout the 1940s and 1950s. It was former ATLU officers who organized the island's first two political parties; the Antigua Labour Party (ALP) and the Progressive Labour Movement (PLM). It was out of the ATLU that the oppositional union, the Antigua Workers Union (AWU), would emerge in the late 1960s. Trade unions continue to be an important training ground for political leadership on the island, and those who can trace their lineage to the original ancestors, the '39ers, are more likely than others to experience political success on the island. The assertion of trade union manhood after 1940 is acted out in reference to trade union womanhood, mainstream womanhood and perhaps also in relation to British womanhood.[10]

The emergence of trade unions with the right to engage in collective action on behalf of its members and to direct the actions of the working people dramatically changed the history of the Caribbean. In Antigua and Barbuda the legislation of 1940, which legalized such organizations was an important turning point not only for labour organization but also for

9 For more on the issue of masculinities readers are encouraged to look at Karen Beckwith, 'Gender Frames and Collective Action: Configurations of Masculinity in the Pittstone Coal Strike', *Politics and Society*, 29:2 (2001): 217. Beckwith argues that to discuss 'masculinity' is problematic because masculinity is not a singular characteristic. In addition she argues that 'masculinities' is a more appropriate term. See also R. W. Connell term 'mainstream masculinities' which he argues exists in advanced capitalist countries. This is linked to power, and is generally organized for domination and as a form of resistance to change in power relations.

10 See Karen Beckwith and Rhoda Reddock for their discussions of configurations of masculinity among workers. While both examine gender within different contexts the Beckwith's discussion of masculinity and the Trinidad context which is the focus of Reddock's work have contributed to my awareness of the theory and practice of gender in the Antigua and Barbuda context.

political participation of the population. Under the influence of the TUC, Caribbean workers restructured their organizations and strategies. This TUC model and British organizational leadership had a great impact on the life of activists, their gender, and their relationship to the state and to each other. By 1951 the change was noticeable in the working class organizations and in working class expressions of manhood.

Two Generations of Leadership

The fact that men are selected for leadership roles and have been the sole sex selected for positions of president and vice president is well documented by the ATLU. Juvenile branches of the union formed the early training ground for the role men and women would play in the organizations. In his speech at the funeral of the late V. C. in 1999 Baldwin Spencer, leader of the United Progressive Party (UPP), recalled that his political career began at the age of 10 as a member of the Juvenile branch of the ATLU. He had been ten years old when he joined the Juvenile Branch of the ATLU and it was at this point that he first met and developed a relationship with V. C.

> His immediate impact was profound, by age 14 through his inspiration I was making my main political speech at the West Bus Station in support of his candidacy in the rural west constituency. The fact that I am now the parliamentary representative of the said constituency is not an accident, Sir Vere in appointing me as one of the two representatives on the political committee of the AT&LU from the rural west constituency at age 16, he had predicted it. Even when I felt compelled to break with him in 1968 and to vigorously oppose him politically he continued to have my greatest respect and admiration as a giant in the industrial, political life of this country.[11]

Both boys and girls were members of the Juvenile branches of the union but the organizations constructed different roles within the organizations

11 State Funeral, tape B.

for both sexes. Leadership was confined to men and boys, but recruitment and other important organization activities were performed by women. In labour action both before and after the forming of the ATLU and legalization of trade unions both male and female members were involved in workers actions against landowners. These actions included civil disobedience, striking, setting fire to cane fields. The techniques employed have a long tradition with the Caribbean workforce and predate the 1938 formation of the ATLU and the 1940 legalization of unions. They have traditionally been used to challenge colonial authorities and to make demands for better wages and better work conditions of landowners.

Women were active participants in these techniques, as the history documents not only in the 1918 riot but in subsequent labour disturbances as well. In recalling these conflicts with the colonial government in 1999 both speakers and the MC's recalled the 'men and women who took up the challenge to free them-selves from the yoke of colonialism.'[12] The list of names of these comrades of V. C. included only men.[13]

While different masculinities existed in the context of Antigua and Barbuda society through the first half of the century, it is possible to see the connections between all of the different masculinities regardless of class, ethnicity, race and background. All are linked by characteristics such as, heroism, leadership, agency, physical prowess, strength, stamina, access to power, and by the exercise of power. While race and class influenced the access of the population throughout the colonial period, gender is perhaps one of the most important factors influencing experience. The enforcement of traditional roles for men and women in British society is replicated in the island colonies through the first half of the century. In a population where women comprise the majority, they experience enormous limitations to personal and professional growth. Throughout the colonial period women are absent from the top professions of administrators, medical personnel,

12 State Funeral, tape B.

13 State Funeral, tape B. The MC's at the funeral of V. C. provided the following list of the Trade Unionists and Political leaders – Reginal Stevens, Lionel and Denfield Hearst, Levi Joseph, Buntin, Donald Shepherd, Earnest Williams, Bradley Carrott, William Robinson, Edmond Robinson, Edmond Lake, Joseph Myers.

and landowners. Women were not represented in the local legislature of the entire Leeward Islands in 2002. Among the coloured population the restrictions were the most chafing. Driven by the desire to maintain the respectability that was the cornerstone of middle class status, this group like their counterparts in Britain and the United States made enormous personal sacrifices to achieve middle class respectability. But while the coloured middle class assented to the sex restrictions of traditional roles, working women suffered patriarchy with few benefits.

In *State Funeral*, the tributes of V. C. contain very little of the family history of V. C. There is mention of his humble beginnings but his family history remains shrouded in mystery, there is no father, no pictures or images of his mother at the tribute.[14] The island's first family began in the 1930s with V. C. and is continued by his sons – some six of them legitimate and natural alike. The tributes are of a piece; they glorify V. C. and exaggerate his contributions, not only by fellow trade unionists and colleagues but also by the priest presiding over the service. It was the priest who set the tone with his description, with strong overtones of the Christ story. A man born of humble beginnings, who becomes a local and national hero.

'It is in spite of his humble beginnings, it is because he dreams and because he made his dreams a reality. It is because of all this that he became a trade unionist, liberator, national hero, Caribbean statesman, and father of our nation [...] beloved father.'[15] He further spoke of V. C.'s 'amazing power to accomplish so much in so little time'.[16] V. C.'s regional contributions were acknowledged by this speaker who though not Antiguan, proclaimed 'We are all beneficiaries of his untiring labours and we thank him for the legacy. Freedom to work, freedom to grow, to achieve, to worship, to become what

14 It was V. C.'s younger brother who proudly showed me a picture of their mother in the summer of 2001 when I interviewed both him and his wife in relation to women's activities on the island during their youth in the 1940s.

15 State Funeral, tape B. Speaker unidentified but represented Salvation Army Organization.

16 Ibid.

we can become. An example to old and young alike. His ability to master circumstances instead of letting circumstances master him.'[17]

A former officer in the Salvation Army, V. C. was honoured for his contribution to this social progressive organization. The tribute from a former colleague identifies his contributions to the Salvation Army in military terms calling him 'a veteran soldier'[18] and acknowledging his many years in the ranks of the Salvation Army. Yet it was his description of V. C.'s trade union and political career, which carried strong religious overtones. He described his colleague as having been called to his role as leader, and despite the power of the state and its coloured middle class collaborators, V. C. emerges victorious. 'Called to deliver his people from the bondage of poverty and oppression, V. C. like Moses answered 'let my people go'. He also addressed his message to those members of the black middle class who gave aid and comfort to an oppressive system designed to prevent the upward mobility of our people; 'let my people go', he said, 'so that they may create a society where children who were born out of wedlock, and were the children of poor working class could not be prevented from attending Grammar school or Girls High School'. He was anxious to eliminate malnutrition. He called to defenceless working men and women and together they 'marched like a mighty army'.[19]

Not to be outdone by those who spoke before him, Lester Bird, a natural son of V. C. and himself Prime Minister of the island in 1999 addressed the gathering crowd with descriptions of his father which included 'Indisputable national hero and visionary titan.'[20] To his father he ascribed confrontations with 'the powerful sugar barons' a man who with the support of the people 'faced the might of the British Empire without fear and sent colonialism packing.'[21]

It is true that people tend to become larger than life in death, particularly in obituaries. But this was not the case for V. C. In life he had

17 State Funeral, tape B.
18 Ibid.
19 State Funeral, tape B.
20 Ibid.
21 Ibid.

loomed as large in the minds of local trade unionists and politicians as well as the people of Antigua and Barbuda. From the 1970s when his political monopoly was shattered by the emergence of a competing union and political party on the island, V. C., no longer sole commander of the army of labourers; would instead use history, imagery and of course money to maintain his party's place in power.

Throughout much of the western world men define themselves in relation to their jobs (income earning potential), their social hierarchy, their families, and land/property ownership. In addition, in Antigua and Barbuda as elsewhere in the Caribbean womanizing is also an important field for defining male identity. The act of womanizing in the British Caribbean context involves the keeping of a wife and several mistresses if not at the same time certainly over time. These relationships produce multiple households some more dependent than others upon the financial support of the man, and they often produce large numbers of children, of varying status. Traditionally natural children were denied equal status to those born in wedlock. Historically colonial laws denied them their father's surnames, and legal protections for inheritance. These children experienced limitations in their quest for education and respectability. An illegitimate child himself, V. C. Bird would make one of his first political tasks the breaking down of the barriers against illegitimate children in Antigua and Barbuda.[22]

Trade union men see their work as a service to humanity, as national service for which they expect to be able to count on the recognition and support of the nation's common man and woman as well as their colleagues. Trade unionists and politicians often battle it out among themselves for these positions and political debates often become heated and rancorous verbal battles between political parties and individual politicians. It is the rancorous nature of politics that is often used to explain women's absence. Both men and women in Antigua insisted that no woman's honour could survive this kind of battle.

22 Interviews with Mrs Edris Bird and Adolphus Freeland discussed in Chapter 5 of this dissertation.

Women: Their History of Work

Both working men and women had been active in the creation of trade unions and in the struggles against capitalist oppression and British colonialism. The local resistance on Antigua was focused against local planters and the commercial class who dominated the land and the commercial market. The language of exclusion, in relation to women's role in unions and independence struggles has been growing stronger among trade unionists who articulate contradictory views on women's role in the island's labour history and struggles. In these views women either did not participate in labour and nationalist struggles, or where they were credited with participation, this participation is described as limited. On Antigua, through the 1990s few people, women included, questioned their exclusion from the island's labour history.

It remained clear to me, despite the rhetoric of a male workforce, a male union and of women's supportive role that it was not likely that Antiguan women had stayed on the sidelines while men (the workers) engaged in labour and political struggles. I was aware that only two generations ago women worked in the cane fields, at the sugar mills and factories and laboured on plots of land assigned under peasant development schemes. I knew they washed other peoples clothing at home and cleaned the houses of others. I knew that the notion that women – all women on the island occupied some 'sheltered domestic sphere' and that men occupied this other public place of employers and colonial administrators was wrong even before I saw the bluebooks and the census. Before the prison records exposed the activities that landed women in prison sometimes in greater numbers than men, for bad language and assault.[23] It was the scars on Selma Brodies' legs from a childhood working in the cane fields – the

23 Report of the Central Prison of the Leeward Islands 1921; document the anomaly of women's presence in the Leeward Prison and reflect that something was going on in the region where some of the highest incarceration numbers for the overall population is reflected.

broken body of Adelaide Charles, her mother who had struggled to feed seven children working in cane-fields, factory and other entrepreneurial ventures that helped her support her family barely. It was the fires in their eyes, the defiance in their shoulder that told me, they were not the kind to stand by and that nobody had ever needed to fight their battles for them. It would have been nice though, how different my life could have been had theirs been less difficult.

It did not seem right that the women in Antigua living under conditions that had barely changed since 1834, would suddenly become transformed into cheerleaders for the men – when they had not waited for men to champion their cause in slavery. In fact the chief complaint of owners of the enslaved population had been of enslaved women, who challenged their authority, continuously.[24]

It did not seem right to Patrick Lewis either, and even after he had stated 'no woman jump out'[25] when asked about the role of women in trade unions. He would correct himself and mention a number of women of labour and in addition he told stories of the women involved in the 1918 strike, and of the women who had willingly stayed in the background while their brothers, husbands and other male colleagues took credit for their work. He explained it as an Antiguan female tradition this unwavering loyalty to their men.[26] It was not familiar to me but I was glad that he had become aware of the problem; if only to explain it away so quickly after recognizing it.

24 See the works of Barbara Bush, Verene Shepherd and Mindie Lazarus-Black about enslaved women in the Caribbean and their defence of themselves and their families.

25 Patrick Lewis, meeting in New York 19 January 2001: A University of Cincinnati trained historian Patrick A. Lewis Ph.D. was director of the Antigua and Barbuda Mission to the United Nations. In addition to his role of ambassador Dr. Lewis serves the Antiguan government as a labour historian. Much of his work since his unpublished Ph.D. Dissertation, focused on trade unionism and politics in Antigua. In my first meeting with him in the Mission to the United Nations in New York in 2001 Dr. Lewis in response to my question on the role of women in trade unionism in Antigua and Barbuda responded, 'no women jump out'.

26 Ibid.

When I explained in the 1990s to my Antiguan friends who were all my age and many, of what I assumed was solid middle class background, that I was interested in looking at women in the trade union movement and they constantly responded that women did not do those sorts of things. I was taken aback. Not that I had not expected resistance, but I had not expected it from my working class friends. From Thibou, Weston or an O'Reilly, and other members of the coloured middle class whose history of work differed substantially from that of rural and urban working class, I would have understood, but I had assumed that everybody else knew the way I knew that our grandmothers had laboured, had been less than passive bystanders in any struggle that involved labour, the ability to feed their families, to achieve upward mobility through education – the right to a living wage; to self-determination; to leisure time. Any struggle that involved having a choice in employment had been women's struggle as well.[27]

The history of the Antigua and Barbuda working class as it is written and known particularly in relation to social class is wrong. The coloured middle class, so much bandied about by trade unionists as colonial collaborators barely existed in Antigua and Barbuda particularly after 1898, and by the late 1930s they were in no position to lead the working class in Union organizing. Much of the talk and the locally published literature about a coloured middle class in partnership with white Creoles have overstated a class role where individual actors should have been identified as acting in defence of their individual interest. Many other sources have assumed that Antigua and Barbuda history follows that of the rest of the region, a history replete with collaborations across colour between upper and middle class coloured and whites. Yet in Antigua and Barbuda as Susan Lowes clearly demonstrates in her dissertation, coloured or black,

27 Susan Lowes, provides a list of middle class coloured families for the nineteenth and twentieth centuries, making connections between groups and providing very useful genealogies of families. It is important to note her discovery that many twentieth century persons she interviewed did not know of their predecessors or of their contributions to the middle class history of the island. These families represent some of the best known of that class in Antigua today.

legitimate or natural, there was too small a 'middle' and certainly nothing solid about the place of nonwhites in Antigua and Barbuda through the first half of the century.[28]

On the issue of gender Antiguan women have been written out of local history and placed as background props in other sources. Yet this population, the island's majority, both in nineteen and twentieth-century Antigua, was a large presence in the sugar cane and cotton fields, whether on estates or on lands allotted to them under schemes for peasant development.

Despite the shrinking labour market of the twentieth century which reduced women's roles in the agricultural workforce, large numbers of women on the island worked as peasant producers. They were predominant in the fields of the cotton estates, worked in factories where they were paid lower wages than men. Women entrepreneurs were engaged in other enterprises including higglering and huckstering to support their families. Educated nonwhite women of the middle class continued to play a crucial role in the development of educational and social institutions and thereby to the growth of the middle class and to expanding literacy among both the middle and working classes.[29] Despite their embrace of traditional middle class ideology, especially that of women's limited public roles, educated women of colour (and their illiterate working class and peasant counterparts) made enormous contributions to trade unionism and to other political movements on the island colony in the decades following union legalization in 1940.[30]

28 Ibid. Lowes argues that contrary to assumptions about class that the middle class in Antigua and Barbuda was relatively new as social and economic conditions on the island had wiped out this class in the nineteenth century. By the 1930s this class remained small and powerless in relation to the white plantocracy. How then could it have given 'aid and comfort' to the colonial system?

29 See my discussion later in this chapter on Women's role in education. From the late nineteenth century through 1930s Antiguan women, four in all opened Private schools on the island. These four schools served black and coloured students from Antigua and the region.

30 The Commission Report produced by the 1938 Royal Commission documents clearly women's participation in the labour force of the region and makes clear recommendations regarding improved work conditions and opportunities for women and children in the labour market.

While the plantocracy dominated the political economy and influenced the social ambitions of the middle class they exerted far less control over the lived lives and the decisions of most of the common order. Where gender ideology was asserted it affected white women and those of the middle class who were invested in legitimacy and respectability. These were luxuries which the men and women of the common order could not afford. It was not until the 1920s that colonial administration and the churches began an active effort to enforce middle class gender ideology among the masses. It was the ATLU however which contributed to the spread of traditional roles among the island's majority by its practice of limiting women's role in the union leadership and supporting discrimination in the pay of women workers in favour of their male counterparts.

Education and the Construction of a Middle Class.

Despite the small size of their class and the social control exerted by the white oligarchy, middle class coloured women played a central role in education on Antigua and Barbuda. Gender ideology had long imposed severe restrictions on the coloured middle class, yet despite the restrictions of class, colour and gender in colonial society, Antiguan women, made important contributions to the spread of education in the Leeward Islands. These efforts by coloured women in Antigua to advance the interest of their class date back to pre-emancipation nineteenth century

Beginning with the efforts of the Hart sisters in the nineteenth century, the tradition of coloured female philanthropy and contributions to the black and coloured population of the island was continued by eighteen year old Nellie Robinson in 1898, with the founding of the first private high school for the black and coloured population of the region. Nellie would name the school in memory of her brother Thomas Oliver Robinson (TOR) and the TOR Memorial School would become associated with the brother as founder rather than Nellie the true founder and educator. This tradition of female dominance in education would continue throughout the first half of the twentieth century with the growing need for secondary education for middle class coloured and black students coupled with the commitment of administrators of publicly funded schools to exclude the majority of this population through high fees and social restrictions. Ernestine Stephens in 1926 founded the high school that bore her name.

In 1930 the Faith and Hope High School was founded by Agatha E. Goodwin and in 1938 Hilda Davis founded the Foundation Mixed School. It was these schools which provided access to all children whose parents could pay the required fees (in all cases substantially less than publicly funded schools) that were crucial to maintaining the existence of a middle class in the island. In addition to low fees, these schools did not have a 'respectability' requirement – and children were admitted irrespective of their parent's marital status.[31] By 1950 the *Plan for Development and Welfare*, a report constructed for the Colonial Office, would report that in the area of secondary education there were five proprietary schools on the island catering to paying scholars. The education department exercised no control over these schools and of the five schools existing on the island four were provided for annually by public funds.[32]

I did not realize who she was when I reached out to Cecile Davis in the summer of 2001 asking for an interview. I wanted to talk with her because while examining materials of The Antigua Girl's High School at the Antigua Archives, I had been impressed by her achievement, and having mentioned her name was told that she was back on the island. Cecile Davis had been born in Antigua in 1938 into a household of educators. Her father was a Rawle graduate[33] and her mother was also a teacher. She had been raised

31 Keithlyn Smith, *No Easy Pushover*, 206–207. Also copies of the Antigua Girls High School files at the Antigua Archives.

32 HC 157 B7: List of those receiving Grants-in-aid includes the Antigua Grammar School, Antigua Girls High School, the Thomas Oliver Robinson Memorial High School, and the Faith and Hope school. From Antigua: Plan for Development and Welfare, 1949 (hereafter HC157 B7).

33 Rawle was the training school in Barbados where select young men from the Leeward Islands were sent for education training to be teachers.

in a family household with her grand-parents, and aunt in addition to her parents. Her aunt Hilda Davis had begun a private school the same year Cecile was born, and at least three generations of Antiguans and other Leeward Islanders received their education through Davis School.

But Cecile Davis stood out not because she was the niece of an educator as much as because she was a Radcliff graduate and former U. N. worker. She was in my estimate an exception, an example of the kind of academic excellence which black and coloured women of the island could achieve despite the social limitations placed upon them.

At the interview Cecile is unsure about why her life experience is relevant. I explain to her what my book interest was and that I had read at the archives from her updates to her alma-mater the Antigua Girls High School. I mentioned that I had been surprised and quite impressed with what I had found out about her. She was one of three young women of colour at Radcliff College in the United States in 1954 and was the only woman of colour from the Caribbean to attend Radcliff that year.

For me the questions about what Antiguan women did in the 1930s and their true contributions to Antiguan society rested in her generation's accomplishments. How had she, a member of the 'common order' gone so far so fast? I did not ask this question directly, but stayed true to my script, asking her about negative perception of women during her childhood. She argues that she left the island at seventeen for college and never really returned until her retirement, at age fifty-five. But at seventeen Cecile had been equipped by two generations of Antiguan women to succeed academically and professionally. I looked for the solid middle class background to justify her success but found instead that the two generations that nurtured her had only just arrived at their lower middle class status.

INTERVIEWER: what were your earliest images of women?

RESPONDENT: role model stuff? Family women and teachers were most prominent

INTERVIEWER: What role did your mother and grandmother play?

RESPONDENT: Grandmother was interesting person. A nurse/midwife actually. She delivered many famous people including papa Bird. She was also a great storyteller.

INTERVIEWER: What was her name?

RESPONDENT: Rhoda Buckley. A great storyteller, on moonlight night she'd gather all the children together and tell us 'anancy' stories and that sort of thing.

INTERVIEWER: where was she from?

RESPONDENT: St. Johns, city area

INTERVIEWER: This was your maternal grandmother

RESPONDENT: No, My mother was from Barbados

INTERVIEWER: Do you have a lot of connection with the family in Barbados as a child?

RESPONDENT: Well yes, we visited.

INTERVIEWER: Was the Buckley family influence greater than that of your maternal grandparents?

RESPONDENT: Well yes, because my grandmother Buckley lived with us, or we lived in the same house.

INTERVIEWER: She must have represented a strong influence on you in terms of image of women.

RESPONDENT: Except you know that aahm, we are not ... growing up ... how to put it ... when we are growing up we weren't conscious of that sort of thing ... and so I don't recall thinking of my life ... of reinforcing ... or being ... I am saying it's a more recent thing to look at people in your life as models. O.K. so you have my grandmother who was a midwife and the other women, were my mother who was a teacher, she was an excellent teacher.

Cecile's aunt Hilda Davis, was eighteen years old when she began a private school to prepare black and coloured children for access to High School and for urban jobs. Hilda has remained a spinster all her life. She had started the Foundation Mixed School in 1938, one of four women on the island who from 1898 to 1938 opened their own schools to prepare the next generation of black and coloured workers and professionals. These schools played a crucial role in building a middle class on the island and as such Antiguan women, were crucial in this effort, working as teachers and role models to generations of Antiguan black and coloured boys and girls. Davis School remained in operation throughout the 1980s. While she dodged the question of images of women by arguing that the idea of role model was a more recent thing and that when she was young this idea was not important she readily identified her grandmother, mother and aunt and headmistress as positive role models. As the second child in a large family of seven children Cecile recalls:

> Academically we had to make it, that this was our pathway to life and [...] because there was seven of us we were encouraged to find our amusements within the family [...] we tend to support each other and look out for each other and so on. Its one of the things that impresses the Antiguans most, a lot of people who I don't know talk about that, about our being such a close-knit family.[34]

And so in 1954 when Cecile went off to Radcliff her brother went off to Harvard. Two Ivy league scholars in a family where they were the first generation to attend college and pursue not teacher training but degrees in higher education. There is no doubt that her family preparation, the preparation at Davis school contributed to their acceptance to local high schools in Antigua which were the Antigua Girls high school for girls and the Grammar School for boys, was extremely important in their academic success.

INTERVIEWER: How have women changed from when you were young?

RESPONDENT: I don't remember being very conscious of women's roles and being told for example that women can be this and not that. I always grew up with the sense that you can be what you want to as long as you excelled and got educated and all that, there wasn't any barrier to what you could achieve, that is something that I grew up with.

INTERVIEWER: You don't recall having any sense that there was a higher expectation for your brothers in your family than for you and your sisters?

RESPONDENT: Not really. They certainly [...] didn't[...] academically we were expected to do as best as we could [...] we all went to university, all seven of us. The eldest to Suffolk my brother and I to Harvard and Radcliff and

34 Cecile Davis interviewed by author, June 2003.

the two boys to University of Hartford and the Youngest sister to the University of Waterloo in Canada.
INTERVIEWER: all on scholarships?
RESPONDENT: Yes

(Mrs. Edie Sowerby-Labadie interview)

I knew of the Labadie family before I had developed a friendship with the youngest daughter Edie. They were well known and highly respected middle class Antiguans. Until our interview I had never really met Mrs. Labadie, but she was a legend in many ways. Both Edie and other friends who had grown up around the family were very much in awe of Mrs. Edie Labadie and she was a legend on the island, recognized as an educator and a national treasure.

In all of the cases of middle class families in Antigua I interviewed, I came to realize that there were no ties to the middle class other than those they had forged in their generation of the 1930s. There was no history with the plantocracy but with the working people of Antigua and Barbuda. In many cases one of the parents of my subjects was from another of the Caribbean islands, often a Leeward Island except in the case of Hilda Davis's family, whose mother was from the island of Barbados.

Edie Sowerby had been born in Antigua in September of 1917. Her mother had married a widower with three children. That marriage produced Edie and a sister. As a well known and highly respected educator on the island Edie's knowledge and opinion on issues regarding women on the island is widely sought. Asked about her childhood she recalled that both men and women influenced her path to education and she also explained that one of the restrictions she and her sister experienced in their family had to do with attitudes about daughters leaving the island and the protection of their families, in particular their fathers. Her sister had demonstrated a gift for nursing very early but was unable to get the training required to be a nurse because in the society 'fathers never sent away their daughters.'

As an adult her sister moved to the nearby island of Dominica where she became a midwife and received medical training for her practice in Scottshead, Dominica.[35] Edie also recalled that in the society in which she

35 Mrs. Edie Sowerby-Labadie interviewed by author, April 2003.

grew up, an informal regulatory body or network of people including government workers, police, parsons, teachers and midwives, existed to keep people in check. This network played an important role in regulating behaviour and ensuring that the values of the community were practiced, as Edie explained – 'if you were not on your p's and q's they would call you down – the parson would talk about it and the police and midwife would come to see you.'[36]

She recalls her career of teaching and that even after retiring from teaching in the public system she continued to teach opening up her own school inspired by observing day workers struggle with young children in the morning as they rushed to their jobs. She had retired at age 55 and from her house located on one of the main transportation routes in and out of St. Johns she recognized the need for a child care centre to serve working people who came to the city from the rural areas for work. She explained that she observed in the early mornings, parents rushing with young children (whom she suspected had not been fed). She decided that if she offered these working parents her home that she would meet a great need and she felt so for the children. She said she began to approach these parents telling them they would not have to take the children any further. This child care service mostly served the needs of airport workers and other 'town' workers. She kept the day care centre until 1981 when she became ill.

Asked about her social class, Edie referred to her profession, as a teacher and recalls that early images of a woman's role in Antigua society included women as homemakers, as mothers who took care of domestic duties as well as their role in agriculture which she identified as field work. Women, she recalled, worked in the fields growing food items such as corn and yams. Both on the plantations as well as their own lots they grew cotton. Women and children were the primary labourers on the cotton estates in Antigua through the first half of the twentieth century. Edie recalled that occupations for women when she was a girl were primarily as domestics and doing fieldwork. Edie noted that the Syrian immigrants to Antigua had black and coloured women as nannies in their households and were the first white group to build true relationships with black people on the island.

36 Ibid.

Edie's teaching career began as a result of the generosity of a friend of the family. She recalled that Thomas Ambrose, a friend of her parents and a school teacher offered to train her on Saturdays at no cost to prepare her for teacher training school. He also recommended her to the Moravian College for training. Edie studied for two years and was successful in getting her teaching diploma through the Moravian Teachers College, an institution she recalled had been formed by Tim Riley over a hundred years ago. The college served all of the islands of the Leeward Island presidencies. Each year one student from each presidency was accepted via entrance exams into the teacher training and education program. The college offered all subject areas including music, art, geometry and arithmetic. After her training, Edie was placed in the village of Liberta as her first teaching assignment. New teachers placed by the Teachers College were not paid on their first assignments so they were placed in areas where they had family members to support them. In Liberta village she stayed with her great aunt, a sister of her grandmother, while she taught for six months unpaid.

Asked about what she recalled of negative images of women and what role the Moravian church played in forming ideas of femininity for her she responded that modesty was expected of young women at the Moravian church school. The Moravian church in particular played a greater role in the lives of the non-white population, especially where education and education training were concerned. Neither the official Anglican church, nor the Methodist offered access to education and certainly no scholarships were available through their denominations. The Moravian church did show preference in their selection of scholarship recipients to their members and those who wanted to improve their social and professional status sought membership in the Moravian church because it offered access to teaching careers.[37] Asked about what generational changes she has observed in women she responded.

> Today women have learned that they are not just here for reproduction alone, for being servants, serving men. They realize that they are human beings, god made them and they have a place, and talents to develop. They [...] can learn like men,

37 Ibid.

> get things done like men. They used to stay at home and push them [men] forward but they by themselves could not stay up there, and they got all the credit and they never mention the misses. The dependence is turning around. Women are now being recognized with men, in the past they did not get recognized, or were given credit for contribution to men's work.[38]

By twenty-seven, married and expecting her first child Edie found herself engaged in a battle for her professional life. She recalled that married women teaching at a school for boys, especially pregnant ones were discouraged from teaching. She had to defend herself and remind them that she had training and certification to teach. 'After we got married they started up the prejudice. They did not want you, because you making baby, didn't want you because it was a school with all boys they didn't want to see a pregnant woman in the school.'[39] Her struggle to remain a teacher despite marriage and motherhood was with a local administrator and educator who insisted that teaching was not a place for married women especially pregnant women. But, Edie put up a fight for her job which she won, largely she believed because of her family connections, and her husband's position in the police force of the island.[40]

Trade Union Ideology and its Impact on Gender

> Women in the union are well-regarded by men, who see them as essential workers and strong supporters. They see them as capable of playing important roles in the workhorse position of secretary or treasurer but not in the top leadership roles of the official structure. While there is no overt prohibition of access, there is also no active encouragement for women to assume higher level positions.[41]
>
> — CAROLINE CARMODY, *First Among Equals*

38 Ibid.

39 Ibid.

40 Ibid.

41 Caroline Carmody, 'First Among Equals', 288.

Women have been confined to a limited space in trade union organizations. As early as 1981 anthropologists Caroline Carmody who had spent several years investigating the rise and nature of local leadership patterns in Antigua for her NYU dissertation noted the disparity between women as active trade union members and their absence from positions of trade union leadership.

In 2003, I expected little change and found instead that the literature of the ATLU did include women in reference to the history of the Union and women's historical participation, but while the men were recognized in a section of the Union publication celebrating its 60th Anniversary, as heroes, the women, many of whose contributions were no less heroic than those of the men, were listed in a section titled 'long service awards.' In 1999 when the Union celebrated its 60th anniversary, there stood at its helm for the first time a woman, the first female General Secretary of the ATLU organization. In her address to a packed audience of Union supporters and members the Senator and general secretary addressed the history of the union by stating 'I am aware, and in humility, understand that I stand on the shoulders of women and men of previous generations who toiled and sacrificed to build our mighty union'.[42] After meeting with Natalie Payne, I was convinced that the inclusion of women in her speech and the placement of women before men in her speech was no accident. It was clear to me in 2003 that a divide existed in Antiguan society between those women who wanted to continue to give all credit to men and those who insisted on correcting the record and allocating an equal place for women in the society.[43] Interviewed in the summer of 2003 Natalie recalled her history with the union began when she was a young girl. At eight years old she was enrolled by her parents in the Juvenile branch of the ATLU. She also recalled both from her long history and current level of participation in the union that the imbalance in women's participation in the union has

42 *AT&LU: Antigua Trade and Labour Union Diamond Jubilee 1938–1999*. 60th Anniversary magazine (Antigua: Antigua Printing and Publishing Limited, 1999). Also from personal interview Natalie Payne, Senator and former General Secretary of ATLU interviewed in April 2003.

43 Ibid.

remained in place at the executive level. She argued that the absence or exclusion of women from the executive level was ironic given the difference in leadership and management styles of men and women. 'women deal and men overlook, men are irrational while women investigate.'[44]

Explaining her unusual rise to the top in the ATLU she recalled that 'I asserted myself.'[45] As an active participant in all levels of union activity from compositor to letter press, as a journalist in the newspaper and then running the newspaper and handling accounts. 'I worked in all areas from bottom up.'[46] Historically in the union men are brought in to fill top positions especially positions of executive, a body for which men are elected or endorsed by the members of the union executive. This structure has kept the executive a male preserve. This was one structure which she attempted to change during her tenure as secretary, yet she lamented the fact that 'I unfortunately do not see more involvement for women in the union. Men have reasserted themselves. I sort of cleared a path that has since been closed.'[47] Like the other women interviewed Natalie recalls that her teachers played a large role in her life as mentors. As a Methodist, she denied that the Methodist church would have played any role in forming her gender ideology. In schools her teachers were both male and female. George Messiah and another female teacher, Ms. Brodie, were the two most influential educators in her life. Born and raised in the village of Bethesda where Mr. Messiah was head-teacher he influenced her drive for education. He instilled values – he would say 'I am so proud of you. I think people don't succeed because they fail to recognize the worth of other people.'[48] She recalled that she had no problem getting a job after school and that family connections played an important role both in her finding a job in government as well as in the union. Recruited in 1967 by a relative to fill the role as recording secretary she would spend the next thirty three years of her life involved in all levels of union work.

44 Natalie Payne, interview by author, April 2003.
45 Ibid.
46 Ibid.
47 Ibid.
48 Ibid.

CHAPTER 7

Politics and Labour Unions

This final chapter makes a methodological shift towards examining the impact of dramatic political changes on the social structures in the island colony during the twentieth century transition from Crown Colony to local government. Clearly by 1960 local leaders realized and utilized their power vis-à-vis mass support. They used it in negotiations with the Colonial Office, as well as international support for de-colonization to negotiate for internal self-government. They used this power aggressively, rejecting proposals from the Colonial Office that were not directly beneficial to workers and thus weakened their power on the island. The proposed federation of the Leeward Islands by the Colonial Office was rejected by local politicians.[1] By 1960 Antigua and Barbuda had returned to limited internal self-government but it was clear to local union and political leaders that more local control could be won with mass mobilization and internal pressure. This period of transformation was also a period of internal conflict as the oligarchy – whose interest had long been protected by the colonial administration, fought to maintain the colonial structure that had long protected their economic and social interests. The first part of this chapter examines this highly contentious period in the colony; the twenty year period following adult suffrage in 1951. Struggles over labour and politics largely took place between two classes of Creoles, classes that divided easily by race and ethnicity. The tensions between Creole men

1 CO 1031/4554 'Federation: Antigua Withdrawal and Collapse, 1965.' When Antigua rejected Great Britain's plan for federation of the Leeward Islands, the proposal collapsed and Great Britain was forced to establish individual plans for all of these small islands of the Caribbean. Some of the smaller islands, for example the British Virgin islands were maintained in a smaller federation.

over control of the state intensify in the 1950s and until 1960 this is at the heart of the industrial conflict which the Colonial Office had to mediate on the island. Additionally, the Colonial Office also found itself embroiled in conflict with union leaders/ministers, whose political and social visions clashed with those of the Colonial Office particularly on the issue of federation over individual self-government for each of the small colonies. This debate and the conflict among Creole men is the focus of the first part of this chapter. The second part of the chapter updates the political history of the island to the 1970s using the life of V. C. Bird, whose own biography reflects the political history of the island nation. By 1967, black union leaders and political leaders/ministers, regained the political power ceded by middle class coloured and white men in the late nineteenth century with the adoption of Crown Colony government. Universal adult suffrage and mass mobilization of the population ended white Creole hegemony, and white Creoles were completely excluded from political leadership in the island colony under full internal self-government.

Yet the struggle in Antigua was far from over by 1971 as key factors such as labour, gender and politics forged a new yet constrained sociopolitical reality. In post-1970 Antigua despite important social and political advances, the imperial legacy and gender exclusion (in addition to corruption and other problems which were not the focus of this book) continued to exist.

Colonial Office documents at the United Kingdom national archives at Kew expose growing tensions between Creole groups in Antigua by the late 1940s. The tension between these groups for control of the political and economic future of the colony manifested itself in the form of industrial unrest, as labour was the primary site of battle between black and white Creoles. Because Antigua and Barbuda was a colony built and maintained by patriarchy the battle was one between contending male groups; that of the hegemonic power of Creole white males and the contending power of black and coloured men. The defining characteristics of the contenders were race, class and colour. All of the participants be they administrators, union leaders, employers or investors were male. Not that this struggle did not involve or have an impact on women, only that women were excluded from direct participation in this struggle just as they were excluded from direct involvement in other areas of social life in the colonies. The struggle for control of the state was a struggle officially between men. In their campaign to wrest control of the state from white Creoles and the British Colonial Office, Antiguan men themselves embraced much of the ideology of the hegemonic male dominance of their white allies and nemesis.

By the 1940s they had already embraced domination of women as an important function of their role as men. In addition to the domination of women as demonstrated by their exclusion from leadership roles in the trade union organization, the ATLU, the union leaders had also insisted that their wives play traditional roles as homemakers even when their financial needs demanded otherwise. The interrogation of the role of European patriarchy in Caribbean societies and the role of Caribbean men in the subordination of Caribbean women is a topic that is currently receiving a lot of attention from Caribbean scholars. Patricia Mohammed insists that scholars need to dispel the popular notion that patriarchy was introduced by white colonial ideology.[2] She encourages scholars of gender studies to examine the complexity of gender identity in Caribbean history, in particular, to look at the larger picture of gender relations between men and women in Caribbean societies. These relations, she argues, are continuously undergoing transformations as are the societies themselves. To exclude black and coloured men from discussions of women's subordination in Caribbean societies is to miss the larger picture of these societies. Within the parameters of these recommendations I examine the archive materials from the late 1940s with a view to understanding how the struggle for state control was manifest through two particular groups of men engaged in this struggle.

As I noted above the struggle was between two groups of Creole men: the small white minority that had dominated British colonial societies since the seventeenth century, and coloured and black trade unionists, who at

2 Patricia Mohammed, 'Unmasking Masculinity and Deconstructing Patriarchy', in Rhoda E. Reddock, ed., *Interrogating Caribbean Masculinities: Theoretical and Empirical Analyses* (Kingston, Jamaica: University of the West Indies Press, 2004): 38–65.

least for a decade since the 1938 Royal Commission had come under the tutelage of the TUC and the Colonial Office. Population numbers for the island have remained consistent in that there is little growth and much loss. Colonial administrators have long attributed population loss from emigration to the island's unstable economy. In difficult years the out-migration is great particularly among men both black and white but particularly black workers who leave for other islands including Cuba, the Dominican Republic and the United States. Certainly similar struggles were underway in other parts of the British Empire where the British were seeking to divest themselves of their political and social control. In the middle east and Africa the struggles were clearly racial and cultural and the dynamics in many cases were quite different as much of the British settlers had only arrived in these colonial enclaves in the twentieth century, many after World War I, and in many cases their population was quite large in relation to the white Creole population in Antigua. These conflicts are well addressed by other scholars and will not be a focus of this book.[3]

Antiguan history from the late 1940s to the 1970s is one of transition and of struggle. Transition suggests change to which there is always resistance. Within the context of Antiguan history this transition from Crown Colony to local rule to independence and the struggles triggered by the political changes instituted by the colonial administration is reflected through the representative groups and individuals from labour (trade union leaders) and employers (employers association leaders and estate owners). In the Caribbean colonial context these are necessarily racial conflicts as white Creoles are overwhelmingly the employers and labour completely black and coloured. I am aware that I interrogate only a small part of the very complex set of transformations taking place in this island Colony, for in addition to the struggles between Creole men (employers and union leaders) there are the actions of the men of the Colonial Office that are crucial as well to events from the 1940s to the 1970s.

3 See for example Dane Kennedy's *Island of White: Settler Society and Culture in Kenya and Southern Rhodesia, 1890–1938* (Durham, NC: Duke University Press, 1987).

Because the actors are all male in the Antiguan context this period must necessarily then be examined through the construct of masculinities(s), the plural or multiple construction of identity based upon sex.[4] Male identities were multi-dimensional, reflecting the diverse class, race, and gender structures of Caribbean societies. One the one hand white males whether Creole or Europeans have historically been constructed in these societies as the norm against which all other male identities are measured. The others in this context include women as well as other men. White masculinity is therefore the hegemonic ideal against which both femininity and other masculinities are judged and is therefore the hegemonic masculinity which is dominant and subordinates and marginalizes all others.[5] While black, coloured and white males are all privileged in relation to women, they are not all equally positioned or privileged in the society. The subordination and marginalization of coloured and black men has long been underway in Caribbean societies and by the late 1940s white Creole males still continued to dominate Caribbean societies despite the fact that their numbers had diminished dramatically.

Creole masculinity in the context of the colonial Caribbean (both hegemonic and subordinate) is under pressure from imperial masculinity and this further complicates the relationship between men in the colonies as both groups of Creoles vie for imperial support for their agendas. In addition to their competition for outside support both sides worked to build a support base among the masses. It was a competition that the black and coloured trade union leaders won handily by the mid-1940s when the Union's existence was secured.

It was the legalization and successful organizing of trade unions that spelled the doom of white Creoles in Antigua and Barbuda and it was the

4 Keith Nurse 'Masculinities in Transition', in *Interrogating Caribbean Masculinities*. Nurse references Connell, 1992 and 1995 – Connell, R. W. 1992 'A Very Straight Gay: Masculinity, Homosexual Experience and the Dynamics of Gender', *American Sociological Review* 57:6 (1996), and *Masculinities* (Cambridge: Polity Press, 1995).

5 This relationship is best described by Foucault *in History of Sexuality. Volume I: An Introduction* (New York: Vintage, 1981). He uses the language of 'disciplinary power' to describe the operation of masculinism.

union that they attacked viciously during its first decade in the Leeward Islands. The Colonial Office expressed concern over rising industrial unrest and sought new solutions to the deepening labour crisis. Both sides, employers and union leaders sought to gain sympathy within the West Indies Department Colonial Office and the numerous communications that passed between Leeward Islands and the Colonial Office document clearly the Colonial Office's desperation to please both sides, a losing proposition.

By 1949 trade union leaders throughout the British Caribbean colonies were an organized group working in concert against employers and white Creole legislators. This was thanks in large part to the legalization of trade unions and the growth of workers organizations throughout the British Caribbean colonies. In addition to individual unions a regional community of trade union leaders had emerged. This group of largely male leaders represented the millions of working people in the Caribbean and they would use their strength in numbers in the region and in their islands in ways that clearly demonstrated to regional employers and their white Creole counterparts that a power shift in the political arena was imminent. Leeward Island's trade union leaders in concert with union leaders throughout the British Caribbean colonies sought to wrest political control from the old-guard ruling class whites and their coloured allies through organized labour, access to legislative councils and other political instruments. In addition they advocated directly through the Colonial Office and other international organizations for more political access and for an expanded franchise.

St. Kitts labour leader Robert L. Bradshaw[6] and Antigua's V. C. Bird were part of a region wide community of male trade unionists whose leadership skills were being developed under the TUC and through association with larger unions in islands such as those in Jamaica and Trinidad. The

6 Bradshaw's labour activism began in 1940 with his involvement in the strike of sugar workers. He was then at the time an apprentice in machine shop, a job he held since 1932, when he became active in the Workers' League. He would become a prominent labour activist, and was elected to the Legislative Council in 1946. As the president of the St. Kitts-Nevis Trade and Labour Union, he dominated politics until his death in 1978 (Bolland, 430 quoting Richardson 1983: 167–168).

relationship between Bradshaw and Bird evident by 1948 was the product of their shared regional experience and of their common mentoring under the TUC and the Colonial Office. As both were leaders of the two largest regional unions that they would collaborate with one another is no surprise. The two created an effective regional tag team against sugar estate owners and white Creole legislators. Their struggles with these groups over the course of the next decade reflect the heightening tensions of race, class, colour and gender on St. Kitts and Antigua. The battles recorded in memos to the Colonial Office address sensitive issues such as the attempt on the part of white Creole legislators and their allies to solve the industrial problem by deportation. The first of such plans is exposed in 1949 when Bradshaw notified the Colonial Office from St. Kitts that the Antiguan legislators were developing secret plans to introduce 'repressive legislation' to deport union activists from the colonies.[7] It was a letter which was of course met with grave concern by the Colonial Office and the secretary of state for the colonies the Right Honourable A. Creech Jones.

These claims were alleged at a time when the Colonial Office was working with black and coloured union leaders to advance constitutional reform for Antigua and Barbuda. The U.K, and the Colonial Office in particular, was under great pressure from the Caribbean as well as from the international community, through the United Nations, to advance towards more self-government for their colonial possession. Early in 1948, Creech Jones had had discussions on this matter with Bird and the fact that the Presidential Legislative Councils of the Colony, still heavily controlled by white Creoles had failed to pass the appropriate reforms to gain the support of both the Antigua and Barbuda and St. Kitts-Nevis councils had only increased tensions in the Leeward Islands between the two groups, black and coloured labour leaders and white Creole legislators. These issues were at the heart of the struggles of white Creoles in the Leeward

7 CO 152 520 4: Memo on repressive labour legislation in the colonies in 1949. Memo written by Robert. L. Bradshaw to Mr. H. Beckett West Indies Department Colonial Office dated 25 November 1949. Bradshaw exposed plans to deport those who disturbed the peace by way of strikes etc. This legislation had been drafted and proposed to the executive council in Antigua.

Islands to maintain their social and political dominance, a dominance threatened increasingly by imperial plans to move towards local control of political affairs in the colonies. The presidential council of the region, an organization comprised of and representative of white Creoles was slated for elimination by the Colonial Office by mid-1950.[8] White Creoles had forestalled their demise once before in 1898 when they reverted to Crown Colony; they sought to forestall their demise again throughout the 1940s and 1950s, struggling even after the passage of universal adult suffrage to maintain their hegemony within Antigua and Barbuda. It was an instinctive act done perhaps more out of habit than of any real belief that they could maintain their place in the new world order that was British colonialism in the second half of the twentieth century. By 1951, it was clear that the age of white Creole dominance had ended, making way for a new order in Caribbean societies. The new order maintained the patriarchy as white Creole males were replaced by black and coloured males. It was the final colonial legacy, transferring power from one group of men to another, this despite the fact that the granting of suffrage in 1951 did not limit the suffrage to males only. Women in Antigua and Barbuda gained full citizenship at the same time as did the men, as sex was not one of the limitations barring suffrage. Yet, despite suffrage women did not achieve their full place as political citizens in Antigua and Barbuda. This would have to wait until 2004 when for the second time in its history the Labour party is defeated at the polls and for the first time in the history of Antiguan politics since 1951 a woman is elected to the post of minister of government.[9]

8 CO 152 520 4 Legislation that was enacted was 'a shockingly scandalous far cry from what was demanded by the councils' The legislative councils of Antigua and St. Kitts-Nevis has refused to cooperate with Government and 'a serious impasse now exists'.

9 The story of women's long absence from political leadership, a bar not broken until the 2004 elections is a different story for another time.

Political Progress 1940–1951

For Antigua and Barbuda, the political progress of the colony can be tracked through the political history of V. C. Bird. In 1943 V. C. became the second president of the Antigua Trades and Labour Union (ATLU) and in 1946 foreseeing the legislative changes and the move towards universal adult suffrage Bird and other union leaders formed the Antigua Labour Party (ALP), the first political party formed by black and coloured people on the island colony. The formation of the ALP was the first stage of the battle for political control by black and coloured men of the island colony. As union leader and a member of the executive council, Bird found himself caught up in a conflict over loyalty to workers and loyalty to the colonial government which he served as a member of the committee. His determination to maintain both positions, that of union leader advocating for the Antiguan masses and state representative with responsibilities to the imperial mandates of the Colonial Office, brought him into increasing conflict both on and off the island.

In the second half of the 1940s once the trade unions had survived their shaky beginnings, industrial unrest had become standard. That unions were blamed by employers and white Creoles as the sole source of such industrial unrest was understandable, as the labour strikes and the contentious negotiations between labour and employers disrupted social order and the export economy. In many cases of industrial unrest it was the actions of employers that provoked labour to action. While they were forced by law to recognize the legitimacy of trade unions, many employers in the colonies, particularly white Creoles resisted the new assertiveness and new demands of their employees and the union representatives who spoke on their behalf. But the great danger by 1948 was that even the Colonial Office, an office which during wartime had demonstrated an unusual resolve to work with the new trade unions rather than against them, was by 1948 demonstrating less of the earlier resolve. The greatest of these threats was on the issue of collective bargaining, a matter at the heart of the industrial crisis of the late 1940s. On this matter the Secretary of State, seeking to end the ongoing disruptions in St. Kitts and Antigua, was articulating support for the creation of a labour board. Labour saw the board as a grave threat to the existence of trade unionism – the very organizations which black and coloured men were using to make their political claims in the colonies.

> The Secretary of State considered that the constant industrial discontent in the LI indicated that the present system of voluntary collective bargaining was inadequate and that the arguments in favour of machinery which would minimize the risk of strikes on wages questions should be emphasized to the governor whose attention should also be called to circulars on this subject.[10]

This was then V. C.'s great challenge in 1948, the prospect of the Colonial Office, the same office which had worked closely with the TUC since the 1938 Royal Commission, to establish trade unions in the colonies as a means of solving the industrial problems facing British colonies in the region. That ten years later the Colonial Office itself would seek to destroy these very same unions was unimaginable. Bird attacked this matter quickly and effectively in the Minority report to the Soulbury Report.

> Mr. Mark Moody Stuart of Messrs. Henckell Du Boisson and Company called on Mr. Beckett and myself this morning. He began by saying that he had come with what he supposed was a forlorn request, to know whether there was anything that could be done 'about the administration in Antigua and Barbuda.[11]

The subject of white Creoles' response to the changing social and political climate has not been heavily investigated for Antigua. The post 1938 historiography has focused largely on the actions of black and coloured men and on the constitutional reforms implemented by the British government through the 1960s. How these impacted and were responded to by white Creoles is often overlooked in the literature. Even the seminal work of Caribbean labour historian O. Nigel Bolland failed to deal with white

10 Ibid., see source in notes and reference both notes 4 and 5 Documents/circulars and memos on the nationalization of the LI Sugar Industry.

11 CO 1152 520 4 Memo from Sir Charles Jeffries, Colonial Secretary on nationalization of the LI Sugar Industry. Dated 17 October 1949.

Creole resistance.[12] The document on the meeting in the Colonial Office with Moody Stuart expanded on the concerns of Moody Stuart, those of his employers and other white Creoles in Antigua. Stuart had arrived at the Colonial Office to complain about the financial impact of an earlier strike on the island's sugar industry of 1948. The meticulous note-taking of the Colonial Office on this meeting lists Moody Stuart's concerns for 1949 in response to the prolonged strike which the sugar industry has recently experienced. Sugar estate operations was Moody-Stuart's business and his concerns regarding past and future disruptions to the sugar operations and their financial impact is listed in numbers which he may not have been quite precise about documenting. The 1948 strike, Moody Stuart complained, had resulted in a deficit of some 60,000 pounds (this was handwritten in the margin of his record, he didn't absolutely commit himself to the figure – but it was in that order).

Moody-Stuart further complained that in 1949 while labour was not engaged in direct strike it was his contention that go-slow methods had been widely practiced, and that this action may have had an impact on the prior year's deficit as well. The actions of labour, with strikes and go-slows were threatening the sugar industry. Moody-Stuart speculated in reports to the Colonial Office that the collapse of the whole economy of Antigua and Barbuda would result if labour actions were not curtailed. Mr. Moody Stuart further pointed to the person on the island, identified by Moody Stuart and other employers to be at the heart of the trouble, Bird, who was described as 'engaged in campaigns in the villages doing his utmost to set the workers against both the estate owners and the Government.'[13] The

12 O. Nigel Bolland, *The Politics of Labour*, 449. In spite of the frequent repression of many political and trade union activities under emergency wartime regulations, the British government initiated some important constitutional reforms in the Caribbean during World War II. These reforms, which included the granting of universal adult suffrage in Jamaica in 1944 and Trinidad and Tobago in 1945, moved these colonies decisively towards democracy and self-government. Most of the smaller colonies followed a similar pattern of democratization shortly thereafter and all had entered the period of mass politics by the 1950s.

13 Ibid.

Colonial Office administrator documenting the meeting expresses some sympathy for Moody Stuart and his comrades noting in his report that 'Mr. Bird, whom we know well, was entirely out for political ends, and had recently got rid of certain more moderate men from the management of the Labour Union'.[14] The document further noted his concern that the next cropping season, in February 1950, might be marked by further prolonged ruinous strikes, if not by violence. This last suggestion that violence was threatened by labour and by Bird was no doubt designed to make a strong point with the Colonial Office, which Moody Stuart clearly thought had not done nearly enough to control the labour union. More directly the suggestion was that the Colonial Government ought to be doing something to counteract Mr. Bird's propaganda, and one such action ought to consist of placing before the people the real facts of the situation. By the 1940s, every peasant in the Caribbean clearly knew these facts regarding the dependence of the colonies upon the sugar industry. But unlike Moody Stuart, who assumed that there were no alternatives to sugar for the Caribbean colonies, and Antigua in particular, and that a resolution in the interest of estate owners and employers was the only kind of resolution to be arrived at, most labourers in Antigua had come to believe and advocate quite the opposite. Change was quite imminent by 1950 and the days of exploitation at the hands of estate owners and factory owners were numbered. Moody Stuart's claims, therefore, to the Colonial government that labour and the island colony faced dire consequences if labour continued to refuse to agree to the terms established by employers rang hollow, especially in light of the minority reports of the Soulbury report in which labour proposed social and economic alternatives which would make such employers obsolete.

Not surprisingly Moody Stuart did not confine his complaints to labour and trade union leaders but also directed concern at the governor's performance on the island. He accused Governor Lord Baldwin of indifference to the current and future situation and complained that the governor was primarily concerned with 'such things as presenting new standards

14 Ibid.

to the steel bands.'[15] As the representative of syndicate estate interests, an investment group which included not only white Creoles but also British investors as well, Moody Stuart was assured by the Colonial Office that his concerns would be reported to the Secretary of State. His level of satisfaction at this meeting is unknown although it was certainly not his first and would not be his last visit to the Colonial Office to complain about the labour and political situation on the island. While Moody Stuart was sent off with not much of a promise in terms of the response which the Colonial Office intended to take to the situation described to them, the administrator made note in his report to the Secretary of State reminding him of the earlier conflict between the union and employers in both 1948 and 1949 when there was concern of a strike during the cropping season. The Colonial Office in the effort to reduce the damage of these conflicts had called the then governor Lord Baldwin back to London for consultation. At the start of the 1950s cropping season there was to be more industrial conflict as suggested by Moody Stuart's visit. Based upon his meeting in the Colonial Office the office administrator concluded in his report to the secretary that because the cropping season for 1950 seems to be one of the largest on record that the union may take this opportunity to call a strike as such a strike would hold employers hostage where labour is concerned at a time when they were hoping to recoup losses from the 1948 and 1949 cropping season.[16] Yet while he made this observation clearly as a result of Moody-Stuart's discussion he is also quick to insist in the records that he is cognizant of the struggle between both groups in Antigua represented by Moody Stuart and V. C. Bird.

> Mr. Moody Stuart of course presents only one side of the picture; but I am inclined to think there is a need for the Government to show some initiative in good time before the next season, if only by way of making sure that the public have a real understanding of the situation and are not wholly led astray by Mr. Bird's distortions, designed to further his own political ambitions.[17]

15 Ibid.
16 Ibid.
17 Ibid.

This conclusion at the end of the 1949 meeting with Moody Stuart, written by a colonial administrator who demonstrates a knowledge not only of the industrial situation on the island colony but also of the primary actors. Not unaware of the tensions of the two Creole groups and caught between both groups and their respective support base was the Governor, who was constantly called upon by the Colonial Office to resolve disputes or give full accounts of activities taking place. As such, the role of Governor of the Leeward became the forum through which the Colonial Office managed the contending groups and by 1949 Lord Baldwin found himself in a difficult situation as he was trusted by neither Creole group and was limited by his job description to following the direction of the Colonial Office in negotiating relations between the two groups. No wonder Lord Baldwin sought to focus on the steel band arrangements in 1949 above negotiating industrial relations between two contentious groups.[18]

> From the Secretary of State for the Colonies to the Officer Administering the Government of Leeward Islands date 14th September, 1949: Secret and Personal. Soulbury Reports, Press Statement.[19]

As a result of the contentious industrial relations in the Leeward Island colonies of Antigua and St. Kitts in 1948 the Colonial Office organized a Commission to investigate and submit recommendations. The report the product of this Commission investigation, has been entered into history as the lesser known of three Soulbury reports. All three Commissions were chaired by Lord Soulbury who investigated conditions in British Ceylon and Trinidad in addition to the Leeward Islands in the 1940s. The Soulbury report for the Leeward Islands of Antigua and St. Kitts has proven to be an invaluable document, for it is produced at a crucial time in the history of British Caribbean colonies, and for Antigua and Barbuda and the Leeward Islands the document positions the future of the colonies and exposes the

18 Ibid. Moody-Stuart also complained to the Colonial Office in the same visit that Lord Baldwin was ignoring his responsibilities on Antigua to focus instead on steel band arrangements.

19 CO 152 520 49.

gap between Creole groups and the Colonial Office over the future of the British colonies. The Commission itself would further heighten already high tensions between Creole groups and labour and employers.

The Antigua/St-Kitts Commission provided a forum for labour leaders in Antigua and St. Kitts to articulate their proposals for their islands and to engage some of the most pressing issues for the region's working people, the issue of employment, access to land and the future of sugar in these small colonies in the Caribbean. The reports, especially the minority section of these reports, represent a local vision for the future, one by labour leaders Bird and Bradshaw. This alone places it among the most important of twentieth-century Commissions (second only to the 1938 Royal Commission). Local leaders for the first time in the history of British colonialism are asked to contribute to an imperial report and to have their contribution considered along with those of neutral parties on the Commission.

Soulbury Commission History

Appointed by Governor Baldwin in July of 1948 to investigate the ongoing tensions between the union and the syndicate estates and sugar factory the Commission was comprised of experienced Commissioners. As a matter of fact the majority of the members of the Antigua/St. Kitts Commission had only just completed a similar assignment in Trinidad earlier the same year.[20] The investigation consisted of interviews on the island of parties on both sides in order to find out the cause of industrial unrest and propose solutions to the Colonial Office.

20 Ibid. The members of the Commission were Lord Soulbury, as Chairman, Captain Mackie, Mr. Holmes, Mr. Turner, Mr. Cuke, Mr. Bird (for the Antigua report), Mr. Bradshaw (for the St. Kitts Report). Report is item 49 in folder. Antigua Report is 191–234 (TUC document summary at TUC Archives HD 9111 1948).

In light of their investigation into the problems between employers and the union the Commission report recommended the creation of an industrial organizations such as a wages board of council, the improvement of arrangements for land settlement and improvement in land use such as addressing the use of under-cultivated land and improvement in workers' pay and conditions of work. The recommendations however fell short of the union's expectation and recommendations as the minority reports demonstrate. Local trade union leaders called for the nationalization of the sugar industry in their respective islands and the breakup of syndicated estates to provide arable lands to peasant settlements, and supported the development of secondary industry.

While the governor supported many of the recommendations of the majority and minority reports he indicated to the Colonial Office his unwillingness to support any recommendation contrary to the recommendations of the Commission such as those to be found in the minority report. The committee did not recommend the nationalization of the sugar industries nor did they support the breakup of the syndicate estates, but rather stressed their efficiency in the case of Antigua. Governor Baldwin indicated in his public announcement of the committee report that the report had been presented to the British Parliament by the Secretary of State on the 25 May. He further stated in his local announcement that the general pattern of the Antiguan system of land tenure and agriculture follows the line of the agreed agricultural policy of combining large estates and peasant settlements. Any proposed change of emphasis must be considered by the local legislature.

This was one of the first changes that Bird and ministers of government would move to address by 1960 when they gained control of the island: the breakup of syndicate estates and the creation of the largest peasant land ownership program in the Caribbean. This has been one of his most defining legacies in the region.[21]

21 Ibid.

Minority Reports – Relevant Facts and Recommendations

Tim Hector, the late political critic and journalist of Antigua and Barbuda was both Bird's biggest admirer and his greatest critic. In addition Hector has written the most on Bird's personal and political life. While I have found little to criticize of his prolific writings on Antiguan politics and on Bird – his claim that Bird never wrote anything is far from correct. The *Minority Report,* a thirty page manifesto for post-colonial Antigua, was certainly V. C. Bird's brainchild. Requested as a supplement to the full report which included a majority report presented by the other members of the Commission it is clear that Bird did not appreciate that local recommendations were to be housed in a separate report titled 'minority' and did not trust the other members of the Commission to understand local conditions. In his cover letter he suggests differences of opinion between him and other committee members. 'I find myself forced to submit certain relevant facts and recommendations to you.'[22] He further complained that the committee rejected suggestions from Union and from workers but that they offered no alternative to these proposals.

His report sought to remedy the defects of the majority report which Bird suggests failed to meet its responsibility to make suggestions on improving the sugar industry. His eight chapter report dealt with economic and political and social conditions on the island at the heart of which lay the issue of industrial conditions. By 1948 the tensions between employers and employees had reached contentious heights. The employers, the syndicate estate and the sugar factory, the largest employers on the island, consistently describe the Union as the source of their troubles. They were far from blameless. They consistently complained of the behaviour of labour leaders and identified Bird and 'the Ministers' as 'dishonest characters'[23] who lacked the skills necessary to run a country. Their complaints were

22 Ibid., 191.

23 CO 1031 2280 – *Constitutional Development in Antigua*: Letter of complaint about conditions in Antigua.

aimed at stopping the impending social changes in Antiguan society. Bird himself spoke clearly to the colonial authorities on what he saw was at the heart of the planters' behaviour towards the union and non-white ministers.

> It is apparent [...] that the attitude of the plantation owners is deeply rooted in slavery and that they are interested, not in seeing the land reorganized for production which will accrue to the benefit of the community as a whole, but actually in opposing and obstructing any rearrangement of land ownership which will assist in building up an independent peasantry likely to deprive them of using a large standing body of unemployed, serf like, landless workers to keep down wages with the object of keeping sugar profits up.[24]

Moreover, Bird, in his report on Industrial Relations, while he diplomatically described relations between the Union and employers as having 'gone as well as might be expected',[25] described relations from the late1940s as ones in which employers attempted to continue to impose their will upon the workers and refused to recognize the union.[26] The change which had occurred after five years involved the attempt (recommendation by investigator Professor Richardson that negotiations precede crop season in January by three months) by the union representatives to negotiate with employers three months prior to the crop season in January of each year. Bird described the 1947 crop season as the beginning of this friction when employers declined to meet the Union's representatives and negotiate with them. Only the intervention by the government forced the employers to relent and even then they created further delays by demanding from Bird an apology for having said they were out to destroy the union. Employer's representatives in the meeting walked out because of Bird's refusal to apologize for his comment.

From the employers' perspective the story of the 1947 conflict was slightly different. Its cause lay not in their refusal to negotiate with the union but with union leader's intransigence. Mr. Moody Stuart, manager of the Syndicates Estates, a collection of sugar estates which included some 29 estates on some of the island's most fertile lands, insisted in reports to the

24 CO 152 520 49, 194.
25 Ibid., 213.
26 Ibid., 213.

Colonial Office that something had to be done about Bird and his spreading of propaganda among the peasants to turn them against employers. By the 1950s Moody Stuart and his colleagues, other estate owners and managers, as well as Sugar Factory administrators were engaged in propaganda to discredit Bird and other black and coloured Ministers of Government.

In response to these accusations Bird in his minority report recorded that the employers in their newspaper, the *Antigua Star*, engaged in incitement of the workers who they had encouraged to demand strike-bonus from the Union. He proudly relayed that the workers staunchly refused to press the Union for a strike bonus and upheld the strike. Bird proudly reported that by 1946 there was clear class solidarity in Antigua among the workers.[27] This solidarity would be evident for the next twenty years as the labour union and the Labour party came to dominate the political landscape of the island.

Bird quoted the assessment of Lord Oliver whose book *White Capital and Colored Labour* had examined the situation of industrial relations in colonies such as Antigua and Barbuda. Bird insisted that Commission members and the Imperial government acknowledge that the tradition of slavery more than one hundred years later still hung heavily over the island. He further insisted that this tradition 'imbues the attitude of the European employers towards the coloured workers. Hence the employers are unfavourably [sic] disposed to meeting on common ground as equals the leaders of the Union, who are men from among the ranks of the workers.'[28] While both the employers and business interests on the island aggressively addressed the topic of labours' responsibility to the estates and the island economy they spoke less passionately if at all of their obligations to workers. This was Bird's thesis in his statement on industrial relations; the need for employers to take some responsibility for workers and for the society. The report was compiled prior to the granting of universal adult suffrage in 1951, and Bird addressed the issues of racism and segregation and the power differentials in Antiguan society, in a surprisingly direct and eloquent manner.

27 Ibid., 212.
28 Ibid.

> Like most of the other islands of the Caribbean Antigua produces mainly sugar, again a relic of slavery. This industry has been owned for centuries by Europeans, whose arrogant superiority is bolstered by the predominant position their race, particularly the British section of it, has held in the world over a long period of time, as well as the fact that the island is a colony, a 'possession' of the Mother Country. This attitude […] is manifested in a number of different ways calculated to make the coloured man feel that he is an inferior being ineligible to be treated on a basis of equality.[29]

This then was the heart of Bird's problem as Union leader and spokesperson for the some 14,000 registered members of the Union, a union of black and coloured workers, the descendants of slaves, now seeking to establish relations of equals over one hundred years after slavery was abolished and experiencing strong resistance. He described the Antiguan social structure as pervaded by racism and segregation.

> The Europeans in Antigua have their own club to which men of colour, however eminent in their professions, are not admitted […] (he identified some men as including the Honourable S. T. Christian, the Honourable E. E. Harney, the Crown Attorney; and the Federal Treasurer Honourable A. Thompson). There is a separate white people's tennis club just across the road from the coloured upper class tennis club. The whites live in one section of a district, the coloured in another. With the racial line so sharply drawn when it comes to coloured people of ability, it can easily be imagined what sort of relationship existed between the workers and their masters.[30]

In addressing the argument of employers that things were quiet on the island before the union was formed, Bird replied in agreement to this assertion adding 'this it is possible to concede, for circumstances did not permit otherwise. After all, there is peace in a graveyard.'[31] He argued that the people were cowed by the overwhelming power of employers and saw the colonial administrators as allies with their employers therefore they saw no recourse to their abuse regarding the employers as rulers to be obeyed. And employers no doubt embraced this power completely and resisted any change to this social and political monopoly which they had enjoyed since the seventeenth century.

29 Ibid., 212–213.
30 Ibid., 212–213.
31 Ibid., 213.

But Bird had not arrived at his present state without learning diplomacy and despite his frank presentation on the racial issues in Antiguan society he made clear to state the need for changes in the society and describe a future society with both white employers and black workers in a better working and social relationship with each other. A new approach in industrial relationships was clearly desirable, but he noted:

> But this means a change of heart and the white capitalists must come to regard the indigent workers not merely as their employees to whom scant attention need be given, because they are in any event easily replaceable, but as human beings and fellow citizens, in a common political entity – the British Commonwealth [...] all the races – Indian, Chinese, European, Negro, must grow to live and work in mutual respect.[32]

Bird also noted in his report that the social relations on the island were also greatly impacted by the economic conditions, and that this played a role in increasing the friction between employers and workers. He pointed out that in the Antiguan sugar economy, like sugar economies worldwide, wages are based upon the market price for sugar. Irrespective of the market price, employers always seek to keep profits as high as possible and as a result it is the workers who pay in the form of their low wages and low rates for the sugar in the case of the Antigua Sugar Factory where peasant producers of sugar cane are forced to sell their sugar cane often at little profit. But the real economic hardship faced by peasants was in their cost of basic necessities, food, clothing and other items, all of which were imported. While the cost of these imported items constantly increased, workers wages never increased enough to make it possible for them to earn living wages. In the colonies, and in the agricultural economy of Antigua in particular, Bird reported that the gap between cost of living and wages for workers was an ever growing one. The role of trade unions in the island was one unique in many ways to the situation in Europe and Bird and other Caribbean trade unionists had a difficult time convincing their allies in the TUC and the colonial government that their situation was unique. The colonial status of the island and its history created a different set of relations and expectations between union leaders and the workers they represented. Bird insisted that

32 Ibid., 213.

workers in the colonial territories as members of trade unions expect their union leadership to work to improve their condition. Contrary to the position of those in the Colonial Office and white Creoles who insisted otherwise, Bird suggests that it was the Antiguan workers and union members who drove him and other union leaders, and who were impatient with any attempt or suggestion of the union working to create peace with employers rather than to advocate primarily in the interest of workers.

This, Bird argued, was one of the major differences between unions in Europe and those in the colonial territories, the expectations and demands of the union membership that their interests as they perceived them take priority over any other social and political interests for union leaders. He reiterated in his report that if workers perceived that union members were working for interests other than those of the members that this 'would do more to break the union than any other impression that workers could have.'[33] Employers resentful of the union and of any changes to the status quo had successfully advocated in 1948 for a wage council or Board to be set up to fix minimum wage rates. This action clearly would have had the intended consequence of eliminating the principle of collective bargaining won by the union with the legalization of unions in 1940. Surprisingly the Soulbury report made such a recommendation, much to the resentment of Bird who in his minority report chastised his colleagues for supporting employers' attempt to destroy the union. 'The proposal strikes at the very foundation of trade unionism, particularly in a country like Antigua and Barbuda, where trade unionism has been recently introduced and its roots not yet imbedded among the people.'[34] He further warned the Secretary of state for the colonies 'If the right of collective bargaining is withdrawn trade unionism will cease to exist.'[35]

Despite efforts begun in the nineteenth century at diversifying the Antiguan economy by the end of the first half of the twentieth century the economy remained focused on sugar cane as the dominant agricultural pursuit. Sugar estate owners by 1950 were a small minority on the island

33 Ibid., 215.

34 Ibid.

35 Ibid., 215.

but it was a minority that dominated the economic life of the island and which sought to continue to influence political life. For the black and coloured workers agricultural diversification was crucial to changing the pattern of dependency and exploitation established under British colonialism. Additionally, alternatives to the sugar monoculture economy were imperative to expanding peasant agriculture on the island and to reducing the poverty and dependency of workers on the estates. This awareness is clearly articulated by Bird whose suggestions in the report included agricultural supplements or partners to sugar. While the legislative council in 1949 was still describing sugar as the most suitable crop for the island; Bird advocated support for cotton, tomatoes, maize, arrowroot and other crops currently grown on small scale by peasant farmers. He also suggested experimentation with new crops such as tobacco, sisal and pineapples.

To the cause of peasant access to the land he attacked modernization in particular the mechanization which he argued was being used in Antigua 'chiefly for the sake of being independent of organized manual labour.'[36] His position while it begins to sound a bit paranoid especially where he argued that the mechanization was introduced as reprisal in response to the departure of workers for the US base. It is clear those estate owners in particular the Syndicate Estates were determined to control the labour market and to maintain high profit margins for investors.

But while Bird does not see mechanization as imperative to the sugar economy of the island, he advocated industrialization as a supplement to agriculture. The move to industrialization would begin with an investigation of the resources the island possessed that could be used in industry, then further investigation regarding exploiting these materials and the employment opportunities such industrialization would entail. Industrialization was not seen solely as an alternative to sugar but as another important source for work, a dire need faced by Antiguan workers despite the best efforts of employers to cover the large un-employment and under-employment faced by the population.[37]

36 Ibid., 220–221.
37 Ibid.

Table 8 Exposing the Unemployment and Underemployment in the Soulbury Report

Population 1947	Men employed in sugar cane	Women employed in sugar cane	Young persons employed in sugar cane
44,000	1,324	1,616	119
Out of crop employment for same year	1,085	1,523	145
Source: Soulbury Report			

What these figures show and what Bird articulated in his report was the ongoing crisis among the working population where the bulk of the 'able-bodied male population' remained unemployed most of the year. He insisted that the claims of employment by employers be closely interrogated for the true nature of employment and underemployment in Antigua and Barbuda. For instance employment figures provided by employers to the Commission were deceptive as they did not explain that the jobs are staggered and the factory and plantations employ workers alternatively to spread out the little available work. The payroll records on the other hand demonstrated large employment numbers, and some employers even gave Commission members the impression that they had difficulty hiring workers. The commitment on the part of employers at both the factory and estate to give the impression to Commission members, all of whom (with the exception of V. C. were unfamiliar with the work conditions in the region and of the historical relationship between employers and labour), reflect the ongoing attempt to discredit the complaints of union leaders and workers that any change was necessary in the economy and society of the island.

> In actuality, as the volume of evidence supports, the present situation of mass unemployment is deplorable and calls for immediate action. The thousands of able-bodied people willing to work and finding themselves more or less permanently unemployed, constitutes one of the biggest social problems facing Antigua.[38]

38 Ibid., 221.

Bird recommended that a record of the unemployment on the island be made and kept by the Government. This was proposed as part of the larger proposal of solutions to the unemployment program supported by the union. He noted in his report that one solution supported by the Union but undertaken by the government was the securing of temporary employment for workers outside of the island. In 1947 workers had been sent to Florida and Curacao. These were temporary arrangements however, and he was sure to note in his report that once the work contracts terminated that these workers would be obliged to return to the island and to the state of unemployment from which they had been temporarily rescued.

Bird insisted on a longer-term solution to the unemployment problem on the island, one which went further than temporary work abroad. He advocated that such a move begin with the collecting of statistics on employment, and move on to government sponsored projects to provide gainful work for the unemployed. One such project could involve using peasants to prepare land for permanent settlement for these same unemployed. The report also advocated for a government-sponsored program for reclaiming lands for use through irrigation, swamp reclamation and other soil culture programs.

The proposed suggestions by Bird and which were supported by the Union would indicate some knowledge of Roosevelt's WPA and other government-sponsored projects in the United States during the 1930s. These projects had successfully lessened the unemployment and economic crisis for many urban and rural workers during the world depression and had created important infrastructure for the nation. Bird was proposing the colonial government become involved in social programs and more hands-on administration. He was also calling for more financial investment by the Imperial government at a time when the economic value of the Caribbean colonies was at a historical low point. No wonder the Imperial government moved with such speed to divest itself of the colonies, putting in place systems for self-government and instituting universal adult suffrage in 1951. The cost of maintaining Empire and the pressure to divest were powerful motivators to end colonialism.

The Period 1951–1960

Antigua. No. 3 of 1951[39] was perhaps the most far-reaching of ordinances where the continuance of white Creole dominance was concerned. The ordinance to provide for the registration of voters in the island colony may as well have been titled an act to end the dominance of a small land owning elite in the presidency for it spelled the doom of white Creole dominance of the Legislative Council for the presidency and opened up the Council for domination by black and coloured elected members. This was a major threat to the white Creoles because the number of elected members was much smaller than the elected membership and while white Creoles were no longer guaranteed an elected place they were certain of being the minority on the council as they were through 1957 the only group nominated by the governor to the council.

The second blow to the white Creole population in Antigua in the 1950s was administered by the Colonial Office in 1956 with the implementation of the *Ministerial System of Government* in Antigua. This represented an additional step towards local political control and while there had been some talk both on the island and in the Colonial Office regarding delaying the implementing of ministerial system because of the ongoing industrial unrest, the governor received clear instructions from the Colonial Office that nothing was to delay the implementation of this system. The Governor K. W. Blackburne in a speech broadcast in Antigua 18 January outlined for the Antiguan population the changes which the ministerial system brought to the method of government in the colony. Legislative Council elect four of the elected members to the Executive Council and governor assigns three of the members of the Executive Council with portfolios as Ministers.

The outline of new governance for Antiguan affairs under the ministerial system established two main organizations; the Legislative Council – responsible for making laws, for voting money for government works, and the Executive Council (works like the Cabinet in the UK), which was

39 CO 152 540 8; Antigua No. 3 of 1951, Registration of Voters.

responsible for preparing the policy of the government and also responsible for the general direction of the work of Government. Laws of the Legislative Council give power to the Executive Council to carry out those laws. The Executive Council was the most powerful of government organizations and was in effect the Government of Antigua and Barbuda.

The ministerial system introduced in 1956 made two major changes to the political system: first, the local council was no longer merely an advisory unit. Decisions of the council were reached by majority vote and were binding on all the members including the governor and administrator, an exception was inserted to protect from bad government which provided an exception to the decisions of the council 'unless the governor or the administrator deem it expedient to do otherwise in the interest of public faith, good order or good government'.[40]

Secondly, the elected members of Council had a majority vote. This vote was to be the basis for all decisions made by the government. The three ministers, all elected members of the council, took over much of the responsibilities handled prior by administrator. After 1956 only finance and legal matters remained as administrator responsibilities. Threc elected members of the executive council held posts of ministers for Trade and Production, Social Services and for Communications and Works.[41] All that remained of the old Crown Colony system were the Crown Attorney and Financial Secretary. The transition of power was evident with the ministerial system as the entire civil service under the ministerial system fell into the hands of local ministers, who alone issued directions to the departments that fell within their ministry. Ministerial system set up in addition a Public Service Commission in each Presidency whose role was to manage the administration of the civil service, handling appointments, retirement, dismissal, promotion and discipline within the civil service. This then became an important base for labour union leaders who dominated the ranks of ministers from 1956. Whether intended or not by the Colonial Office, the ministerial system was the first step in de-federalizing

40 Ibid.
41 Ibid.

the region. The ministerial system made each of the Presidencies separate colonies. Forced to institute the ministerial system in the island in the midst of industrial unrest the governor declared in his address to the island colony that the change in government was the 'last step of the ladder to fully responsible government.'[42]

The industrial, class and race struggles continued through the late 1950s as white Creoles sought to gain the ear of the Colonial Office and to discourage the growing move in that office towards local government. Antigua's white Creoles and their allies used a variety of tactics to delay the inevitable political shift to black and coloured Creoles. In the Colonial Office they tried to use guilt and sought to tarnish the reputation of the black and coloured ministers. Locally they attempted propaganda directed at the working people.

With political and social changes being rapidly advanced by the Colonial Office in the 1960s, white Creoles became increasingly desperate as the political changes more and more relegated them to a role befitting their class size in Antigua. Whereas it had been enough in the past to send a letter or visit and suggest impropriety on the part of administrators and others in order to influence the actions of the Colonial Office, these actions no longer seemed to have any effect on the Colonial Office where administrators politely listened and ignored the requests, advise and gossip of white Creoles. Yet the group persisted through the 1950s. Perhaps the most aggressive of such actions by white Creoles was the 1957 joint deputation seen by the Colonial Office on 14 December. This deputation included members of the Antigua Employers' Federation and the Antigua Livestock Association. Not surprising the group seems to have been led by the managing director of the Syndicate estates as well as the managing director of the Sugar factory. These were from the primary industries, the estates, sugar factory, hotel, livestock producers, and importers/exporters.

42 Ibid.

Table 9 White Creole Deputation 1957

1957 JOINT DEPUTATION TO COLONIAL OFFICE	INDUSTRY REPRESENTED
Mr. A. Moody Stuart	Managing Director, Antigua Syndicate Estates
J. M. Watson	Managing Director, Antigua Sugar Factory
S. T. Hawley	White Sands Hotel
F. H. S. Warneford	Retired superintendent of Agriculture, and Livestock producer
R. Cadman	Dew and Sons (importers/exporters)
Major Medhurst	Secretary of either the Employers' Federation or the Livestock Association or both.
Source: Report of 1957 Joint Deputation (CO 1031/2280)	

The meeting was attended by both the acting governor of the Leeward Islands, Mr. Macdonald, and the Administrator, Lieut. Col. Lovelance. While the members of the deputation came with business specific concerns, which included concerns over the meat and milk prices and hotel licensing, the Colonial Office administrators were frank in their assessment of the real reason for the visit, noting that 'what they really wanted was the chance of blowing off generally about their dissatisfaction with the Antigua Government.'[43]

While the group addressed their specific complaints regarding the ways in which local government decisions impacted them negatively and sought intervention by the colonial secretary to protect their interests, they received little support for the colonial administrators. In fact their complaints seemed to draw belligerent responses from the Colonial Office. The nature of the complaints though seems to have confused the Colonial Office. Moody Stuart complained that one important reason

43 CO1031 2280: Notes of Meeting of Joint Deputation.

why Ministerial government was not a success in Antigua was that there was no proper financial responsibility. Yet Antigua was embraced by the Colonial Office as one of their greatest success stories in the Caribbean, and colonial administrators were not likely to fall for unsubstantiated claims of financial impropriety in this case.

In addition in seeking to play the race card, Mr. Hawley of the White Sands hotel stated that the federation included blacks and whites – more blacks than whites and complained about the racial situation on the island claiming that he was speaking as a minority of oppressed whites on the island.[44] Hawley made the most direct appeal to the Colonial Office for white Creoles and by the end of the meeting he is noted to have stated to the office that he and the other white Creoles had lost all confidence that anyone was looking after them and they felt abandoned. He claimed that in Antigua the government was dictatorial, and racially biased, and that in addition 'some of the members of government had in the past stolen from Salvation Army funds.'[45] The colonial administrators in the United Kingdom remained unsympathetic to the complaints of Hawley and other white Creoles even recommending to the group that 'one has to learn to live in the world one finds oneself in.' No wonder Mr. Warneford's closing remark was that 'Great Britain was throwing away her Empire bit by bit to the natives.'[46]

Despite the absence of encouragement to the deputation in 1957, white Creoles continued to attack the local government, constantly challenging their decisions and questioning the integrity of black and coloured ministers

44 Ibid. Hawley, a white Creole who was a member of the deputation meeting with the Colonial Office, was a hotel employer who sought to deny access to the beaches at his resort to local blacks and who had developed antagonistic relations on the island with both his employees and union leaders.

45 Ibid. While this comment about the Salvation Army clearly refers to Bird, there was no information available regarding any financial scandal with Bird and the Army. It is true that the reasons for his sudden departure from the Army in the 1930s has never been disclosed, but sources have suggested more personal reason associated with his Grenada appointment.

46 Ibid.

and union leaders. Their complaints to the Colonial Office continued into the 1960s and included complaints over the method of the introduction of legislation into legislative council; conversion of electricity as a government undertaking. This particular undertaking was targeted by Moody Stuart and the other nominated members of Legislative Council, who were committed to showing the Colonial Office that their black protégé's were nothing if not incompetent and financially dishonest. Despite their actions the Colonial Office was far from convinced especially as Mr. Lake, the present Minister for Social Services was Chairman of the Electricity Board before he became a Minister in 1956.

The actions of Creoles in attempting to undermine local government contributed further to their loss of esteem in the eyes of the Colonial Office and their loss of political power. By 1957, Moody Stuart actions included violating an important principle of his membership in the Executive Council. His constant attacks on local government and his exposure of information discussed in secrecy by the Council drew censure from the Colonial Office and eventually the loss of his position on the Council. The Colonial Office grew increasingly concerned by his behaviour of opposing the Government outside of Executive Council. They also noted that his action played right into the hands of Antiguan ministers who were beginning to call for the abolition of nominated members of the Council. In 1959, Moody Stuart resigned his position on the Council and was replaced by a coloured Creole Dr. L. R. Wynter.[47]

47 Ibid. The remaining three nominated members of the Legislative Council of the island were white Creoles: Moody Stuart, L. R. Wynter and S. R. Mendes.

The Final Blows to White Creole Dominance

The final blow to white Creole dominance came with additional change to the legislature of Antigua in 1961. The change increased the number of elected seats in this organization from eight to ten and provided the colony with a political status which was largely self-governing associated state with Great Britain. This was a halfway stage between colony and nation, with ministers who controlled the state able to gain economic advantage from the political power which came with change in political status. With control of the economy came the final act of removing white Creole control over the society. Engaged in a contentious battle with estate owners that resulted in both sides called to mediation in London, V. C. Bird, the island's first prime minister, in a surprising move, bought the remaining estate lands from the Syndicate Estates, making their role and presence in the island colony irrelevant. In a bold and unanticipated move, V. C. instituted in 1966, the largest land acquisition in post-emancipation British Caribbean. Additionally, the state under V. C. took full control of the island' sugar industry.

Despite the protests of white Creoles the British government moved, in 1960, to grant important political changes to the island. This move occurred under the secretary of state for the colonies The Right Honourable, Iain Macleod. The political change made Bird the island's first Chief Minister and Minister of Finance and Planning. The new political structure further created three additional ministerial positions including ministry of trade, of social services, and public works and communications. It was a move which black Creoles embraced wholeheartedly but the granting of small bits of autonomy only served to make black Creoles and their labour allies all the more determined to wrest full control from the Colonial Office and sever British colonial ties.

Table 10 Political Change of 1960

1960 Political Change in Antigua
Hon. V. C. Bird : to be Chief Minister (Minister of Finance and Planning) Hon. L. Hurst: to be Minister of Trade, Production and Labour Hon. E. H. Lake: to be Minister of Social Services Hon. E. E. Williams: to be Minister of Public Works and Communications Hon. Dr. L. R. Wynter, M.B.E.: to be Member of Executive Council without Portfolio
Source: CO 1031/3216 – Government under new Constitution 1960

As the Chief Minister of Antigua, V. C. appointed the other ministers of Government in 1960 and these men were all loyal trade unionists and nationalists because Bird did not court any other political or ideological allies. The battle for sovereignty continued apace in the colony and by 1964, barely four years later, the Antiguan ministers lead by V. C. were in conflict with the Colonial Office regarding constitutional advance and their efforts to take a bigger step towards independence from Great Britain. The matter becomes one debated aggressively between Antiguan ministers and the Colonial Office as the Colonial Office insists that its delay in rejecting the proposal was based on nothing more than their efforts to keep a uniform system in the Leeward Islands and their commitment to advancing Federation for the region. That Antigua and Barbuda, the largest of the Leeward Islands was seeking to advance its political interests ahead of and independent of the other islands of the region was a problem for the Colonial Office whose plan was to create a political Federation of the islands that would allow the British to grant independence to a larger political entity than to small islands with limited resources. The federation constructed initially by the British for the Leeward Islands in 1871 had been dissolved in 1962 largely the result of the withdrawal by Antiguan politicians from such a federation.

V. C., Hurst, Lake and Williams stood their grounds on the issue of constitutional changes and when the Colonial Office, in moving ahead with its plans for a federation, proposed to create in the region a common services organization and unified public service, the Antiguan ministers responded with written protests and a visit to the Colonial Office in late 1965 to voice their unhappiness. As noted in the Colonial Office notes of the meeting of 15 November 1965 by an administrator: 'We had not expected to find Mr. Bird and his colleagues in such an angry mood, and it looked for some time as if we might come to grief at this first stage of our mission.'[48] In addition to expressing anger at British plans for federation the Antiguan ministers expressed additional concern at what they saw as the British government's attempt 'to revive, or impose, federation, and thus to retain its imperialist hold on the small islands of the region'.[49] The response of Antiguan ministers to the issue of Federation was that the issue was premature and not one for the UK government. Further, they insisted, as documented by the Colonial Office administrator, that from their perspective the Colonial Office should be focused on settling constitutional issues first; and that the creation of long-term arrangements for regional co-operation should be left for later time and that further such initiative would be driven solely by the local population and not imposed as the Colonial Office. The strongest statement in response to efforts at federation by the Colonial Office however by Antiguan ministers was that the Antiguan Government would under no circumstances accept the system of federation imposed by the British government or any system which made it possible for any external authority to appoint administrators other than Judges and Magistrates to positions of authority on the island.[50] In notes taken by Colonial Office administrator regarding constitutional development in the island in 1964 was duly noted the fact that 'Mr. Bird and his colleagues are nothing if not emphatic and tenacious in their views.'[51]

There is further note that this group, black and coloured Creoles, was unified in their refusal to contemplate another local election for obtaining endorsement from the United Nations on the matter of the island's request for internal self government. It is clear that the Colonial Office was

48 CO 1031 4431: Constitutional Development Antigua, 1964.

49 CO 1031 4431: Confidential Memo 52 documenting meeting with Antiguan Ministers 15 November 1965.

50 Ibid., CO 1031 3216: Formation of the Government of Antigua under the New Constitution; CO 1031 4431.

51 CO 1031 4431.

recommending such a delay and that local politicians were adamant in their refusal insisting that their most recent election campaign had been run on the very same issue and that their intentions were well documented in their Manifesto and elaborated in public debate during the election campaign.[52]

It was clear that the Colonial Office tactics for delay were losing effect on Antiguan politicians who were quick studies in local, regional and international politics and they continued to press the colonial government on the issue of 'internal self government', an issue the Colonial Office itself admitted it had little grounds on which to delay the Antiguan request. Yet it did delay the process in its attempt to solve the 'problem' of the Leeward Islands in one move. Holding out still on its plan to create a political federation of the islands of this region in order to effect a more politically justifiable pullout of Great Britain from the region.[53]

52 Ibid.

53 Ibid. Communications included a memo dispatch No. 149, 5 June 1965; which was an application from the administrator to the Secretary of State regarding request for internal self government for Antigua. The communications were from V. C. Bird and other Black Ministers of Government V. C. Bird, Lake and McChesny George.

Conclusion

Although most British Caribbean labour history sources have as their beginning the 1930s, labour's power relations and dominance structures are rooted in the post-emancipation period of the nineteenth and early twentieth centuries. Antigua and Barbuda is of central importance in the history of free labour in the British West Indies because this island was the proving ground for post-slavery labour laws and later became the site of the first conflicts between large numbers of former slaves and former slave owners. Many of the other islands in the area, not all of them British colonies, modelled their labour codes and social controls after the ones instituted in Antigua in 1834. Antigua's significance in this context has been long overlooked.

Labour developments, in particular, the rise of an independent labouring population with class consciousness, progressed differently in the smaller and larger islands. The small size of Antigua and its on-going dependence on sugar cane production as the primary agricultural activity greatly retarded the development of an independent labour force and a true peasantry. The yearly production figures rose and fell, never entering the continual decline that occurred in Jamaica, between 1838 and the end of the nineteenth century.

In Jamaica, the decline of sugar provided opportunities for ex-slaves to become tenant farmers and landowners. This new, rising peasant class was able to introduce new products, in particular bananas, at the end of the nineteenth century, stimulating the lagging export economy.

Gender and race are very intertwined with labour and have been so dating back to the construction of plantation slave societies in the Caribbean region in the seventeenth century. Yet this book covers only the nineteenth and twentieth centuries, 1834 to 1970, the long period between emancipation and adult suffrage, to the emergence of distinct labour and political organizations in Antigua and Barbuda. This overview perspective provides a better historical base from which to understand twentieth-century labour, gender, and politics in Antigua and Barbuda. The colonial documents identified in Chapters 3, 4 and 5, shows evidence of the daily experiences of the islands' majority. These documents include the census and reports such as bluebooks and prison reports. Colonial documents such as these are supplemented by oral and written sources, acquired from direct interviews and from archival searches, and have together provided a fuller, and more accurate story of Antigua's labour history.

This book not only contributes to the story of the Antiguan working people, colonial history, and labour history, it also provides a significant study of other groups, especially women who have been excluded from the islands' history. In my examination of the colonial and post-colonial economy, what has become clear for the case of Antigua, is not only the significance in size of the female population, but also the significant role that this female population has played and continues to the present, to play in the economy of the island.

The book interrogates the meaning of gender for women across the three racial groups, white, coloured and black, and across social classes of middle class and peasantry among the coloured and black racial groups. The female experience varied in Antiguan society where gender wage systems and professional discrimination based upon gender were heavily enforced. The 1911 and 1921 censuses, prison reports and oral accounts are used to highlight the experience of the islands majority, the female and poor population who suffered under the gender, race, and class discrimination that was enforced by law and by local practice. The challenges faced by rural women are exposed through oral accounts of two generations of Antigua women. The central role of the TUC is exposed, not only in terms of its alliance with local workers in building viable unions, but also its role in imposing and promoting traditional roles for men and women workers in the ATLU. The gender exclusive practices endemic in the ATLU have their roots in TUC structure as well as in local grassroots organizations.

Chapters 6 and 7 address the key issues of labour organization, and political participation in Antigua. Trade Union leadership has its origins in local level organizations such as the lodges. These purely social organizations reflected gender exclusive leadership which would be retained in the established trade union organization, the ATLU after 1940. This book began as part of an effort to answer the question of women's role in trade union organization and in union struggles from 1940. Following on that question was the effort to understand how women's contributions became forgotten or marginalized in the labour history of the region today.

Antiguan women despite the gender exclusion that sought to limit their social and political contributions played a crucial role in institution-building in Antigua and Barbuda. They were the educators who single-handedly reconstructed the middle class of the twentieth century. As the island's majority they struggled to assert some control over wages paid and work conditions in the sugar and cotton fields. As single parents and head of households, and as partners to male workers in the Antiguan twentieth century economy they suffered the oppressive workplace rules, punitive fines for lateness and absence which included public floggings and imprisonment in estate dungeons. These were the twentieth-century work conditions against which they organized in the 1940s.

The struggles to legitimize their labour organization the ATLU in the 1940s is a struggle fought and won by a partnership of workers which reflected the gender structures of the early British trade union movement. The early union limited women's participation only at the top. Throughout the rest of the organization, in membership, recruitment, and support, women were present in great numbers. They fought no battles to claim their place at the top believing that their first battle against poor labour conditions was the most important struggle. Then the second battle against colonialism ensured their full support to union and political leaders – male.

The final chapter of this book focused on exposing the true history of labour. It is clear that to tell the full history is to include all of the stories, all of the actors, irrespective of their gender. In a colonial environment where race, colour and gender, social class and religion mattered enormously to one's experience, this male-centred story, the story of legends, barely touches the surface of the complex realities on the islands. The nucleus of social history of the eastern Caribbean is labour, the struggles for control of the labour of the black and coloured population, dates from the seventeenth century. Through the nineteenth century until emancipation, women were a significant factor in this group. Their roles continue to grow over a century later, as the male population continued to shrink. Yet the gender inheritance of British patriarchy, the internalization of gender exclusion as part of the British middle class values by coloured and black men and the patriarchal exclusionary practices of the colonial authorities limited women's place both in the working class and middle class organizations. It is no surprise then that much of the history post 1950 and adult suffrage, involved conflict between Creole men, union leaders and employers for control of the state. It was the imagery which resulted from the construction of masculinity between these two groups that further contributed to women's exclusion and to the 'motherlessness' of the Antiguan nation. As a result of the battles between white, black and coloured Creoles for control of the state in the 1950s, competing masculinities emerged and came to dominate the political landscape.

Not gender but the posturing of white Creole masculinity in contestation with black and coloured masculinities, dominated the national struggle. Gender played little role in the debates over suffrage in 1951, as all adults (persons 18 and over) irrespective of gender, caste or class were given the vote. This was the last good opportunity for a gender discussion to be addressed in Antigua. Because it was not, Antiguan men comfortably maintained their leadership over trade union and political spaces. Leadership discussions were limited to men debating each other over issues of honesty, responsibility and union qualifications.

The absence of debate on questions of gender from the 1950s to 1970s further served to marginalize women from the national stage. Therefore gender and women played no central role while masculinity and class dominated during this period – not much importance was attached to women's role in the nation. The single parent imagery of the 'father' dominated the political landscape and the motherless nation emerged. The other edge of the double edged sword has proved no less dangerous for women in Antigua. In Antigua the twentieth-century nationalists were not embroiled in any ideological battles over identity – gender, race, class or otherwise and therefore they were called upon to 'imagine' no role or place for self or other. The middle class constructs of male head of households and respectable stay at home wives – remained entrenched. Because women in the unions occupied no leadership place white Creole men never had to engage in attacking the morality of the women of labour or of the Black Creole nations.

Little importance was attached to women's role as mothers of the nation – and as a consequence, very little attempts were made to control their sexuality outside the confines of social class and religious restrictions. Black Creole nationalists were not overly concerned with attempts to control women's sexuality and imagery. Rather it was the imagery of black Creole masculinity that emerged as a central imagery during this period.

Combined, the lack of importance of controlling women, particularly their sexuality, and the construction of nationalists and leaders as men only had by the 1970s normalized women's exclusion and made the nation a single parent household, even as women laboured to ensure the survival of the nation.

I encountered the problem continually in Antigua while I conducted research at the Archives, spoke with subjects about their experiences and engaged in discussions in social environments. The women were there. In 2002 when I returned to the island to look at the trade union materials, I was told that a new publication of *The Struggle and the Conquest*, Novelle Richards's monograph on the labour struggles, was about to be released.[1] I spoke to two of the people central in the re-release of the work and asked about how they had handled women's invisibility from the original. They paused, looking at me perplexed at the question. They could not rewrite the book. No, but I suggested the new introduction could have handled that issue. They had not thought of it, despite the roles their female relatives have played in the ATLU. One organizer later confided her embarrassment at not having done this – not having thought it important to fill in the gap of women's contribution. Her grandmother had been an early leader of the trade union movement and had been an organizer in the women's branch of the movement. Women have remained active and loyal union members and political party supporters. They have also emerged in Antigua and Barbuda as the driving force behind the economy, and are active in every sector of the economy and society. Yet the picture of national leadership does not clearly reflect this participation. Despite the expectation that Caroline Carmody recorded from informants in the 1970s that things would change, evidence of this change have yet to be truly manifest.

1 Novelle Richards, *The Struggle* (New York, Seaburn Publishing, 2004).

Select Bibliography

Archival Sources

Antigua and Barbuda Archives (Antigua Archives) St. Johns, Antigua.
Antigua Public Library (APL), St. Johns, Antigua.
Antigua and Barbuda Museum, St. Johns, Antigua.
Library of Congress (LOC), Washington, DC USA.
London School of Economics (LSE), London, UK.
New York City Public Library (NYPL), 42nd Street and 5th Avenue, NYC.
New York Public Library Science, Industry, and Business Library (SIBL), NYC.
Schomburg Center for Research in Black Culture (SCRBC), Harlem, NYC.
Trade Union Congress Archives (TUC Archives) at London Metropolitan University United Kingdom, London, UK.
United Kingdom National Archives London Public Records Office (UK National Archives/PRO).

Books, Theses and Articles

Alexander, Jack. 'Love, Race Slavery and Sexuality in Jamaican Images of the Family'. In Raymond T. Smith, ed., *Kinship Ideology and Practice in Latin America*. Chapel Hill: University of North Carolina Press, 1984.

Amin, Shahid. *'Peripheral' Labour?: Studies in the History of Partial Proletarianization*. Cambridge: Cambridge University Press, 1996.

Anderson, David and David Killingray. *Policing the Empire: Government, Authority and Control, 1830–1940*. New York: St. Martin's Press, c1991.

Antigua and Barbuda National Report for the United Nations: Fourth World Conference on Women Beijing, China 1995. St. Johns, Antigua: Antigua Printing and Publishing 1995.

Antigua Girls' High School Centenary Celebrations Committee. *Antigua Girls's High School Centenary 1886–1986: A Tribute to Our Alma Mater*. St. John's, Antigua: Antigua Printing and Publishing, 1986.

Aronoff, Marilyn. 'Community in an Industrial Society: A Study of a West Indian Labor Movement'. Thesis at Brandeis University, 1973.

Auchmuty, Rosemary. 'Spinsters and Trade Unions in Victorian Britain'. In *Women at Work*. Ann Curthoys et al., Canberra, Australia: Australian Society for the Study of Labour History, 1975.

Baker, E. C. *Guide to the Records of the Leeward Islands*. London: Basil Blackwell. 1965.

Baker, Maureen and Mary-Ann Robeson. 'Trade Union Reactions to Women Workers and Their Concerns' *Canadian Journal of Sociology*, Vol. 6, No. 1 (Winter 1981). JSTOR. State University of NY Westchester Community College Library, Valhalla, NY. 20 October 2006 <http://www.jstor.org/>

Beckwith, Karen. 'Gender Frames and Collective Action: Configurations of Masculinity in the Pittsburg Coal Strike'. *Politics & Society*. June 2001. Vol. 29, No. 2, 297–309.

Benn, Dennis. *Ideology and Political Development: The Growth and Development of Political Ideas in the Caribbean, 1774–1983*. Kingston, Jamaica: Institute of Social and Economic Research.

Bertram, Sir Anton. *The Colonial Service*. Cambridge: Cambridge University Press, 1930.

Bolland, O. Nigel. *The Politics of Labour in the British Caribbean: The Social Origins of Authoritarianism and Democracy in the Labour Movement*. Jamaica, WI: Ian Randle Publishers, 2001.

——. *Struggles for Freedom: Essays on Slavery, Colonialism and Culture in the Caribbean and Central America*. Jamaica, WI: Ian Randle Publishers, 1997.

Bolles, A. Lynn. *We Paid our Dues: Women Trade Union Leaders of the Caribbean*. Washington, DC: Howard University Press, 1996.

Boyd, Rosalind E. et al., *International Labour and the Third World: The Making of a New Working Class*. Great Britain: Gower Publishing Company, 1987.

Brereton, Bridget. 'Society and Culture in the Caribbean'. In Franklin W. Knight and A. Palmer, eds., *The Modern Caribbean*. Chapel Hill: The University of North Carolina Press, 1989.

Brereton, Bridget and Kevin A. Yelvington. *The Colonial Caribbean in Transition: Essays on post-emancipation Social and Cultural History*. Gainesville: University Press of Florida, 1999.

Brereton, Bridget, editor. *General History of the Caribbean. Volume V: The Caribbean in the Twentieth Century*. UNESCO Printing and Macmillan, 2004.

Brown, Neville Cleofoster. *The Emergence of a Bishop: Memoirs of Neville Cleofoster Brown: Bishop of the Moravian Church*. Trinidad: Granderson Bros. Ltd, 2000.

Carmody, Caroline M. 'First Among Equals: Antiguan Patterns of Local-Level Leadership'. Thesis at New York University, New York, 1978.

Chaney, Elsa and Mary Garcia Castro eds. *Muchachas No More: Household Workers in Latin America and the Caribbean*. Philadelphia: Temple University Press, 1989.

Christian, Sydney T. Editor. *St. John's Lodge. St. John's Lodge of Antient (sic.) Free and Accepted Masons, Centenary Commemoration Celebrations*. St. Johns Antigua: Antigua Printing and Publishing, 1944.

Citrine, Walter McLennan. *Men and Work: An Autobiography*. Westport, Conn.: Greenwood Press, 1976, c1964.

——. *Two Careers*. London, Hutchinson, 1967.

Cooper, Frederick *Decolonization and African Society: The Labor Question in French and British Africa*. Great Britain: Cambridge University Press, 1996.

Cross, Malcolm & Gad Heuman eds. *Labour in the Caribbean*. London: Macmillan Caribbean, 1988.

Cruse, Harold. *Crisis of the Negro Intellectual*. New York: Quill, 1984.

Curtin, Philip D. *The Atlantic Slave Trade: A Census*. Madison: University of Wisconsin Press, 1969.

Davis, J. Oliver. 'How Workers in Antigua Were First Organised: Recollections'. Ralph Prince, ed., *Antigua and Barbuda: From Bondage to Freedom*, Antigua: Antigua Printing and Publishing, 1984.

Davis, Nira Yuval and Athias Floya. *Woman, Nation, State*. New York: St. Martin's Press, 1989.

Dirks, Robert Thomas. 'Networks, Groups and Local Level Politics in an Afro-Caribbean Community'. Thesis at Michigan State – Ann Arbor, 1972.

Douglass, Lisa. *The Power of Sentiment: Love, Hierarchy, and the Jamaican family Elite*. Boulder, Colorado: Westview Press, 1992.

Duignan, Peter and L. H. Gann. *Colonialism in Africa 1870–1960. v4* 'The Economies of Colonialism'. Cambridge: Cambridge University Press, 1975.

Dyde, Brian. *A History of Antigua: The Unsuspected Isle*. London and Oxford: Macmillan Education Ltd. 2000.

Eklins, W. F. 'A Source of Black Nationalism in the Caribbean: The Revolt of the British West Indies Regiment at Taranto, Italy': *Science and Society* 35:1 (1970):99–103.

Fage, J. D. *A History of Africa* 4th ed. New York: Routledge, 2002.

Ferguson, Moira. *The Hart Sisters: Early African Caribbean Writers, Evangelicals, and Radicals*. Lincoln: University of Nebraska Press.

Fieldhouse, David Kenneth. *The Colonial Empires; A Comparative Survey From The Eighteenth Century*, 1st American ed. New York, Delacorte Press 1967, c. 1966.

——. *Colonialism, 1870–1945: An Introduction*. New York: St. Martin's Press, 1981.

——. *Economics and Empire, 1830–1914*. Ithaca, New York: Cornell University Press, 1973.

——. *The Theory of Capitalist Imperialism*. New York, Barnes & Noble, 1967.
——. *Unilever Overseas: The Anatomy Of A Multinational 1895–1965*. London: Croom Helm; Stanford, Calif.: Hoover Institution Press, c1978.
Flax, Olva. *Antigua Grammar School: One Hundred Years of Service to Antigua, 1884–1984*. St. John's, Antigua: Antigua Archives Committee. 1984a.
——. *The Influence of Church and School upon the Antigua Society: A Study of the First Fifty Years After Emancipation.* St. John's, Antigua: Antigua Archives Committee. 1984b.
Fog-Olwig, Karen. Editor. *Small Islands, Large Questions: Society, Culture and Resistance in the post-emancipation Caribbean*. London: Frank Cass, 1995.
Franck, Harry A. *Roaming Through the West Indies*. New York: The Century Co., 1920.
Fraser, Peter. 'Some Effects of the First World War on the British West Indies'. *Caribbean Societies 1, Collected Seminar Papers*, No. 29. University of London, Institute of Commonwealth Studies, 1982.
Gann, Lewis H. 'The Economics of Colonialism'. In Duignan, Peter and L. H. Gann. Eds. *Colonialism in Africa 1870–1960*. London: Cambridge University Press, 1969–1975.
Gaspar, David Barry. *Bondmen and Rebels: A Study of Master-Slave Relations in Antigua*. Baltimore: The Johns Hopkins University Press. 1985.
Geoff, Eley Ronald Grigor Suny. *Becoming National.* New York: Oxford University Press, 1996.
Gilbert, Erik and Jonathan T. Reynolds. *Africa in World History: From Prehistory to the Present.* Upper Saddle River, New Jersey: Pearson Prentice Hall, 2004.
Goveia, Elsa V. *A Study of the Historiography of the British West Indies to the End of the Nineteenth century*. Washington, DC: Howard University Press, 1980.
——. *Slave society in the British Leeward Islands at the end of the Eighteenth Century.* New Haven: Yale University Press, 1965. Caribbean Series 8.
——. *The West India Slave Laws of the Eighteenth Century*. Barbados: Caribbean Universities Press, 1970.
Greenwood, R. and S. Hamber. *Emancipation to Emigration*. London: Macmillan, 1980.
Guha, Ranajit. *Dominance without Hegemony: History and Power in Colonial India.* Cambridge, MA: Harvard University Press, 1997.
Hall, Catherine. 'Missionary Stories: Gender and Ethnicity in England in the 1830s and 1840s', in Catherine Hall, *White, Male, and Middle Class: Explorations in Feminism and History*. New York: Routledge, 1992.
Hall, Douglas. *Five of the Leewards, 1834–1870: The Major Problems of the Post-Emancipation Period in Antigua, Barbuda, Montserrat, Nevis and St. Kitts*. London: Ginn and Company, 1971.

Hamshere, Cyril. *The British in the Caribbean*. Cambridge; Massachusetts: Harvard University Press, 1972.

Hartman, Grace. 'Women and the Unions'. In Gwen Matheson, ed., *Women in the Canadian Mosaic*. Toronto: 1976.

Helg, Aline. *Our Rightful Share: The Afro-Cuban Struggle For Equality, 1886–1912*. Chapel Hill: University of North Carolina Press, 1995.

Henry, S. A. 'Historical Notes on Education in Antigua, 1837–1984'. In Ralph Prince, ed., *Antigua and Barbuda: From Bondage to Freedom, 150th Anniversary of Emancipation*. St. John's, Antigua: Antigua Printing and Publishing, 1984.

——. 'Riot in Antigua 1918'. In Ralph Prince, ed., *Antigua and Barbuda: From Bondage to Freedom, 150th Anniversary of Emancipation*. St. John's, Antigua: Antigua Printing and Publishing, 1984.

Hine, Darlene Clark and Jacqueline McLeod. *Crossing Boundaries: Comparative History of Black People in Diaspora*. Bloomington: Indiana University Press, 1999.

Holt, Thomas. *The Problem of Freedom: Race, Labor, and Politics in Jamaica and Britain, 1832–1938*. Baltimore Maryland: Johns Hopkins Press, 1992.

Ilife, John. *Africans: The History of a Continent*. New York: Cambridge University Press, 1995.

Isiche, Elizabeth. *A History of Nigeria*. New York: Longman, 1983.

Jeffries, Sir Charles. *The Colonial Empire and its Civil Service*. Cambridge: Cambridge University Press, 1938.

——. *Partners for Progress: The Men and Women of the Colonial Service*. London: George G. Harrap. 1949.

Jones, Jacqueline. *Labor of Love, Labor of Sorrow: Black Women, Work, and the Family from Slavery to the Present*. New York: Vintage Books, 1995. Reprint. Originally published: New York: Basic Books, c1985.

Klubock, Thomas Miller. *Contested Communities: Class, Gender and Politics in Chile's El Teniente Copper Mine, 1904–1951*. Durham N.C.: Duke University Press,1998.

Knight, Franklyn. *The Caribbean: The Genesis of a Fragmented Nationalism*. London: Oxford University Press, 1990.

——, and Colin Palmer. *The Modern Caribbean*. Chapel Hill North Carolina: The University of North Carolina press, 1989.

Lanahan, Mrs. *Antigua and Antiguans: A Full Account of the Colony and its Inhabitants*. Vol II. London: Saunders and Ottley, 1844. Reprinted. London: Macmillan, 1991.

Langford, Oliver, Vere 'Caribbeana [microform]: Being Miscellaneous Papers Relating to the History, Geneology, Topography, and Antiquities of the British West Indies'. London: Mitchell, Hughes and Clarke, 1910–1919.

Lazarus-Black, Mindie. *Legitimate Acts and Illegal Encounters: Law and Society in Antigua and Barbuda*. Washington, DC: Smithsonian Institution Press, c1994.

Lewis, Patrick A. 'The Emergence of the Union Party System in Antigua'. In Ralph Prince, ed., *Antigua and Barbuda: From Bondage to Freedom, 150th Anniversary* of Emancipation. St. John's, Antigua: Antigua Printing and Publishing, 1984.

——. 'An Historical Analysis of the Development of the Union Party System in the commonwealth Caribbean, 1935–1968'. Thesis (Ph.D.) University of Cincinnati, 1974.

Lewis, P. Cecil. *The Revised Laws of Antigua*: Prepared under the Authority of the Revised edition of the Laws Ordinance, 1959. London: Waterloo, 1965.

Lowes, Susan. 'The Peculiar Class: The Formation, Collapse, and Reformation of the Middle Class in Antigua, West Indies, 1834–1940'. Thesis (Ph.D.) Columbia University, 1994.

Lugard, Frederick John Dealtry. *The Dual Mandate of Tropical Africa*. 5th ed. Hamden, Connecticut: Archon Books, 1965.

Macmillan, William M. *Warning from the West Indies: A Tract for Africa and the Empire*. London, Faber and Faber, 1936.

Mallon, Florencia. *Peasant and Nation: The Making of Postcolonial Mexico and Peru*. Berkeley: University of California Press, 1995.

Massiah, Jocelin. *Women as Heads of Households in the Caribbean: Family Structure and Feminine Status: UNESCO: Women in a World Perspective*. United Kingdom, 1983.

Merivale, Herman. *Lectures on Colonization and Colonies*. New York: A. M. Kelley, 1967.

Mevis, René. *Inventory of Caribbean Studies: An Overview of Social Research on the Caribbean*. Royal Institute of Linguistics and Anthropology, 1974.

Mullings, Leith. *On Our Own Terms: Race, Class, and Gender in the Lives of African American Women*. New York: Routledge, 1997.

Nicholson, Marjorie. *The TUC Oversees: The Roots of Policy*. Vol 1. London: Allen and Unwin, 1986.

Nurse, Lawrence. *Trade Unionism and Industrial Relations in the Commonwealth Caribbean: History and Contemporary Practice and Prospect*. Westport, Connecticut: Greenwood Press, 1992.

Palmer, Colin. Eric Williams. *Eric Williams and the Making of the Modern Caribbean*. Northern Carolina: University of North Carolina Press, 2006.

Parsons, Timothy H. *The British Imperial Century, 1815–1914: A World History Perspective*. New York: Rowman and Littlefield Publishers, 1999.

Philips, Sir F. *West Indian Constitution: Post Independence Reform*. New York: New Oceana, 1987.

Post, Ken. *Arise ye Starvelings: the Jamaican Labour Rebellion of 1938 and its Aftermath*. The Hague; Boston: Nijhoff, 1978.

——. *Strike The Iron: A Colony At War: Jamaica, 1939–1945* Atlantic Highlands, NJ: Humanities Press; The Hague: Institute of Social Sciences, 1981.

Prince, Ralph. *Antigua and Barbuda: From Bondage to Freedom. 150th Anniversary of Emancipation.* St. Johns, Antigua: St. Johns Printery, 1984.

Randall, Stephen J. and Graeme S. Mount. *The Caribbean Basin: An International History.* New York: Routledge, 1998.

Rawley, James A. *The Transatlantic Slave Trade: A History*. New York: Norton, 1981.

Reddock, Rhoda. *Women, Labour & Politics in Trinidad & Tobago: A History* New Jersey: Zed Books, 1994.

——, ed. *Interrogating Caribbean Masculinities: Theoretical and Empirical Analyses.* Kingston, Jamaica: University of West Indies Press, 2004.

Richardson, Bonham C. *The Caribbean in the Wider World, 1492–1992: A Regional Geography.* New York: Cambridge University Press, 1992.

Richards, Novell. *The Struggle and the Conquest: Twenty Five Years of Social Democracy in Antigua.* St. Johns, Antigua: Published by the author, 1981.

Safilios-Rothschild, Constantina. *Women and Social Policy*. Englewood Cliffs, NJ: Prentice-Hall, 1974.

Scott, Joan Wallace. *Feminism and History*. Oxford; New York: Oxford University Press, 1996.

—— *Gender and the Politics of History*. New York: Columbia University Press, 1988.

Shepherd, Verene. *Women in Caribbean History: The British Colonized Territories.* Princeton; New Jersey: Markus Weiner, 1999.

Shepherd, Verene. Bridget Brereton and Barbara Bailey. *Engendering History: Caribbean Women in Historical Perspective.* New York: St. Martin's Press, 1995.

Smith, Keithlyn B and Fernando C. Smith. *To Shoot Hard Labour*. Scarborough Canada: Edan's Publishers, 1986.

Smith, Keithlyn B. *No Easy Push-o-Ver: A History of the Working People of Antigua and Barbuda 1834–1994*. Scarborough, Ontario: Edan's Publishers, 1994.

Spivak, Gayatri Chakravorty. *A Critique of Postcolonial Reason: Toward a History of the Vanishing Present*. Cambridge, Mass.: Harvard University Press, 1999.

St. Johnston, Sir Reginald. *From a Colonial Governor's Note-Book*. London: Hutchinson, 1936.

——. *Strange Places and Strange Peoples or, Life in the Colonial Service*. London: Hutchinson, 1936.

Stoler, Ann. 'Making Empire Respectable: The Politics of Race and Sexual Morality in 20th Century Colonial Cultures'. *American Ethnologist*, Vol. 16, No. 4 (November). 1989.

Tongue, Gwendolyn M. 'Policy of the Women's Desk Antigua and Barbuda', *Unity for Development*. St. Johns, Antigua: Antigua Printing and Publishing, 1985.

——, 'Women: Antigua and Barbuda', *Unity for Development*. St. Johns, Antigua: Antigua Printing and Publishing 1984.
Wallace, Elisabeth. *The British Caribbean: From the Decline of Colonialism to the End of Federation*. Buffalo: University of Toronto Press, 1977.
Weylen, Georgina. *Gender in Third World Politics*. Boulder, Colorado: Lynne Rienner Publishers, 1996.
——. *Women and Empowerment: Illustrations from the Third World*. New York: St. Martin's Press, 1998.
Williams, Eric Eustace. *Capitalism and Slavery*. London: Deutch, 1987.
Yuval-Davis, Nira. *Gender and Nation*. Thousand Oaks, CA: Sage Publications, 1997.
Yuval-Davis and Athias Floya. *Woman, Nation, State*. New York: St. Martin's Press, 1989.
Zin, Henry. *Labour Relations and Industrial Conflict in Commonwealth Caribbean Countries*. Trinidad: Columbus Publishers, 1972.

Interviews (Interview, unpublished)

Cecile I. G. Davis, personal interview, June 2003.
Rufus and Hildred Lewis, personal interview, June 2003.
Evelyn Rosetta Etinoff, personal interview, June 2003.
Sheila Rousseau, personal interview, June 2003.
Gwen Tongue, personal interview, June 2003.
Bridget Harris, personal interview, June 2003.
Edris Bird and Mr. Bird, personal interview, June 2003.
Nathalie Payne, personal interview, April 24, 2003.
Adolphus Freeland, personal interview, April 23, 2003.
Edie Labadie, personal interview, April 2003.
Evelyn Edwards, personal interview, April 2003.
Selma Brodie, personal interview, March 2003.
Enid Brodie-Joseph, personal interview, March 2003.
Patrick Lewis, Ambassador – Antigua/Barbuda Mission to United Nations, personal interview, January 2001.

Misc. Print and Non-Print Sources

Antigua Trade and Labour Union 40th Anniversary Magazine. Antigua: Antigua printing and Publishing, 1980 (AT&LU Headquarters, 2002 and Antigua Archive).

Discographies

'State Funeral of Sir Vere Cornwall Bird: KNO, ON, OCC. 9 December 1909–28 June 1999' (Antigua: Government of Antigua-Barbuda, 1999), 2 videocassettes A and B.

Newspapers and Magazines

Antigua Magnet. St. John's, Antigua. 4 January 1930, December 1932; 1 August 1933–30 July 1938; 3 January–24 November 1939; 10–26 February 1940.

Antigua News Notes. St. Johns, Antigua. 1909.

Antigua Official Gazette, various.

Antigua Observer. St. John's, Antigua. 30 November 1848. 9 December 1870–27 December 1888; May, July, 26 September–26 December 1889. 9 January 1890–11 June 1903.

Antigua Star (Antigua), 1 April 1937–30 July 1938; 4 January–24 November 1939; 10–26 February 1940; 4 January-24 November 1939; 11 February 1957; 6 January 1966.

Antigua Sun (Antigua), various.

Website

Hector, Leonard Tim. 'Hail Bwana, Farewell Papa!' Fan the Flame, 9 July 1999. Web. 15 June 2005 <http://www.candw.ag/~jardinea/ffhtm/ff990708.htm>

Index

Trade Unions Past, Present and Future

Edited by Craig Phelan

This series publishes monographs and edited collections on the history, present condition and possible future role of organised labour around the world. Multidisciplinary in approach, geographically and chronologically diverse, this series is dedicated to the study of trade unionism and the undeniably significant role it has played in modern society. Topics include the historical development of organised labour in a variety of national and regional settings; the political, economic and legal contexts in which trade unionism functions; trade union internationalism past and present; comparative and cross-border studies; trade unions' role in promoting economic equality and social justice; and trade union revitalisation and future prospects. The aims of the series are to promote an appreciation of the diversity of trade union experience worldwide and to provide an international forum for lively debate on all aspects of the subject.

Volume 1 Craig Phelan (ed.): Trade Unionism since 1945: Towards a Global History. Volume 1: Western Europe, Eastern Europe, Africa and the Middle East.
467 pages. 2009. ISBN 978-3-03911-410-8

Volume 2 Craig Phelan (ed.): Trade Unionism since 1945: Towards a Global History. Volume 2: The Americas, Asia and Australia.
364 pages. 2009. ISBN 978-3-03911-950-9

Volume 3 Pablo Ghigliani: The Politics of Privatisation and Trade Union Mobilisation: The Electricity Industry in the UK and Argentina.
293 pages. 2010. ISBN 978-3-03911-961-5

Volume 4 Heather Connolly: Renewal in the French Trade Union Movement: A Grassroots Perspective.
260 pages. 2010. ISBN 978-3-0343-0101-5

Volume 5 Magaly Rodríguez García: Liberal Workers of the World, Unite? The ICFTU and the Defence of Labour Liberalism in Europe and Latin America (1949–1969).
354 pages. 2010. ISBN 978-3-0343-0112-1

Volume 6 Jeffrey Sluyter-Beltrão: Rise and Decline of Brazil's New Unionism: The Politics of the Central Única dos Trabalhadores.
481 pages. 2010. ISBN 978-3-0343-0114-5

Volume 7 Craig Phelan (ed.): Trade Unions in West Africa: Historical and Contemporary Perspectives.
288 pages. 2011. ISBN 978-3-0343-0117-6

Volume 8 Forthcoming.

Volume 9 Tracy Carson: Tomorrow It Could Be You: Strikes and Boycotts in South Africa, 1978–1982.
325 pages. 2011. ISBN 978-3-0343-0119-0

Volume 10 Laura Ariovich: Organizing the Organized: Trade Union Renewal, Organizational Change and Worker Activism in Metropolitan America.
310 pages. 2010. ISBN 978-3-0343-0132-9

Volume 11 Indira Palacios-Valladares: Industrial Relations after Pinochet: Firm Level Unionism and Collective Bargaining Outcomes in Chile.
268 pages. 2011. ISBN 978-3-0343-0136-7

Volume 12 Zhining Ma: The ACFTU and Chinese Industrial Relations.
260 pages. 2011. ISBN 978-3-0343-0205-0

Volume 13 Quenby Olmsted Hughes: "In the Interest of Democracy": The Rise and Fall of the Early Cold War Alliance Between the American Federation of Labor and the Central Intelligence Agency.
218 pages. 2011. ISBN 978-3-0343-0212-8

Volume 14 Hans-Wolfgang Platzer and Torsten Müller: Global and European Trade Union Federations: A Handbook and Analysis of Transnational Trade Union Organizations and Policies.
949 pages. 2011. ISBN 978-3-0343-0744-4

Volume 15-16 Forthcoming.

Volume 17 Christolyn A. Williams: NO WOMEN JUMP OUT! Gender Exclusion, Labour Organization and Political Leadership in Antigua 1917–1970. 248 pages. 2013. ISBN 978-3-0343-0863-2

Volume 18 Akira Suzuki (ed.): Cross-National Comparisons of Social Movement Unionism: Diversities of Labour Movement Revitalization in Japan, Korea and the United States. 355 pages. 2012. ISBN 978-3-0343-0868-7

Volume 19 Stefan Rüb, Hans-Wolfgang Platzer and Torsten Müller: Transnational Company Bargaining and the Europeanization of Industrial Relations: Prospects for a Negotiated Order. 333 pages. 2013. ISBN 978-3-0343-0909-7